creating a **COME AS YOU ARE** culture in the
CHURCH

JOHN
BURKE

GRAND RAPIDS, MICHIGAN 49530 USA

Willow Creek Resources

ZONDERVAN.COM/
AUTHOR**TRACKER**

ZONDERVAN®

No Perfect People Allowed
Copyright © 2005 by John Burke

Requests for information should be addressed to:
Zondervan, *Grand Rapids, Michigan 49530*

Library of Congress Cataloging-in-Publication Data

Burke, John, 1963–
No perfect people allowed : creating a come-as-you-are culture in the church / John Burke.
    p. cm.
Includes bibliographical references and index.
Summary: "Discusses ways church leaders and congregations can reach out to and connect with postmodern, post-Christian society"— Provided by publisher.
    ISBN-10: 0-310-25655-0
    ISBN-13: 978-0-310-25655-7
    1. Pastoral theology.   2. Postmodernism—Religious aspects—Christianity.   I. Title.
BV4011.3.B87 2005
253—dc22   2005000359

Interior design by Tracey Walker

Printed in the United States of America

---

06 07 08 09 10 11 12 • 12 11 10 9 8 7 6

CONTENTS

Part Five: The Struggle with Brokenness

Part Six: The Struggle with Aloneness

Part Seven: The Struggle Forward

I dedicate this book
to the core group of Gateway.
You dreamed of what God might do in our city.
Through your prayers, sacrifice, and service
you created a culture
where God made that dream a reality.
You are my heroes of faith.

Artist: Patrick Shinn

All artwork has been contributed by artists at Gateway Community Church.

INTRODUCTION: GOD'S STORY IN OUR STORIES

People ask me how long it took to write this book. The truth is—about fifteen years.

I left the business world for campus ministry fifteen years ago because I wanted to help my generation find authentic faith like I was beginning to experience. The first seven years of ministry to America's first postmodern* generation were discouraging—I almost lost hope. Since then, God has turned my philosophy of church and ministry upside down. I now believe that only a church full of imperfect people, acting as his Body, can bring the hope and healing needed to change our postmodern world for the better—one life at a time. That's why I've written this book, because I see God powerfully at work in our generation.

A year ago I attended a conference about ministry in a postmodern context. I found myself terribly discouraged and bothered—and tired of modern-church deconstruction! For the past six years, I've read numerous books, attended conferences, and surfed the blogs about the emerging trends of new generations and their new ways of thinking. We have deconstructed everything, identified all the problems with the current church, and proclaimed what we knew would *not work*. We've read statisticians like Barna, Gallup, and Regele warn of the impending doom for our generation and the church in America.

What disturbs me is the absence of a path forward. We don't need more deconstruction, more theories, and more statistics; rather, we need tangible evidence that God is still doing what God has always done in every

---

* The term *postmodern* refers to a worldview that generally assumes there is no absolute truth or morality—truth and morality are only relative terms in the community in which we participate.

generation, constructing his church out of the most hopeless situation. It's not tearing-down time anymore—it's construction time!

All the practical principles of ministry you will encounter in these pages are illustrated by God's amazing work in the lives of the formerly unchurched of Gateway Community Church. You have to experience the feel of a culture to understand it, so I've included these stories to take you on an experiential journey—spanning from our postmodern culture to our church's culture. My goal is to let you see and feel the struggles of nearly a hundred real people who come out of our postmodern context. Most were not Christ-followers when they came to Gateway. Many were indifferent or even hostile to Christianity and had tough questions from a postmodern perspective, yet they found a safe culture within church where they could question, struggle, find faith, and grow.

At the conference that day, I ran into Jack Kuhatschek from Zondervan, whom I had met years earlier. He listened as I shared stories of the amazing things we've seen God doing in a cynical, skeptical, broken generation. I explained the hope I see for our generation in our church and in other churches around the country. Intrigued, Jack flew to Austin later that month and heard many powerful stories from the people themselves. Jack encouraged me to share this with others who desire to see God reaching our broken post-Christian, postmodern culture. *No Perfect People Allowed* gives tangible evidence that God *can and does* reach our generation through his church.

Austin is a window into the future because it attracts so many young adults. A *Forbes* survey called it America's "coolest" city, ranking it the best place for singles in America—singles who move here from all over the country, seeking employment in our high-tech, recreational, artsy capital city.[1]

The stories in this book represent the diversity of our generation across the nation. You'll read about people who grew up on the East Coast and the West and in between, from the wealthy to the poor, from Anglo, Black, Hispanic, and Asian backgrounds, singles and marrieds. This is truly the most diverse generation in American history, and, as you'll see, it's a generation not easily reached by a one-size-fits-all approach. But the people of this generation form the context in which the church must function, and they live all around you right now.

Though I've changed some names and details where necessary to protect the privacy of my friends at Gateway, the stories in this book are about real people dear to my heart. (Those who requested I use their real names are noted with a double dagger—††.) They have willingly shared their struggles, barriers, and brokenness in hopes of helping others find God's goodness.

Some have not arrived at faith but have allowed me to present their stories in process. The hardest part was selecting a few stories to include, since there are hundreds more to be told of God's amazing works in reclaiming our generation as his family.

I've written this book primarily for leaders—church leaders, small group leaders, and ministry leaders—to help them create a come-as-you-are culture to bridge the chasm between the church and our postmodern world.

Yet I believe *No Perfect People Allowed* gives a unique insight into the struggle for faith that will benefit everyone—skeptics and believers alike. You will see in vivid detail how God meets seeking people in mysterious, unique ways, and you will see how no one is too far away or too far gone for God's loving reach.

Whoever you are, I pray this book inspires in you a confidence that God is still at work in our generation. I pray you are motivated to action so that we may see *his-story* continue to unfold through his church for generations to come. My desire in writing is to tell God's story about his work in one church for our generation. I'm amazed at God's great work and what he's showing us. This is simply a gift we've received that we share, and so we pass on what we received in the hope that others might receive the same gift from God. My prayer for this book is that God might use it to give his greatest gift to our generation—and the next and the next—through his church.

PART ONE

The Struggle for Emerging Generations

graffiti artist: Brian Bonniwell

The First Corinthian Church of America

*Look around you! Vast fields are ripening all around us
and are ready now for the harvest.*

Jesus, John 4:35 NLT

*Do not be deceived: Neither the sexually immoral nor idolaters nor adulterers
nor male prostitutes nor homosexual offenders nor thieves nor the greedy
nor drunkards nor slanderers nor swindlers will inherit the kingdom of God.
And that is what some of you were....*

1 Corinthians 6:9–11

What do a Buddhist, a biker couple, a gay-rights activist, a transient, a high-tech engineer, a Muslim, a twenty-something single mom, a Jew, a couple living together, and an atheist all have in common?

They are the future church in America!

Most of them are in their twenties or thirties and became followers of Christ in the past five years. Many are now leading others in our church.

This is the generation the church must reach if it is to survive. It is an eclectic generation on a winding, wayward spiritual quest, and the church has an incredible opportunity to be a guide for the journey.

But time is running out. Unless Christians leading the church in America change, and unless the church begins living out the magnetic attractive force Jesus had on the world, the Christian church in America will be completely marginalized within decades!

So what will it take to become the kinds of Christian leaders in the kinds of churches and ministries and small groups that will truly impact emerging post-Christian America? What will it take to turn the tide that is washing the church off the map of our country? What kind of culture will captivate and compel emerging generations? How do we become the kinds of attractive Christ-followers who draw spiritual seekers into the family of God like Jesus did?

This book seeks to answer these questions. I hope painting a picture of what God is doing through his church will help you see how you can experience the invisible Jesus made visible through his Body, your local church. But I must warn you up front, doing church like this is a mess . . . but it's a beautiful mess!

Messy Lives

Lana came in late. The strained look on her face and the redness of her eyes immediately betrayed her. Something was wrong. "Brad's not coming, he's using again." The words flooded from her mouth with a flow of tears as soon as she reached the safety of our small group. Inside, Lana couldn't believe she was telling all to a church group, yet she had never found such love and acceptance. When they first came to Gateway, Brad and Lana were seeking support. In their late twenties with two kids, it felt like they were slowly unraveling on all sides: parenting challenges, job challenges, and years of drug abuse still stalking in the shadows.

Invited to our group one Sunday by a couple they met after church, they quickly jumped into our small group. From the first, Lana wanted to make sure we understood her views. "I think all religions are equally valid," she burst out one night. "Actually, I'm attracted by a lot of what Eastern religions have to say about peace, and I think Jesus was a good person—a life worth emulating—but I don't know beyond that. Frankly I don't like religious people who judge and look down on other beliefs. That's where I'm coming from, so I hope that's all right with you all."

She wanted to make sure we weren't going to judge her for being "open." As Lana and Brad got to know the group, they soon realized this was not your mama's church. The group was comprised of mostly young couples, in their twenties or early thirties. Out of twelve people, nine had come to faith at Gateway in the past two years.

Marcy and Casey, our biker couple, typically came adorned in black. Marcy's cranberry-red, elbow-length hair sported one metal spike braid in the back, extending down to her waist. Casey's scruffy, long black beard matched his pony-tailed hair. They came to Gateway in a state of spiritual seeking. Casey was tentative and distrustful at first but, over the course of a year or so, came to faith in Christ. His mother prayed a prayer of faith with me while on her deathbed, which helped open his heart to faith. Marcy would have called herself a Christian but did not seem to fully comprehend grace. Her Catholic upbringing gave her hope in Jesus, and she had seen him pull her through a very traumatic childhood. She had lived with a man before meeting Casey, and she and Casey had lived together before finally getting married.

I found out the hard way that living together was the norm. One Sunday, early in our church's history, I gave a message about commitment, which I titled "The C-Word" (due to our generation's fear of commitment). In the message, I talked about living together before marriage, explaining that although it seems like a prudent decision on the surface, it leads to nearly a 50% higher chance of divorce for those who do get married, because there's no sense of commitment. (We'll talk more about this issue in a later chapter.)

That next week I got gang-piled at my small group. All but one couple had lived together before marriage! The reason our group was so safe to explore faith is because *I* was the abnormal one in the group. This is the emerging church, not church *for* a post-Christian culture, where Christians huddle up behind the fortress walls and make forays outside into the messy culture, but a church molded *out of* a post-Christian people—an indigenous church, rising up out of the surrounding culture to form the Body of Christ!

Some group members had skeletons of drug abuse in their past. Jay and Arden were both managers with good careers, but Jay still had a ten-year probation for possession with the intent to sell lurking in his past. Jay felt the grip of addiction squeezing tight. Skeptical about church, unsure of what they believed, Jay and Arden were seeking spiritual support for their battles but had been turned off by more traditional churches. Four years later, Jay and Arden wholeheartedly follow Christ, lead a small group, and help out with our recovery ministry.

Dave, an engineer, and Kim, a teacher, came to Gateway after watching *Touched by an Angel*, which sparked a conversation about wanting to know God. The next night, a local news station aired a segment on a new church in town. Gateway was their first church experience since childhood. When they joined the small group, they had to ask if it was okay to take smoking breaks (at first a quarter of our group would have to take smoking breaks). Their marriage teetered on the edge of the abyss when they came to Gateway. Sexual dysfunction caused by early sexual abuse and promiscuity had slowly severed their marital ties. They desperately wanted to understand if God was real and if he could help them, but they had many questions and feared being judged.

Karla and Greg met in a halfway house while both were recovering from alcoholism. After living together for four years, they found Gateway on our opening day. Imagine my shock after our first Sunday service when the second couple I met said, "We want to get married. Will you do our wedding?" Karla considered herself an atheist converted to agnosticism through recovery, but the Bible and Jesus freaked her out. Greg had lived as a transient for fifteen years. After receiving our postcards and hearing an unconventional ad on secular radio for our church, they hesitantly agreed to try it once—it seemed different. But they made a pact that they would sit in the back row, on the aisle, and if I said one wrong word, they were out of there. Amazingly, they both opened their hearts to Christ during our premarital counseling appointments, realizing Jesus was the Higher Power who had rescued them from the death grip of addiction. Greg sometimes shares his story of hope when our church participates in "church under the bridge" for the homeless in Austin, and Karla, a child development specialist, serves in our nursery.

Daryl and Brianna alone came churched. They represent a bold new genre of missional Christians who are not content to play church by just huddling up with Christians. They wanted to be in a place where real, worldly people, with real messy lives, were seeing the real God in action. But unfortunately, they represent a minority of churched Christians—Christians who, like the apostle Paul, willingly venture out of their comfort zone into the messy, pagan culture of a Corinth or Austin.

Many churched Christians who came through the doors of Gateway in the early days just could not handle the discomfort of having so many seekers around them. They would hang out in the lobby after the service, strike up conversation, and slowly realize that the person they were talking to held none of their "sacred beliefs" regarding abortion, sex before marriage, evolution, or other hot-topics of Christian subcultures. After a conversation like that, they usually scared each other off.

Don't get me wrong, I am not advocating throwing in the moral towel, but why expect a secular society to act like a Christian one? First things first, and according to Jesus, loving God comes first—followed closely by loving people. But it takes a new kind of Christian to live and minister in the mess of Corinth. And that is precisely where we now live!

Our Very Corinthian Culture

As I read about the church in Corinth, I see many parallels to our situation today. Being so near the intellectual hub of Athens, first-century Corinthians prided themselves for their intellectual pursuits. As residents of a large, wealthy metropolitan port city, the people emphasized luxury and comfort. They entertained themselves at the Isthmian games held at the Temple of Poseidon, and they advocated a full indulgence in the pleasures of life.

Corinth was known for its wild party life and sexual freedom. The famous Temple of Aphrodite, the goddess of love, complete with a thousand temple prostitutes, towered above the city, beckoning all to come and feast their sexual appetites. Partying and hedonistic pleasure-seeking was so common in Corinth that they branded the name—"to live like a Corinthian" implied diving into days of drunken, promiscuous living.

Rome proclaimed religious tolerance as a great virtue. In fact, the one thing about Christians that the Greco-Roman culture detested was this antiquated idea that Jesus was the only way to God. And *Truth*? "What is *Truth*?" Wasn't it a Roman governor, raised in the same Greco-Roman culture, who asked this first recorded relativistic question to Jesus?[1] Corinth was a mess!

Yet, as Paul's letters attest, this is precisely the place where God's Spirit built this beautiful mess of a church. And though anything but perfect and tidy, it still held God's hope for the world. And his church, functioning as the re-presentation—that is, an all-new presenting again—of Christ's own Body in the world, prevailed, and changed the whole Roman Empire. And he can do it again today through his local church in our world.

The Death Bells Toll

After studying trends of church attendance in America, pollster George Barna warns of the waning influence of the church on emerging generations, calling for radical change before a postmortem is declared:

> Our goal cannot simply be a timid, powerless survival; it must be the role that Christ called the Church to play, that of a loving, authoritative, healing, and compelling influence upon the world . . . lacking such a turn-about, we may rightfully anticipate the virtual disappearance of the Christian Church in this nation.[2]

Statistically, this has already happened in England and Europe, a continent further down the post-Christian turnpike than North America. Church attendance in England averages about 7% of the population, and Europe as a whole runs a close race.[3] In effect, the Christian Church in Europe has gone the way of the dinosaur, and the North American Church tracks close behind. Barna and others note that the current generation is actually the first generation in American history in which a majority of those seeking faith begin their spiritual journey with a faith group other than Christianity.[4]

Emerging cities of America have much in common with Corinth: wealth, education, leisure, sports and entertainment 24/7, the most religiously diverse population in the world, trumpeting the value of tolerance as the highest virtue, sexually unrestrained like never before, seeking pleasure and personal satisfaction as the prime directive, rejecting absolute truth absolutely!

But much like the church in the pagan, pluralistic, promiscuous city of Corinth, the twenty-first-century church will be messy if it's to be effective. The emerging generations represent the first post-Christian culture in America. Unlike the generations before them, they have no predisposition for Christian faith. Not only do they lack an accurate understanding, but many have a distorted view of Christianity from what they've seen.

What I like to call the "Postmodern Experiment," which we will explore in depth in the next chapter, began in the sixties in America and had a much broader effect than merely the relativistic way people think about truth.

The pragmatic effect of this experiment has been widely missed in the debate about ministry in a postmodern world. But this experiment has undoubtedly spawned a generation of wounded, broken, spiritually hungry people. These people seek spirituality with an openness not seen in decades, and yet the church has completely gone off their radar. As in Corinth, Christianity at best is one among many equally good religious options on the menu.

Leighton Ford indicates that North America now holds the distinguished honor of being the third largest mission field in the English-speaking world.[5] And the United States has more secular, unchurched people than most nations of the world,[6] yet many churches don't seem to operate in light of this fact.

Paul was a visionary church-starting entrepreneur, who sacrificed dearly to dive into the mess of a culture foreign to him. Those of us currently leading in churches need to prayerfully consider this: Are we raising up a generation of leaders ready to lay down their comfortable lives to dive into the muck of cultural America? Or are we just playing church—developing spiritual dependents who consume the goods off whichever church shelf will "feed me," or "puff me up with more knowledge," or even "feel postmodern"?

No longer can we afford to stand on the cliffs high above the cultural mudslide, chastising people for not climbing out of the mess to come up to higher ground. No longer can we feel content throwing our heroic lifelines of propositions intended to save. No longer can we idly sit by, bemoaning change and wishing to turn the clock back to nostalgic days gone by.

No, it is time for Christian leaders, tethered to the lifeline of God's Spirit and a community of faith, to gather up courage and plunge into the swirling mess of the cultural flow. Just as Paul said he did in Corinth, we too must "try to find common ground with everyone so that [we] might bring them to

Christ."[7] We must emulate the God who dove right into the sewer of life himself in the body of Jesus. And we must reawaken his dream—God's dream of swimming this rescue mission on earth through a new Body—the Body of his Church—Christ's Body re-presented.[8]

This great mystery of God, re-presenting himself in the world through those who truly trust in him, must come alive through us. This must be the first priority for leadership of the church in a post-Christian world: making the invisible Body visible.

Seeing Jesus

Brad showed up late that night. He confessed to the group what we already knew. I was amazed that he would be willing to admit using crack again, but even though he was not yet a Christian, he knew we cared about him. He sensed the mysterious hand of God's Spirit reaching out to him through this Body of new believers, and he knew he needed help.

Lana had opened up her heart to Christ during the past year. Now it was Brad's turn. That night this unlikely small group, now morphing into Christ's Body in the world, wrapped his arms around Brad with love and truth—at times confronting, as only those who have been through addiction can—at times encouraging, as wounded healers who have seen God's overcoming power. Brad prayed and asked for God's forgiveness. With his group surrounding him, touching him, praying for him . . . Brad told God, "I want what Jesus did to count for me. I need your power to do your will. Help me overcome so I can be the husband and father you intended." That intervention began the long journey for Brad and Lana we have seen many take, off the path of the addict and onto the way of Christ.

As I drove home that night, thinking about the miraculous life-change God had accomplished in that entire group, tears of gratitude filled my eyes. How many times I would drive away from a night with my small group, thanking God that I get to see Jesus alive—seeking and saving those who are lost, proclaiming the time of God's favor among the poor, the oppressed, the broken, the spiritual misfits of his day and ours. And I must say, God has used those people in my life as much as he has used me in theirs—for I too am a spiritual misfit. Through my friends, God reminded me that no one is more or less worthy of his grace, we all need it. And we must all grow up together into the community of people he intended us to be.

My small group is not an aberration, not even an extreme example. When we launched Gateway Community Church in 1998, we used to joke about our "Corinthian core." From ten people, the church grew to a couple thousand in the first five years, and I would say the lives of the people you just met are pretty typical. We keep seeing God draw hundreds and hundreds to faith in Christ every year out of similarly messy, broken, spiritually eclectic backgrounds. My small group lives in your city all around you, and if you have not gotten to know them yet, maybe it's because you're not looking up at the fields before you. This state of the union calls for a new kind of Christian leader. Are you ready? Look up! The harvest is great but the workers are few![9]

But God Causes the Growth

If the thought of reaching our post-Christian culture scares you, take heart! God can use anyone, because it's not ultimately up to us—it's up to him. But we do have a responsibility. Paul reminds church leaders in his letter to the Corinthians:

> I planted the seed, Apollos watered it, but God has been making it grow. So neither the one who plants nor the one who waters is anything, but only God, who makes things grow. The one who plants and the one who waters have one purpose, and they will each be rewarded according to their own labor. For we are God's co-workers; you are God's field. (1 Corinthians 3:6–9 TNIV)

As Christians in a post-Christian society, our job is to become cultural farmers. Church leaders, ministry leaders, and small group leaders must come to trust the God who is already at work all around us, making things grow. Our responsibility is not to make people grow or change. Our task is to create the right soil, a rich healthy environment, in which people can grow up in faith until the invisible God is made visible through his Body, the church.[10]

But how do we create soil in which the invisible is made visible? This is the art of culture creation and the focus of this book. As we labor in the field with him, creating a healthy come-as-you-are culture, God will cause the growth. As wise cultural farmers, we must realize God has given us responsibilities as his fellow laborers to create healthy cultural soil.

Jesus often used agricultural metaphors to describe the kingdom of God. I believe he did this not just because they related well in an agrarian society but also because there are general principles of growth to which they refer.

All life requires the right soil for healthy growth. Clearly this is true of plant life. Though the farmer never causes the growth, if he neglects the soil and it becomes hardened, or lacks nutrients or water, no growth will occur. If he does not protect the seed from the birds, before the plant ever has a chance, his adversaries will destroy his work. Conversely, if the farmer does his part to create the right soil, growth happens!

Children, psychologists tell us, also need the right soil in which to grow. Research confirms that children in loving, secure, truth-speaking family environments tend to thrive. It is the family culture that most influences healthy growth toward maturity.

But have we considered the soil needed for a healthy Christian community in a hard-packed, post-Christian society? God is responsible for the growth, for changed hearts, but the soil is the responsibility of the leaders and Christ-followers who make up that church. Creating a come-as-you-are culture is the most important task leaders can undertake to engage a post-Christian society, and yet we often give culture creation little mental effort. In fact, because culture is largely unseen, we are mostly unaware of the cultural soil we have created in our churches, small groups, or ministries.

In discussing the effect of culture on organizations, business consultant James Alexander notes how "the culture becomes highly ingrained to the point of becoming invisible to the members of the organization. That is why it is so difficult for group members to talk about their culture, because it operates at a level below our normal consciousness."[11]

But this explains why several churches may be trying to reach the same group with the same methods, but one just "feels" completely different than the other. That intangible "feel" is the culture. The culture is what seekers pick up on immediately, though it may be imperceptible to regular members. But the culture makes all the difference in the world in a post-Christian society. This is why effective leadership must be synonymous with creating the right culture.

Yet all too often, leaders implement new "seeker" services or "post-modern" services with cool music, candles, art, aesthetics, or whatever the latest conference hypes up, but miss the most essential nutrients for healthy Body-growth.

When I was Executive Director of Ministries for Willow Creek Community Church, I would see leaders come to conferences and get excited about leading people to Christ. But they would tragically assume it was the music and drama or other visible elements they were lacking, and they would go home to start a drama team or "contemporary" service with a new band and less worship, assuming "if we build it, they will come." But many missed the all-important culture created specifically to effectively reach one particular culture of Suburban-Chicago Baby Boomers. Much of the criticism aimed at the "seeker church" for being entertainment-oriented derives from this common mistake.

One time a staff member at Willow walked into the auditorium during a conference to witness a team of visiting church leaders measuring the auditorium. Curious, he asked them what they were doing. They said, "We love what's happening here, so we're just going to copy every last detail of it." Unfortunately, I suspect we could make the same error with emerging generational trends. We may end up with cool-looking candlelit venues, hip sounding music, a mosaic of "postmodern" do-it-yourself art in the service, or some other fad, and yet not really engage or penetrate our postmodern, post-Christian society at all! It's not the visible but the invisible that needs attention. It's not candles but community, not art but attitude, not liturgy but love that makes the difference in our broken world.

Are you planting and watering, tilling and fertilizing the culture of your church, small group, or ministry? Do you see the fruit of God's Spirit as secular people find faith and grow in your particular region? What does a come-as-you-are culture need to look like in a post-Christian society? What does it need to look like in your unique region or city? These are the meta-questions we will seek to answer in the following chapters. And I believe pondering these questions of culture creation can be beneficial regardless of whom you are reaching.

Whether you are in an emerging church or a church for the Boomer or Builder generations, whether a point leader or small group leader, understanding how culture gets formed and reflecting on your current culture is an essential task of leadership. But let me give you an overview of the threads of culture creation that will weave throughout the chapters that follow.

Defining Culture

First, what exactly is culture? Culture could be defined as the glue that holds any organization together. In churches, it encompasses the normal practices and behaviors of people as they determine what, why, or how they act or interact. But it is also the sum of all behaviors, attitudes, and styles of the people, programs, and services.[12]

Culture creation forms the texture of relational life and community in a local church. The outcome of an effective come-as-you-are culture is an engaging community of faith that God uses to transform individuals, neighborhoods, cities, and societies. It happens when leaders effectively contextualize the message of Christ for the surrounding indigenous culture, and out of the surrounding culture the community of Christ grows.

But we must beware that community alone is not the answer. There are life-giving communities created, but there are also repressive, toxic communities that form in local churches, small groups, and ministries.

Leadership Mindset

Creating a come-as-you-are culture begins with the mind-set of the leadership of a church. The way leaders think about themselves and the church creates the core from which the culture grows. As the leaders interact with others, they model the culture much as parents model the creation of a family's culture.

What do you and the other leaders in your church currently model culturally?

This book will present a vision of the church in culture that may challenge how you've thought of yourself and the church. Or it could be you will discover the culture you thought you or others were creating is not the culture spiritual seekers actually experience. Maybe the greatest value of reading this book will turn out to be not a new strategy or methodology you can implement, but a mindset shift. Instead of new methodology, maybe your views and attitudes that most shape the culture will morph. In culture creation, what happens in the hearts and heads of leaders has the greatest impact. For that reason, this book is more experiential than pragmatic. You'll experience lives and stories intersecting God's story of his church, challenging you to examine your view of yourself and your leadership.

Public Vibe

The "vibe" of the public service or group meeting also serves to create culture. The look and feel, the quality factor, the style of music, the way people speak and dress and interact publicly are very important. These elements signal to others what you are like, what to expect, and how to act. This public aspect of culture must be contextualized more than any other aspect to the tastes of the unchurched around you if you want to reach them.

> *I went through a divorce two years ago and have just recently started to attend mass again, but I feel so much guilt and always feel like I just don't belong. So it was a very big step to walk into your church this past Sunday. I have to say I was very welcomed by everyone, and I loved the service and teaching. I just wanted to thank you and the staff for creating such a warm and loving environment for people to open up to even hear the message, knowing that whatever level they're coming in at is okay—they'll be loved for who they are! I know with any organization that attitude comes from the top and is duplicated by the whole organization, which can be good or bad, but yours is GREAT!*
>
> *—Gabrielle*

In the following chapters, you will get a taste of the worship services at Gateway, and you will catch a vision for the vibe that affects the mood of small group communities. But remember, the visible aspects of a church are only a small part of the overall culture.

Vision-Casting

One of the most overlooked aspects of culture is how the average person, seeker, or believer, captures a vision of how to live and function in the church community. This aspect of vision-casting for culture creation is the most neglected and yet most powerful influence on cultural formation.

What gets communicated over and over and over again? What stories get told? What real-life spiritual journeys are highlighted to reinforce what the church is about? What does the average person think about when they think about your church, what it stands for, and their role in it? As I tell our leaders, we can have the coolest music, the most compelling communication, the most edgy technology, but if seekers don't like the people, they won't keep coming back. Our people are our secret weapon.

But how do you lead people to create the right culture? We will explore this question of vision-casting and storytelling to create the right culture throughout this book.

Organization

And culture creation cannot be divorced from organization. If the church is an organism, the Body of Christ, it must function in a coordinated way.

How do we organize in a way that enhances and supports culture much like a skeleton supports a body? Organization that is too rigid does not allow the flexibility and agility the Body needs to fully express itself. On the other hand, no organizational backbone hinders the Body from forming and expressing itself in a growing diversity of unified parts.

Hopefully you will catch a picture of some of the organizational structures that can be used to support and sustain the Body of the church to live out its cultural mandate and mission.

Understanding Context

Though principles of culture creation translate across cultures, they must be contextualized to the surrounding society in which people live.* So let me tell you a little about the uniqueness of Austin and our church to help you better translate these principles into your context.

Gateway is unique to the context of Austin. At the time of writing this, 50% of the people at Gateway are single, while Austin itself is nearly 60%

---

* For an in-depth treatment of contextualization to the surrounding culture, I highly recommend "The Cultural Perspective" section in *Perspectives on the World Christian Movement*, edited by Ralph Winter and Steven Hawthorne.

single. The majority of people at Gateway were formerly unchurched, but past estimates indicate that Austin's population is over 85% unchurched. On our yearly survey, 60% indicated they were not active Christ-followers when they first came to Gateway, though most say they are now active Christ-followers. The racial diversity of Austin is approximately 30% non-white, while Gateway is around 20% diverse in this respect. Approximately 75% of those attending are under age forty, yet we are watching God's Spirit draw hundreds and hundreds to faith every year of all backgrounds—especially out of this most cynical, jaded cohort of emerging America.

Through the real-life stories of people who have come to faith through Gateway Community Church, you will experience how a come-as-you-are culture can loosen up the hard-packed hearts of emerging generations. But understanding the uniqueness of *your context* is essential for effective culture creation. We will discuss principles of contextualization that can help you determine the way to culturally farm your unique soil—whether in your church, ministry, or small group. And my intent is to inspire Christ-followers and church leaders to overcome fears of diving in and engaging our post-Christian culture whatever the context, and to believe again that God can and will work through his followers in his local church to bring hope and healing to the world around us.

I want to clarify up front, I am not claiming what has happened at Gateway is the only way to reach our postmodern world or that we have the church everyone should imitate. In our diverse world, many diverse methods and strategies must be employed to create the right soil for the right context.

Gateway's not a perfect church—far from it!

Just as there are no perfect people, there are no perfect churches. We definitely do not claim to have all the answers or even know all the questions, but we see God at work, powerfully forming his church out of this broken, lost generation.

So this is simply the story of God's amazing work in our generation, seeking and saving those who were lost, and using his church to do his work. And my prayer in writing this book is that God would use it to help many more find faith through the ministry of local churches, parachurch ministries, and small group communities.

But before we talk specifics of culture creation to form fertile soil, we must first understand the struggles that created the hard-packed soil of the current generation. People hear God's Word, but often the seed lands on hard ground.

So the job of the Christian leader is to first take into account the context creating hardheartedness toward God's Word and Christ's church. What are the sociological struggles arising from the past forty years that keep people from finding faith through the local church? How do we live out and lead out Christian faith so that the soil of the local church becomes a place where people can grow despite these challenges? In the next chapter, we will explore these questions as we trace back to the source of the five greatest struggles our generation has with Christian faith and the church—struggles with Trust, Tolerance, Truth, Brokenness, and Aloneness.

STUDY GUIDE

Culture Check

1. How would people define the "feel" of your church after several experiences? Consider asking an unchurched neighbor to come two or three Sundays and give you raw, honest feedback about what he or she perceives people at your church value and what the experience was like for him or her.
2. Write down what you think your church values in reality. What do you desire it to value?
3. Write down *Leader Mindset, Public Vibe, Vision-Casting,* and *Organization.* As you read the remaining chapters, beside each word, make note of ideas to help create the kind of culture you desire.

Small Group Questions

1. How would we define the "feel" and "experience" of our group? (Is it safe? Like family? Educational? Reverent? Challenging?) Ask your group to write down anonymously on note cards the words that define how the group currently "feels." Have one person collect and read all the cards out loud, then discuss why this culture exists.
2. Now write down on another note card the words that describe the perfect "environment" you all hope to create for one another. Have someone read the words, then discuss why you want that environment and ways to help create that environment.
3. Read 1 Corinthians 9:20–23. What do you think Paul meant by "becoming all things"? How is the culture around us similar to or different than the culture of Corinth? What are some ways we can "be all things" to the surrounding culture without compromising following Christ?

Cynical and Jaded: Results of the Post- modern Experiment

All the diagnostic experts keep pointing backward to the era of . . .
the '60s and '70s as the fatal hour when everything started going to hell.

Howe and Strauss, *13ᵗʰ Gen*

The Egghead's your typical college-town breakfast dive, situated in the middle of Isla Vista, a beach community of students who attend the University of California Santa Barbara.

It was 1991, and I was enjoying the Egghead special, the Breakfast Slammer, as Chris and I talked about Christian faith. As a campus pastor, I often had conversations with spiritual seekers. I don't even remember how we met or got into the conversation that day, but that conversation marked the continental divide in my approach to engendering faith in my generation.

After listening to Chris discuss some of his views on reality and the relativity of perception, I gave him a well-rehearsed four-point outline of the message of Christian faith. He asked some questions, and I used my best arguments in response. He agreed with all of my philosophical, logical reasoning.

Misreading his affirmative head-nods as evidence he might be close to a decision of faith, I asked Chris if there was anything that would keep him from accepting this gift offered in Christ. His reply confounded me.

He said, "I can totally see why that makes sense for you, but it's just not for me."

That response didn't compute with me. "But it is for you," I insisted. "If it makes sense and is true, then why not believe?"

"I can see why it's true for you, but it's not true for me," Chris rebutted.

"But Chris, you just said it all makes sense, and you can see why I believe in Christ—so why wouldn't you want to believe too?" I pushed for clarity.

His reply haunted me for years: "You know, I guess I just don't want to be like you."

Ouch!

I didn't have a good, back-pocket reply for that one. That conversation marked a turning point in my thinking. I don't know if it was simply my breaking point after beating my head against the wall in years of similar conversations, or if it was a divine epiphany, but in that moment I began to sense a shift. A cultural quake was about to alter the landscape of ministry permanently.

It was not so much that Chris didn't like me; after all, he didn't really know me. What he didn't like was what I represented. He didn't like Christians, or should I say, the stereotype of what Christians are like. I'm afraid Chris's sentiments extend more broadly than most Christians care to realize. I've since discovered that the average person has a strong perception of what Christians are against, but little of what Christians are for. I was simply confirming his negative stereotype of a narrow, intolerant, arrogant person who just wanted everyone "to be like me." In our postmodern world, you can't separate the message from the messenger. I think Chris was really saying, "Arguments don't convince me. Show me a faith that's attractive, and I'll consider it. Otherwise, I'm not interested, no matter how 'true' you say it is." Truth had gone relational.

That encounter began a quest and ongoing prayer for understanding of how to reach this generation. As I moved from the West Coast to the Midwest to the Southwest over the following decade, I observed this same shift occur across the country. A confluence of American and global trends has shaped and molded the culture of emerging generations, and we must understand this culture if we are to communicate with them.

In every region and location in the world, there are unique cultures created by the sociological, political, religious, and historical paradigms in which people grow up. If the church is to have an impact on society, the first task for leaders is to understand the broader cultural context. When you study the church within the context of a culture, anthropology and missiology have both demonstrated that the most effective efforts do not try to change the culture but rather contextualize the message of Christ for each unique culture.

My wife and I moved to St. Petersburg, Russia, in 1991, following the overthrow of a seventy-year regime of atheistic communism. After a year of ministry, about one hundred students had come to faith and were connected into smaller growth groups. The students were incredibly open and vulnerable with our American team, but when we turned leadership of the groups over to Russians in preparation for our leaving, the dynamics of the groups changed. Suddenly, we found the students shutting down, talking negatively about each other, and undermining the new Russian apprentice leaders. What we had not taken into account was seventy years of informing on each other. Russians could never trust their own neighbors—for they might be underground communist informants. Until we helped these new Christians overcome this cultural barrier to Christian community, none of our efforts would survive.

In every culture, a leader must consider the factors that have shaped the people he or she seeks to communicate with and reach: What language do they speak? How do they hear this message? What issues are highly sensitive and why? What has happened in the past that put up barriers to belief? What metaphors or symbols communicate in positive or negative ways? What styles of communication or stories or art forms or songs best connect with both the head and the heart? What factors shaped who they are today? And most importantly, the question for every culture: How do we best contextualize the unchanging truths of Scripture in ways they can understand and live out *in their culture*? Answers to these questions are critical for creating a come-as-you-are culture at any time, for every generation, in every place.

These were the questions the early church wrestled with at the Jerusalem counsel in Acts 15. What elements of Jewish custom needed to be stripped from the message of faith for a Gentile culture? Their decision was based on an understanding of the cross-cultural message of faith and the unique Gentile/Hebrew mix of the receiving culture.

Do you understand the unique factors of the broader culture you live within? Are you willing to adjust your customs to be true to the message of God's grace for emerging cultures? To do this, we must not only understand how to draw out the timeless truths of Scripture, we must understand the times.

The Postmodern Experiment

Many books have been written about postmodernity, usually with an emphasis on a relativistic way of thinking about truth and morality. But the broader Postmodern Experiment has most shaped emerging generations. What I define as the Postmodern Experiment began with a generation deciding to test what life would be like living out the philosophy, "If it feels good, do it." This experiment encompassed the sum total of behaviors produced by this way of thinking, and society is just now getting the results. Postmodern thought formed the epicenter of a cultural quake that has rippled out since the sixties in a pervasive way that extends far beyond a mental construct of truth or morality. Its influence has rattled the very identity of a generation and continues to affect successive generations in a multitude of ways. Until we understand its effects, we cannot effectively reach those shaped by it.

From the 1960s to the 1980s in America, radical cultural shifts took place to an earth-shattering magnitude, and global communication exported it worldwide. According to generational experts Howe and Strauss, "All the diagnostic experts keep pointing backward to the era of . . . the '60s and '70s as the fatal hour when everything started going to hell."[1]

As I have interacted with people in counseling situations, most born post-1960, I find myself asking, "What happened to this generation to produce so much chaos?" I hear story after story of neglect, physical abuse, sexual molestation, drug abuse, porn addictions, eating disorders, anger issues, serious crime, abortion, STDs, AIDS, and sexual addictions passing from one generation to the next. Issues once prevalent only in inner-city churches now live on Main Street.

After studying the confluence of shifts and trends, I'm convinced something radical did happen. Americans went out for a three-decade binge on self, and now our country is vomiting up the consequences uncontrollably.

Since the sixties, several cultural seismic waves have rolled through our society, leaving behind an unexpected aftershock for the Christian church. Similar trends can be seen in Europe, Australia, Japan, and other Western countries during this period.[2] The acceleration of life in the last half of the twentieth century produced a Community Aftershock. Air travel, technology, and the globalization of business have increased the speed of life and uprooted the concept of the stable community.

We've also experienced Information Aftershock. Television became a standard fixture of Western civilization beginning in the 1960s, and with it the possibility to acculturate and educate shared values into an entire global generation while entertaining them. Soon after that, the next information wave, the Internet, rolled through, creating a global marketplace of ideas, changing the way we interact with other cultures, differing religious views, and our own beliefs.

And a Generational Aftershock, caused by the shift from an outward building of institutions (with the WWII generation) to an inward building of self (with the Boomer generation), changed the landscape in the family system, in the marketplace, and in our national collective conscience.[3] In 1966, the cover of *Time* magazine shockingly asked, "Is God Dead?" reverberating Nietzsche's foreshadowing of the Postmodern Experiment. A world in which God is dead leads to a casting off of all moral restraints. What evolved from these generational changes can be seen in retrospect as the social self-absorption of this inner-directed era at the expense of future generations and the national collective life. Consider the generational changes Howe and Strauss describe.

> In the 1940s, the very thought of making babies propelled young soldiers and Rosie-the-Riveters to victory over fascism; in the 1950s, baby-making was just standard suburban behavior; by the 1960s, the very thought drove young couples to doctors to prevent it [for fear that babies would cramp their style]. A child's world was unerringly sunny in the '50s, overshadowed by adult arguments in the '60s, scarred by family chaos in the '70s. In the '50s, nearly every movie or TV show was fit for kids to watch; come the '60s, it was touch and go; come the '70s, forget it. The quality of new teacher recruits remained high through the '50s, became suspect in the draft-pressured '60s, and sank (along with teacher pay) in the '70s. Adolescent sexual discovery meant free love in 1970, herpes in 1980, AIDS in 1990.[4]

It was the dawning of the Age of Aquarius, the age of "if it feels good, do it," the age of the "Me Generation," the birth of the Postmodern Experiment. Analysis of all the potential reasons for the cultural shift that has taken place is beyond the scope of this book, but pragmatically, I see five main sociological struggles Christian leaders now face to reach emerging generations: struggles with Trust, Tolerance, Truth, Brokenness, and Aloneness.

Trust

Sonja flinched at the sound of footsteps in the hallway. Dread shot through her veins like morphine, numbing her mind in preparation for another night of horror. The door creaked open. Sonja's mind raced through a time warp, wondering about a world of innocence lost years ago. The same door that had first opened when she was only a child, ten years old, opened the door to pain instead of pleasure, confusion rather than fatherly comfort, the dark nightmare of sexual abuse from the man intended to bring the light of safety into his little girl's nighttime fears.

Now as a teenager, the realization that this was not normal had been crashing into her adolescent mind, producing sharp edges of bitter anger and rebellion. She loved her father and hated him bitterly. She longed for security but now realized he wasn't safe. There was no refuge—no trust-worthy confidant. Not in a family so unstable.

Sonja's mind raced back in a split second across the years of broken trust. Years of sexual abuse, of trying to tell her mom, hearing the yelling it caused, then the anger from her father . . . and in the end, more of the same. She couldn't trust her mother. Snapshots of broken trust flipped through her mind—of mom's half-truths and cover-ups—a family in constant flux, all for the sake of a little better job. And how could she trust parents who treated her like the proverbial unwanted elephant in the room—hugely in the way, largely ignored?

For so many years, she had yearned for security. For someone she could trust. For arms that would hold her to protect her rather than hold her to use her. But they never could be found. Surely not in her dad or mom, not in the boyfriends she had known. Even the oldest, most mature boyfriend turned out to only want to take more of the same. And God . . . the times she had gone to church, she longed for there to truly be a God in heaven who could save her—who could rescue her from the world she knew—but where was he? Stuck somewhere in the stained-glass window looming over the monotony of the Mass? She could trust no one.

As the door opened and her father crept into the room, in a flash she decided, "I'm done with this. If I can't trust in anyone else, I'll trust in myself." It would be her last nightmare . . . at least her last nightmare at home.

Several years after coming to Christ, Sonja still fights against fears of trusting and finds it hard to bond with others. Trust is the cornerstone of relationship and faith. Without it, we cannot engage others or God in inti-mate relationship. Trust comes from a deep conviction that I matter, that I can trust the other person because he has genuine concern for my well-being. The ability to trust often gets established or destroyed early in child-hood. Trust often eludes a large number of Americans who had to be weaned from trusting Mom and Dad at a young age. The impact of this on their abil-ity to trust others, trust religious leaders, and even to trust God severely ham-pers their lives and faith. What trends shattered an eagerness to trust for many in our current culture?

Me-First Mistrust

Many learned early that parents' things are always more important. In the book, *Ourselves and Our Children* (note the title's word order), Silent Gen-eration (pre-Boomer) authors insisted that "consider yourself" be the first principle of good parenting. "By the mid-1970s, bookstores were loaded with popular books (also mostly by Silent authors) warning against the marital resentment, financial distress, and physical discomfort that supposedly resulted from the bearing and raising of children."[5] Nineteen seventy-five marked a record low birthrate since World War II. Welcome the unwanted generation—the Baby-Busters.

Marital Mistrust

Many kids grew up learning their mom's and dad's "love needs" come first. The Sexual Revolution of the sixties proclaimed freedom of sexual expression through *Playboy* magazine, *Love American Style* TV, and Marvin Gaye humming "Let's Get It On." Beginning in 1962 with the mass marketing of the birth-control pill, the media everywhere hailed the age of "free love." The Postmodern Experiment with sexuality turned out to have a high price tag. Successive generations are paying the bill in record levels of sexual abuse, STDs, AIDS, and the highest divorce rates ever seen.

This era of sexual freedom began to give way to increasing rates of adultery and a national epidemic of failed families and disappearing dads. Consider the impact on emerging generations' trust levels:

- From 1962 to 1981, the number of divorces tripled![6]
- In 1962, 50% of adults believed that parents in tough marriages should stay together and work on it for the sake of the kids. By 1980, less than 20% felt that way.[7]
- A child born in 1968 faced three times the risk of parental break-up than a Boomer child born in 1948 faced.[8]
- Less than 50% of the emerging generation reached age seventeen with both biological parents living with them in the same house.[9]
- A 1987 national survey showed that more than 50% of all children of divorce had seen their fathers three times or less in the previous year.[10]

The pain felt from the ripping apart of families can be heard in the lyrics of an Everclear song,

> *father of mine*
> *tell me where have you been?*
> *you know I just closed my eyes*
> *my whole world disappeared . . .*
>
> *i will never be safe*
> *i will never be sane*
> *i will always be weird inside*
> *i will always be lame . . .*
>
> *daddy gave me a name*
> *then he walked away.*[11]

And for millions of kids, the family's fine china of trust shattered, as parental "free love" took priority.

Latchkey Mistrust

Through the 1970s the term *latchkey kid* was coined as the number of children under age fourteen left alone after school roughly doubled.[12] With an increasing rate of divorce and disappearing dads, many moms were forced back into the workplace. At the same time, society as a whole shifted values as sociologists Howe and Strauss note: "As millions of mothers flocked into the work force, the proportion of preschoolers cared for in their own homes fell by half. For the first time, adults ranked autos ahead of children as necessary for 'the good life.'"[13] The idealism of the '60s and '70s morphed right into the "Material World" of the coming '80s "Me Generation." Instead of coming home to milk and cookies, more and more kids were coming home to an empty house and MTV. The underlying message resulted in a subtle distrust of authority figures whose careers and lifestyles often came before kids.

Abusive Mistrust

Kids learned they were not really worth protecting. As a permissive parenting style took root, parent-child relationships became more "egalitarian" than "authoritarian." Author Benita Eisler called them relationships of "uneasy equality." And parents looked more and more to their kids as sources of help and solace, forcing kids to grow up into adults too soon or inadvertently using kids for emotional comfort in the wake of divorce trauma. The net effect— adults became more childlike as children became more adultlike.

Judy Blume, an author popular during these years, unabashedly declared what seemed a pervasive sentiment of the day, "I hate the idea that you should always protect children. They live in the same world we do."[14] Maybe proof of how widespread this societal sentiment became comes from the rash of Evil Child movies that came out during the '60s and '70s. Never before had children, once associated with innocence, been depicted as so evil, yet this new genre of bad-baby-horror-films attracted blockbuster crowds every year for over a decade (see table 2.1).

After 1970, social statistics showed a negative shift in public attitudes toward (and treatment of) children. A new topic suddenly filled the pages of academic journals: family violence. During this era, the homicide rate for infants and children under four rose by 50%, the number of reported cases of child abuse jumped fourfold, the number of kids home alone after school doubled.[15] Statistics for that time seem to point to a subtle yet undeniable society-wide negativity, and even hostility, toward children.

In my experience, adults affected by these trends will not necessarily connect them with their struggles to trust today. Just as children of adult alcoholics never knew their always-drunk father had a problem, in the same way, what we grow up with becomes "normal" for us. The resulting wounds of distrust fester, however, and they affect our ability to trust others and God. Read this email sent to me from a woman in our church that illustrates the issue so well:

> My parents got divorced when I was ten years old due to extramarital affairs my mother had throughout their marriage. Although I don't remember them all, the last one that caused my dad to leave is something I have carried with me for a long time. I've gone to therapists and been put on antidepressants and none of those things helped me. My worries are not just the fact that my mother chose herself over my sister, my father, and me. What I carry with me is that she included my sister and me in the act. She would use us as a reason to get out of the house without any questions from my dad. Since my sister was so young, she made me in charge of making sure [my sister] didn't say anything to my dad. She told me to be extra careful because if my father found out, he would make my mom, my sister, and me leave without any clothes or toys. Needless to say, I was a very scared and stressed out ten-year-old who was sort of forced into an adult world when I wasn't ready. . . . I have been attending Gateway for six months, and I have felt this enormous change in my life since I've started. I was turned off by church and Christianity because of my mother and her never-ending biblical quotes and prayer-chain gossip about friends and family. Gateway has totally changed my mind about all that stuff as I am now seeing it in a completely honest and sincere manner.
>
> — Adrian

Table 2.1
Evil Child Movies

1964 *Children of the Damned*
1968 *Rosemary's Baby*
1973 *The Exorcist*
1974 *It's Alive!*
1976 *Look What's Happened to Rosemary's Baby*
1976 *The Omen*
1976 *Carrie*
1977 *Exorcist II: The Heretic*
1978 *It Lives Again*
1978 *Damien—Omen II*
1978 *Halloween*
1980 *The Children*
1981 *The Final Conflict*
1981 *Halloween II*
1984 *Firestarter*
1984 *Children of the Corn*

[Reproduced with permission, Howe and Strauss, *13th Gen*, 66.]

When you create a culture to deal with these painful issues of trust openly, with sincerity and honesty, you begin to see two things. First, you will hear more and more stories of wounds like this that once remained hidden and festering. But you will also hear increasing numbers of stories of God's healing work as people are brought into the light.

Tolerance

"Hey Sarah, your kids any better?" I shouted, as I rode my mountain bike past my neighbor unloading her three-year-old from her car.

"Mike's better, but Jake's still got a fever—thanks for asking," Sarah shouted back. Then she surprised me. "Hey, what times are your church services?"

I U-turned and pulled into her driveway to keep from yelling.

Sarah, a twenty-something mother of three, had only been married once. Her husband was the father of only one of the children (there were two other dads in the picture before she married Tom). Both Sarah and Tom were extremely warm, welcoming people who lived one street over from us. Their loving nature showed in the way they treated their kids—not to mention how they let Sarah's sister live with them as she struggled to get back on her feet from a crack addiction. Tom worked two jobs, as a software analyst and waiter, to afford their modest three-bedroom suburban life. Kathy and I had built a relationship with Sarah and Tom and invited them to church several times, but this was the first sign of interest in a year.

"We have two services, nine o'clock and ten thirty," I said as nonchalantly as possible.

"We're thinking about coming, but can I ask you a question that might offend you?" she hesitantly inquired.

"Sure! Don't worry, you're not going to offend me." I tried to make myself vulnerable while praying for wisdom for whatever arrow was pointed my way.

"Well . . ." She hesitated. "Are you a loving church? I mean, do you teach people to love others?"

I laughed, feeling some relief and trying to ease her tension, "Of course—that's the central point of the message of Jesus, 'love God and love others.'"

"Well . . . but how do you feel about gays?" she finally spit it out.

Not knowing why this was so important, I decided to try to both ease her mind and understand more, "We feel they are people that matter to God. Is that something you have dealt with personally, or do you have close friends who are gay?"

"No," she replied, "I just need to know you're not one of those hateful churches. I just couldn't go to a church that teaches people to hate others."

To understand how serious this issue of tolerance is for emerging generations, you have to consider Sarah's underlying concern, reflected in many people I meet. During the first two years of Gateway's existence, I consistently was asked two questions by spiritual seekers more than any other questions: "What do you think of other religions?" and "How do you feel about gay people?" I've discovered the real question they are asking is: "Are you one of the narrow-minded, bigoted, hate-filled, intolerant types of Christians I've heard about?" What they really want to know is whether we promote love or hatred. The connection may not seem obvious, but it is critical to understand if you want to communicate effectively.

In a generation raised on so much divorce and disagreement, they long for unity. They want to know, "Can't we just get along?" They want something to unify and bring us together. They're tired of being torn apart and divided. This part of the tolerance equation is good, as truly only the God of love can be so tolerant and willing to forgive the most heinous of sins humankind can commit. And leaders must learn how to communicate just how tolerant and loving God is (which we will always fall short of adequately representing) while not compromising God's righteousness or holiness.

Why is tolerance so important? Remember, we are talking about a media-suckled generation. They have been inundated with news not only of religious scandal and priestly sexual abuse but also with a slew of press reports painting Christians as judgmental extremists banning books, burning down abortion clinics, and carrying "God hates fags" banners. At the same time, this generation was receiving some of the strictest tolerance training through the media and schools. TV consistently presented Christians as narrow-minded, uneducated, judgmental people.

In one episode of *The Simpsons*, Homer sees his born-again neighbor, Maude Flanders, over the fence and greets her warmly, "Hey, I haven't seen you in a couple of weeks. Where have you been?"

"Oh," Maude cheerfully replies, "I've been away at a Bible camp, learning to be more judgmental."

In schools and universities, tolerance education became a mainstay for many programs. Outcome Based Education programs emphasized not just academic performance but specific values, such as tolerance, as outcomes to be demonstrated before graduating to the next schooling level.[16] This tolerance education has formed associations in the post-Christian mind.

Students grow up learning about cultural, racial, ethnic, religious, and sexual diversity. They are often taught that intolerance caused the great wars and hate crimes of the century. Bosnia, Rwanda, the Middle East, Nazi Germany, and Northern Ireland provide examples of the conflicts created by intolerance—often religious intolerance. In reality, these are examples of intolerance Christians should abhor as well.

But Christian leaders must also understand the stereotype we fight against. When our arguments for what is true or right are heard outside of the context of experiencing the love of God mediated through his Body, the church, we are seen in the same light as those who were responsible for so many of the horrific atrocities of our century. It may not seem fair or right, but this is often reality.

And the issue of tolerance will not be going away soon. Nor should it, in most cases. The United Nations now promotes November 16 as International Day of Tolerance to teach all countries to be more tolerant. This will be an increasingly global issue we must learn to navigate as we communicate the message of Christ. The way we must navigate these cultural shallows comes from understanding that in a postmodern culture, the messenger is the message. How we are perceived is every bit as important as the truths we espouse. What they see is what they get. The attitude of the church culture will either convey the person of Christ and his attitude, which was outrageously accepting of and attractive to the "sinners" of his day, or our attitudes toward others will reinforce a stereotype that does a disservice to Jesus. Christ-followers must remember that people are never our enemy, and if we can stand alongside people in the things Jesus stands for (like human rights), we can best undermine the schemes of the real enemy who uses lies to paint Good as Evil and Evil as Good.

We can demonstrate to people how incredibly tolerant God is to not immediately punish all our sins and wrongs. In his love and mercy he willingly overlooks how different we are from him because of the cross of Christ. And we must acknowledge God's tolerance toward our own moral failures as leaders. As the Scriptures ask, "Do you show contempt for the riches of his kindness, *tolerance* and patience, not realizing that God's kindness leads you towards repentance?"[17] And from Jesus' example, as we will see in coming chapters, we can learn to navigate speaking truth in love in a tolerant-obsessive culture.

Truth

I believe that people are truly incapable of objectively seeing truth. Our perceptions are hopelessly tainted by our backgrounds and cultural biases. This postmodern belief is not the cause of people falling away from God. While some people who profess postmodern beliefs have leapt to the false conclusions that our inability to accurately perceive "absolute truth" means that either truth does not exist or if it does, it is irrelevant, this is not a necessary conclusion. In other words, postmodernism is not the cause of our deception, but rather an explanation for how we can be deceived while maintaining the conviction that we are right . . . then again, as a postmodernist, I have to acknowledge I could be wrong about all this ☺   — Josh

As Josh reveals in his email to me, the central watershed issue of postmodern thought divides over truth. Truth has gone relative! Though truth is the central issue of postmodernity, pragmatically, I find it is not the central challenge of everyday ministry. The greater challenges come from the deep emotional impact of living within the Postmodern Experiment (especially struggles with brokenness). Nevertheless, this view of truth still presents a formidable challenge for a faith whose Messiah proclaims, "I am the way, the *truth*, and the life."

I find that most people do not have deeply thought-out convictions like Josh does about truth being relative; it's just an unchallenged given for most. So to talk about truth is not repulsive to them until you appear exclusive or arrogant.

But we must understand their assumed position. The lyrics of songs from the past decade spout forth postmodern doctrine. Jane's Addiction sang, "Ain't no wrong now, ain't no right. Only pleasure and pain."[18] More recently, a popular Travis song proclaimed, "There is no wrong, there is no right, the circle only has one side."[19] What started as an ivory tower academic philosophy of linguistics and epistemology (how we know what we know) has now become a staple in the diet of pop culture. A national survey taken by Barna Research revealed that only one-third of Americans believe moral truth is absolute and unchanging.[20]

After technology and scientific progress not only gave us the telephone, TV, and automobile, but also the Great Depression, World War II, and the threat of nuclear holocaust, academics began reassessing the metanarrative myth of human progress. Einstein's theory of relativity and the Heisenberg Uncertainty Principle illustrated to scientists that when we "objectively" observe, we only observe from a relative position. That even in science, things are not as certain as we once hoped because the observer affects and alters what she's observing.

Postmodern academic philosophers, reflecting on the works of linguists such as Bertrand Russell, began proposing that there is no "truth" fixed by outside reality. That everything people hold as "true" comes from social conditioning. That people really are a product of their culture and only imagine they are self-willed individuals who make up their own minds. So postmodern thought claims there is no "outside objectivity" to any claim of truth, it is relative to your dominant culture. Reason cannot be trusted any more than intuition or feeling. And though most people could not spout off | 41 postmodern doctrine, it has seeped into our culture. Pragmatically, competing worldviews bombard our generation, and people have no clear path to guide them in deciding what's true.

I walked into a music store to buy guitar strings. A twenty-something guy with shoulder-length hair and a pierced eyebrow helped me check out. After revealing that he'd visited Gateway for several months, we had a deep spiritual dialogue about Jesus. He later sent me this email:

> Well, oddly enough, I prayed for GOD to reveal himself to me the night before you showed up. I came about this decision [to start praying] after speaking to some people at my AA club about wanting to define my conception of GOD . . . I guess I just don't like to trust what people are telling me. It gets confusing, actually. You know, one person tells me to believe in Jesus and offers a convincing argument. Another tells me of Buddhism and offers an even more convincing argument. Still another tells me of Judaism. I feel like a spiritual pinball. —Scott

I find our generation incredibly open to spiritual truth and dialogue, but they have grown up in a world of competing beliefs. People just check out when they feel that Christians are arrogant and unwilling to consider the "truth" claims of others as well. But they are very open to hearing expressions of truth and stories illustrating why God's words are true. They long to experience something firm and solid that "feels" true. They don't resist truth; they resist arrogance. But there is a humble way to express truth, as we will see in a later chapter.

Since neither modern nor postmodern culture holds a lock on truth, this cultural transition offers an opportunity for Christ-followers to assess what the Scriptures really teach about truth. Fundamentally, truth is not primarily propositional, but personal. Jesus said, "I am the truth. . . ." The best way to help emerging generations find truth is to introduce them to him.

Generally, emerging generations do not ask, "What is true?" They are primarily asking, "Do I want to be like you?" In other words, they see truth as relational. "If I want to be like you, then I want to consider what you believe. If I don't see anything real or attractive in you or your friends as Christ-followers, I don't care how 'true' you think it is, I'm not interested."

Personally I have found that much of postmodern thought presents a potentially greater opportunity than threat for the church. Why? First, because postmodern thought has made spiritual pursuit culturally acceptable. This provides an opportunity not seen in past decades to nurture the souls of a spiritually hungry generation. They do not fear the mystery of

God; they embrace mystery. They long to experience the deeper realities of a spiritually fulfilling existence.

Second, we can return to the Lord's plan for presenting truth. How can postmodern people best experience Christ, the Truth, re-presented in the flesh? Through his Body! The church is the Body of Christ according to the Scriptures. I believe the church has lost its sense of true identity and mystery under the scrutiny of modern pragmatism. But as you will see throughout the stories to follow, Christ really does convey his truth to spiritual seekers as they encounter and experience truth in us. People experience truth, not just in words, but with hands and feet when his church, "joined and held together by every supporting ligament, grows and builds itself up in love, as each part does its work."[21] This really is the goal of culture creation, to re-present the Body of Christ in the world.

Brokenness

Colleen had always craved the attention of men. She could never get enough. Early on in life, she learned of the pain of having a man leave her, as she watched her father walk out one day, never to return. As an adolescent, she learned how to use her body to get men to stay interested. Finally the payoff came, she met the man of her dreams, and they were married.

Unfortunately, the man of her dreams could not fulfill the deep need for affection and attention that welled up inside her broken soul. Before she knew it, her old tactics of luring, hooking, and reeling in men were operational again. She found a man at work noticing her more and more, and the attention seemed to temporarily meet that craving. One thing led to another, led to another, led to adultery, and the eventual destruction of her dream marriage.

Broken over what she had done, she agreed to come to Gateway with a friend. About eight months later, Colleen opened her heart to Christ. She had been attending a small group, but now she began serving the elderly and the homeless. She found a spiritual growth group with three other women who studied through the Bible, vowed to be totally honest about struggles with each other, and prayed for each other regularly as they journeyed on the way of Christ.

After two years of growth and spiritual fruit, Colleen became an apprentice leader of a small group. She was meeting with the leader for discipleship and training, when out of nowhere, Colleen disappeared! One day, she went off the radar completely. We found out she had moved to another city and moved in with her fiancé. Her growth group had been confronting her about their fast-moving new relationship and his lack of spiritual desire, but Colleen still had a hole in her heart she was determined to fill.

Nothing has been more difficult for me than watching people react in destructive ways to brokenness. Nothing poses a greater challenge and opportunity to the church than the overwhelming emotional pains that drive our generation into so many addictive behaviors. If Christian leaders do not prepare and organize and pray so that healing can occur from the wounds caused by the Postmodern Experiment, we will lose a generation. Trust issues may make them cynical, tolerance issues may make them unwilling to listen, truth issues may confuse them, but acting out of brokenness will destroy them.

Juan was a crack addict who started coming to Gateway, went through a month of in-patient treatment we recommended, and was 130 days clean. Last month he disappeared. Last night, I got a phone call from Del Valle Jail. He had been on a binge, accused of stealing a car in order to fund his addiction, and now he's going through forced recovery. On the phone last night, he asked me one question, "Am I still welcome at Gateway?" He told me he wants to fully surrender his life to Christ. But will Juan automatically be free of the stranglehold of addiction? How can our churches and groups prepare for these challenges?

These are not isolated cases. If God is going to use his church to reach emerging generations, the church must be prepared for these struggles of brokenness. There was nothing "free" about the Postmodern Experiment. It came with a huge balloon payment of broken lives for coming generations. Those who grew up starting in the early '60s set the all-time U.S. youth records for drunk driving, illicit drug consumption, and suicide. "They have been among the most violent, criminal, and heavily incarcerated youth cohorts in U.S. history."[22] If you are going to minister to emerging generations, you must create a culture where broken people are welcome and healing happens.

Broken people are wounded people. Like abused puppies, they often run from those attempting to help them. Leaders must create a safe climate, so the healing work of God can begin in their lives. It will take patience and time. People will come and go, walking toward the light of freedom, then plunging back into the darkness. But they must see the church as a lighthouse; always there to lead them into the safe harbor of God's grace.

Think about it this way, if you are reaching the average person under age forty, more than likely, one out of every three women you interact with will have had an abortion.[23] One or even two out of six women you talk to will have been sexually molested.[24] More than six out of ten people you speak with will think living together before marriage is the wisest way to prevent divorce, and five out of those ten will already have lived with someone.[25] Most will have been sexually active, and the thought of waiting until marriage will sound totally foreign and will need explaining. Most men will have struggled with pornography or serious problems with lust. One in five to ten people will struggle with substance abuse.[26] At least one in five and as high as two out of five people who come to your church will smoke.[27]

These are the people Christ came to seek and save. They are lawyers, construction workers, and doctors, blue collar and white collar, light skinned and dark skinned, from the "good" and "bad" sides of town. We've seen them all. Are they welcome in your church? Are they safe in your small group?

If the church is to be the hope of the world, its leaders must realize what a broken world we live in. We must be prepared to offer the hope and healing Christ offered to Zacchaeus the thieving tax collector, to the Samaritan woman who was shacking up with her sixth man, and to the woman caught in the very act of adultery. Can we lovingly accept them "as is" and offer love, hope, and healing as Jesus did to "go and sin no more"?

To do this, we must begin to see how we too are broken, and in need of a Savior. We must show others how our brokenness leads us to daily dependency on a merciful Savior who brings healing for our souls and hope for our futures.

Aloneness

A new Christian at Gateway writes:

> My entire family is still alive and still delivering me messages of my being a total stupid, weak, and useless loser. The concept of unconditional love is such a dream to me. I want it soooo much. I now believe God is the only one that really loves me unconditionally ... but I can't shed the feeling of confusion. I don't know if I'm smart or stupid, pretty or ugly, lovable or unlovable ... I used to love people. Now I'm so afraid of them. I told my small group that I was afraid of them and I am forcing myself to get involved, and they were cool about it. Although Gateway is a great place and a Godsend in my life, I am so afraid of everyone.   —Lin

The waves of change that have swept through this generation have created a culture of aloneness, of people longing for community, but afraid to get close—surrounded by friends, feeling ever more alone. In his book, *Bowling Alone*, Robert Putnam notes this trend: "For the first two-thirds of the twentieth century," he writes, "a powerful tide bore Americans into ever deeper engagement in the life of their communities." But over the last three decades, "Without at first noticing, we have been pulled apart from one another and from our communities."[28]

Think about it, half of all families break apart, often leaving children feeling abandoned and alone trying to sort out why Dad or Mom left. The other half live in a society fragmented and torn apart by the sheer velocity of twenty-first-century life. No wonder people feel so disconnected and alone. My family has lived on our street for five years now, and we've become friends with the people in the ten nearest houses to ours. In five years, nine families have moved out of those ten houses. While writing this chapter, the tenth put a "For Sale" sign in the yard! Think about your neighborhood, it probably is similar.

We live in a highly fragmented, relationally isolated society. People move, change jobs, get divorced, commute hours each day, travel around the country weekly, then spend all their free time surfing through 1700 cable channels and millions of Internet sites, and all at the cost of relationships. We have increased our financial capital, but it has cost us relational capital. Add to it the other societal trends of the past half-century, and you have a generation feeling painfully alone.

Before technology allowed us to fly, drive, and move so easily, people were far more likely to stay put in a local community. Parents, grandparents, siblings, neighborhood friends, parents of friends, store merchants you regularly interacted with all formed a community support network. Even if children and teens had horrible family lives, there was still the potential for the broader community net to catch them from relational free fall. But that net doesn't exist anymore.

This provides a tremendous opportunity for the church. According to Scripture, the church is to function like family. We are to be that supportive community, that extended family to one another. We have a tremendous opportunity to teach people how to live in healing, life-giving relationships with one another. No one else in society can better meet this need. I find it awe-inspiring to watch the Lord re-parent and grow people spiritually in the safe environment of the church family. I am convinced authentic community provides the context where the majority of spiritual growth and healing can take place.

Emerging generations, like never before, crave this sense of community inside a spiritual family. If they don't experience hope for authentic relational support, I don't care how hip the service, or how rippin' the music, or how vintage the vibe . . . they won't stick. The challenge for leaders is first to learn how to live in community with others, and then to provide ways to ensure that nobody stands alone.

As you can see, the challenge for the church of the twenty-first century has very little to do with the type of music or weekly service or drama or art or candles or coffee we serve. These things are important and may attract people initially, but they will never keep people connected and growing in a faith community. The challenge ahead of us has to do with culture creation: creating a come-as-you-are culture that reflects biblical priorities for the church, functioning as Christ re-presented in community. Only then will we help people overcome their struggles with Trust, Tolerance, Truth, Brokenness, and Aloneness. In the following chapters, we will experience the ways God uses a come-as-you-are culture to lead people past these five struggles. Listen to the waves of doubt washing over Susan as she struggled to trust.

STUDY GUIDE

Culture Check

1. Can you list people you know who have struggled with issues of trust, tolerance, truth, brokenness, or aloneness? Have they connected to your church community or been repelled by it? Ask them why.
2. What would it take for your church community to be willing to change in order to be a light in the emerging culture?
3. Are there young leaders who could be raised up within your church to help you if reaching the emerging culture is not where you best relate personally? Begin to pray for names and list them.

Small Group Questions

1. The society we live in does tend to influence us. What cultural trends do you think have most affected you and those with whom you interact?
2. What issues did you struggle with before coming to faith? How have you (or your friends) struggled with issues of trust, tolerance, truth, brokenness, or aloneness?
3. What do you think will most help people overcome these cultural struggles in order to find faith?
4. The first step of creating a come-as-you-are culture is seeking to understand the surrounding culture. Plan a social or an event for your group to invite unchurched friends from your neighborhood, apartment, or work. Hang out, have fun, and ask a lot of questions. Debrief what you learn together.

The Struggle
with Trust

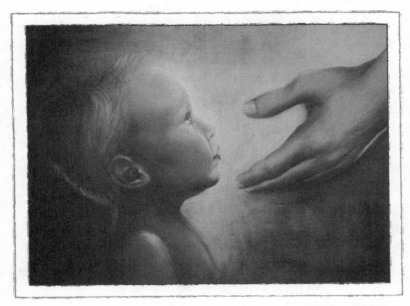

Artist: Heidi Korstad Dwyer

Doubters Wanted: Creating a Culture of Dialogue

There lives more faith in honest doubt,
Believe me, than in half the creeds.

Alfred, Lord Tennyson

I've been attending Gateway for a few months now and am particularly interested in your current series, "I Doubt It." I will probably have some extra questions for you during your free for all, but I was hoping you would address some questions that came up during today's sermon. When people set out to discover that something is the truth they have the tendency to find ways to believe it. You ignore contradictory evidence or dismiss it out of hand and embrace confirming evidence, even that which is full of holes ... you see, you are looking at this entire issue from an entirely different world than I am. We may as well be on two different planets. You have an answer you are trying to confirm. I have no answers and am looking for truth. In my world, when you suggest that God is merciful and loving and yet sends people to hell ... that sounds like a contradiction. Jesus had some neat things to say during his lifetime. Basically it was all about loving people, and that's really cool, but I don't see why you can't love people without believing. Actually, some of the most loving people I've known have been unbelievers. They loved me and accepted me no matter what, which is rarely the case with the Christians I've met who will only love me and care about me if I believe as they do, or if they think there's a chance to convert me. Frankly, I think if we're all going to hell for not being believers, we'll be in good company.   —Susan

Susan is still an agnostic as far as I know, but for some reason, she not only kept hanging around Gateway, she got in a small group and made an | 51 appointment to come talk to me about her issues. Why would someone so seemingly hostile and hurt by Christians get plugged into a community of Christ-followers and want to meet with a pastor? God's Spirit is doing something in her, and she feels safe enough in our community to keep exploring.

When a culture of dialogue gets created, people far from God who do not typically trust Christians feel safe enough to hang out and explore. And as we have seen time after time, a culture of dialogue allows people to put down their guard and seek, and as they truly seek, just as the Lord promises, they will find him.[1]

But how many people outside the family of faith never feel safe enough to even come close? How many people have the stereotype that Christians "love" them only if we sense we can get them to be like us or believe what we believe? Is that what it means to be like the Father, who loves even those who are his enemies and seeks to do good toward them?[2] How do we engage and convince the Susans of the world that the reason to believe is not to avoid hell but to know the love of a Father, a love that transcends all cultures and all hostilities?

Susan is right. Our cultures shape how we view life and each other. We might as well live on different planets. In many ways, we speak different languages and see the world from different perspectives. Going to church for Susan is a cross-cultural experience. As Dr. David Clark says, "Every telling of the Christian story to a non-Christian will cross cultural boundaries."[3] But is it Susan's responsibility to learn and adapt to our Christian subculture, or is it the responsibility of the mature Christ-follower to adapt to her culture in order to clearly communicate? This question is paramount to reaching emerging generations.

What Would Jesus Do?

Let's consider two examples: that of the Pharisees and that of Jesus.

The Pharisees of Jesus' day were absolutely certain of all they believed. If asked, they would say they knew God. They knew what he wanted of them with certainty. They followed the Law of Moses impeccably, and they lived within the walls of their religious culture confidently. And those who did not conform to their culture were cast out, unwelcome "sinners." They had a very "us-them" perception of the world. They often boasted about how wonderful it was to be the chosen, compared to those "messed up" people out there who didn't know the Lord. They subtly, and not so subtly, looked down upon and talked down to those who did not hold their beliefs. And rightfully so they thought, because "We have the truth! We *are* right!" But

Jesus scolded them because they wouldn't lift a finger to help those on the outside.[4] They had no genuine love for people different than themselves. Their chief failure was their failure to see that "chosen by God" never meant chosen for *merit*, but chosen for a *responsibility*.

Enter Jesus, "friend of the worst sort of sinners!"[5] He, whose culture could not be more different than ours, set aside the culture of heaven to enter the culture of humanity. Jesus adapted to the lowliest class to seek, serve, and save people.[6] He chastised the religious leaders of his day who were unbending with their traditions by quoting Isaiah and saying, "'These people honor me with their lips, but their hearts are far from me'. . . . You have let go of the commands of God and are holding on to the traditions [religious culture] of men."[7]

And what are the commands of God? Jesus summed them up in two phrases, Love God, love people.[8] Stop and ask yourself as a Christ-follower and especially if you are a leader: How much do I really love those who are not in the family of faith? How willing am I to adapt my cultural comforts to be able to create a culture of dialogue for those who do not hold my cherished beliefs? Am I comfortable if they hang out and question and doubt in our church or in my small group or ministry? Am I willing to admit where I have doubts or uncertainty as well as where I find confidence in Christ? Do I subtly consider myself "better than" or "more together" than those who are not Christ-followers?* Are nonbelievers attracted to my friends and me just as the "sinners" of Jesus' day were attracted to him?

If the church is truly to be the Body of Christ re-presenting Jesus to the world, what should we be doing to be more like him? Notice that even though Jesus had all the answers, he still respected and valued the opinions and free will of others. He often asked questions to get people to search rather than just telling the answer. He taught in parables to pique spiritual curiosity of those truly seeking. Though he proclaimed truth with authority, he did not force his truth on others. In love he offered what they needed and then was willing to let people disagree and walk away, even though it saddened him.[9] Because of all the baggage and lack of trust in our post-Christian world, people need to be engaged in dialogue. Few people are interested only in a monologue. Instead, if they listen to a message in church, they want to process it. They need to question it and wrestle with it. It needs to engage them where they live life.

---

* "For who makes you different from anyone else? What do you have that you did not receive? And if you did receive it, why do you boast as though you did not?" (1 Corinthians 4:7).

Creating a culture of dialogue means becoming people who truly respect and value all people as worthy of the love and sacrifice Christ demonstrated. It means being willing to respect their thoughts and opinions, making sure they know we value them, even if we differ in belief. An atmosphere of dialogue requires us to take into account the perspective of the other person, seeking to understand her position as much as we want her to understand ours. It is other-centered communication. It creates a two-way street of conversation. This kind of environment respects the free will of individuals and helps people not be afraid of offending us in their exploration and questioning.

Culture creation that allows dialogue requires immense trust in God. It requires letting go of the need to fix, change, or control others' beliefs or actions. It requires trusting that God's Spirit can work behind the scenes in people's hearts as we create a culture where they are free to question, doubt, and explore faith at their own pace. This shifts the burden to change people back where it belongs—with God alone.

This does not mean we hold back telling the story of God's work in our lives and throughout history. Nor does it mean there is not a time for proclamation—for speaking God's truth revealed in the Scriptures. But timing is everything! Creating a culture of dialogue requires us to walk in the shoes of the other person. To consider how it feels to be an "outsider" to faith; desiring to understand, but not having a clue; wanting to ask questions, but afraid to offend; needing to fit in to explore, but not sure of the rules. Nothing sensitized me more to the needs of people "outside" of my faith than being an outsider among faithful others.

Breaking In

Ommmm ... Ommmm ... the low rumble of chanting mixed with the fragrance of incense, filling my mind with new sounds and smells as the ornately painted, towering red-hued wooden doors opened.

It was 1986, and I was traveling across Asia with two friends. All my senses felt on alert for some reason as we entered the dimly lit Gandan Temple. Every sight and sound provoked a new question. We had just passed through the beautifully ornate gate of the largest Buddhist Monastery in Ulan Bator, capital city of Mongolia. The green-tiled roof curved gently down, tipping skyward on every corner. Ornamental carvings and drawings in red, gold, and green decorated the protecting walls and square archways surrounding the temple.

When I walked under the gate, I noticed several ornately decorated symbols over my head—an eight-spoked wheel and a person sitting under a tree—what did they mean? And why did the woman standing by the gate have her head shaved? What was she doing with the beads in her hand?

We tried to be as unobtrusive as possible entering the temple. Hugging the walls, I crept quietly into the dimly lit room behind my two companions. I passed a beautiful waist-high golden statue of a thin man or woman, I couldn't tell which, sitting cross-legged in lotus position with a pointed crown on its head, one hand opening out. Money of various denominations littered the floor around it. I looked around awkwardly; was I supposed to give it money? Would it offend the Lamas if I passed on the offering?

I peered through multiple pillars segmenting a crowded room into candlelit alcoves. Rich, red oriental rugs filled the rooms. Men with shaved heads in red flowing robes sat chanting on golden pillows—eyes closed. No one seemed to notice us, so I tiptoed past the offering statue following my two American friends.

As we stood motionless against one wall, listening to the mesmerizing hum of the chants rise and fall, a thousand questions filled my head. Why do they do this? What does it do for them? Am I an intrusion or will I be welcomed here? Will they be mad that an "outsider," an "unenlightened one," has invaded their sacred space? My mind shifted through my many questions, partly to ease my boredom as the chanting went on and on thirty minutes without a break.

Suddenly, a gong sounded, startling me out of my questioning. Everybody stood. Some walked to statues around the room and kissed them. My heart raced as I scanned the room for clues of what I was supposed to do. All of the people bowed. Were we supposed to bow too? Why are they bowing? Would I be impolite not to bow, even if I don't know what I'm bowing in reverence to? I hated not knowing what to do—I wanted to escape the awkwardness I felt.

Just then, a kind-looking young man in yellow and red robes moved our way—signaling to us with a smile and slight bow to follow. We did.

We made our way out into the courtyard as the Lamas resumed the lotus position. The young monk walked with us, addressing us in English. As we explained our visit from America, I courteously took the risk to ask him to explain what we just witnessed, hoping I wasn't being offensive. Though he spoke perfect English, his words were like a foreign language to me as he talked of the constantly reincarnated Living Buddha, who answers prayers, of Mongolia's last living Buddha, Bogd Gegeen Javtsandamba Hutagt, who was third in the Lama hierarchy after Tibet's Dalai Lama and Panchen Lama. He explained why they kiss an idol of a bodhisattva—an enlightened one who traveled the eight-fold path to Nirvana ahead of us.

It was all so confusing. I had so many questions, but I held back asking, fearing my skeptical inquisition might offend. I so appreciated his warmth and willingness to welcome us, but it would be many years until a course in comparative religions deciphered his coded Buddhist language for me.

■ ■ ■

Every time you enter a new culture or an unfamiliar social setting, instinctively you try to figure out the rules. Most of us steer clear of unknown, cross-cultural settings because we don't like the feeling of being "out of place," not knowing the right things to say or proper ways to act. We like our church or Christian group because we know the rules and feel safe. But consider how others feel trying to break in.

Do you realize that for most spiritual seekers in a post-Christian culture, coming to church is often just as awkward for them as visiting a Buddhist temple would be for you? They don't know the rules so they automatically feel out of place. They don't know when to sit or stand. They don't know the songs—or even if it's offensive to sing or okay to pass instead of miming words they don't believe. They don't know the Scriptures or how to decipher Christian terms and characters they've never heard of before. They don't know if their questions will offend or if it's acceptable to voice their skepticism.

So we must tell them.

From the earliest days at Gateway, we've made it clear from up front that seekers, skeptics, and cynics are welcome. We've tried to let them experience authentic Christianity while minimizing cross-cultural hurdles our traditions might pose. We've made it public that no question is a dumb question. And doubters are wanted because we believe authentic faith has nothing to fear—including doubts. Creating a culture of dialogue means letting everyone know it's okay to be in process.

Room for Doubt?

How can we welcome doubt if our goal is growth in faith? First, we must realize that doubt is not the antithesis of faith. All of us have our doubts because our knowledge is imperfect and incomplete. We must be willing to be honest about our doubts.

Consider John the Baptist. He heard a voice from heaven declaring of Jesus, "This is my beloved Son," yet when life turned south and John was staring through the bars of a prison, he started to doubt. Jesus was not doing things the way he anticipated, so he questions, "Are you the One or should we expect another?"[10]

Isn't this true of us as well? When God does something contrary to what we confidently know his will should be, even leaders erupt with caustic questions and disconcerting doubts. We must be honest with seekers and other believers. There are times when we question and doubt.

But this is the path of authentic faith: to faith that trusts and remains faithful even as it is tested. Consider David who cried out in the psalms, "God, why have you forgotten me?"[11] as his enemies are closing in on him. "God, will you hide yourself forever?"[12] Or how about the words of David reverberating down through the centuries, all the way up onto a wooden cross crying, "My God, my God, why have you forsaken me?"[13] Why? Why?

Questions ... doubts ... struggle ... yet faith!

Creating a culture where questions and doubts can find voice is not only healthy, it's thoroughly biblical. In the Bible, you *do* find those who had absolute certainty. But those who never doubted, struggled, or wrestled with what it meant to do the will of God were not the heroes of faith ... they were the Pharisees who crucified Jesus!

The religious leaders' certainty of what was true and right gave them confidence to crucify the Son of God. Stop and consider that for a second. Do we think we are "above" being deceived by our religious cultural conditioning? Do we feel pretty confident we have faith all figured out? Has our theology boxed out the mystery of God who sometimes works in strange ways?[14] Maybe we should ponder the plight of the Pharisees who crucified Jesus. How about the apostle Peter? In his confident declaration of what he knew was "right," Peter had to be rebuked by Jesus saying, "Get away from me, Satan!"[15]

Questions, doubts, and struggles are not the antithesis of faith. The opposite of faith is a decision to not trust God. The man who cried out to Jesus, "I do believe; help me overcome my unbelief"[16] did not demonstrate faith with zero doubts but a willful decision to trust in God even in the midst of questions and doubts. When leaders come to terms with this interchange between doubts and faith, then we find freedom to create a culture of dialogue. As Bryce's story attests, it's in this kind of environment where even the most hardened skeptic can wrestle through trust issues and find faith.

Finding Faith from Doubt

Seventeen-year-old Bryce Johnson couldn't take the indoctrination any more. His hand shot up defiantly, "How do we know Jesus really did that?"

Father Purcelli, known best as "Father Evil" at St. Mary's High School, was obviously taken back. "Because it's in the Bible!" he retorted, raising his voice.

Bryce was fed up with such ridiculous answers crammed down his throat by such misdirected people. "How do we know the Bible is true?"

"Because God gave it to us." The red rash and protruding veins appearing on Father Purcelli's neck told Bryce he'd better shut up . . . , but this time, he couldn't. Why could no one answer his questions? He'd been asking them since he was seven . . . no answers, just platitudes. Out of the corner of his eye, Bryce could see the grins of his friends urging him on.

"How do we know God gave—"

"Enough, Mr. Johnson," Father Purcelli interrupted, but his attention quickly shifted across the room where Rudy and Paul were whispering and snickering. Walking swiftly past Bryce in the front row of desks and right up to the first of the two boys, Father Purcelli kicked Rudy's shin swiftly, successively sweeping his arm across Paul's desk, sending books flying. "Do you lovers want to shut the &@%# up?"

Bryce should have been shocked. But shin-kicking, ear-pinching, and a good ol' slip of the F-bomb happened almost weekly in Father Evil's theology class—it's how he earned his name. It all reinforced Bryce's long-held belief—"Religion is a bunch of crap!"

In a flash of anger, Bryce's mind traveled back seven years to his grandfather's wake. The only father figure he'd ever known had been ripped from the pages of his life, and its pain pierced his heart again. "There is no God," his conviction from age ten, had only strengthened. "How could there be? What kind of God would take a little boy's father before I could know him, then take my grandfather too, then put my mom through the hell of raising four children alone?"

The only answers Bryce ever got to his greatest struggle, "Why did God take my dad and my granddad too?" was the constant refrain, "It was God's will." As a young boy, the thought of God provoked images of anything *but* a loving being.

"I've seen too much to be fooled," Bryce thought. "If there's such a powerful God who can do miracles, why doesn't he stop the crime I see all over my neighborhood? Why doesn't he feed the poor and hungry of New York I drive past daily? No one can answer my questions because it's a sham—a political ideology used to control and oppress. Where hypocrites hide from the real world in a self-contained cocoon called church. If man's gonna be helped up, it's gotta be by the hand of man."

Bryce lived out his humanitarian atheism devoutly for decades, thinking of God as nothing more than a figurative metaphor. Bryce set his sights on career success coupled with good deeds to help his fellow man. At thirty-two, he moved to Austin to position himself for the Director of Wireless Web

Communications in his firm. After two years of preparation and hard work, Bryce was passed over for an outside hire. Crushed by the decision, the pain only compounded when he quit. He felt worthless, directionless.

Bryce began reading Carlos Castaneda, the Celestine Prophecies, and several books on Buddhism—searching, not for God but for a new philosophy to pull him out of the dark despair he felt closing in on him. They all promoted a means of self-enlightenment that felt empty to Bryce. He knew he couldn't save himself.

One Saturday night, sitting on the couch in the depths of despair, Bryce prayed. "God I don't know if you're out there. But if you are, please help me to help myself to find you." That night, Bryce got on the Internet and searched "Christian churches nondenominational." He didn't even know what nondenominational meant, but it sounded non-indoctrinated, non-political. One website said "Come as you are—whether you are searching for the first time or you lost count . . . you are welcome to join us as we seek God together." "That's the one," Bryce decided. "Gateway Community Church, 4300 Bull Creek Road."

The next morning, Bryce drove himself to church for the first time. "I'm scared as hell," he thought to himself as he pulled into the parking lot. "What's wrong with me?" As a psychology major, Bryce knew how to objectify his feelings, but he couldn't pinpoint this one. It was a subconscious fear . . . almost that when he walked into that building, he would be exposed for denouncing God his whole life and the wrath of the Almighty would fall.

Bryce circled the parking lot. "Good, it's full. Maybe I'll try it next week." Just then a guy standing in the lot signaled an empty space across the street. Bryce felt obligated to stay. He sat in the back of the auditorium, defenses up. But thirty minutes into the service, a photo essay set to music about loneliness ambushed him. The song he knew well overthrew his defenses as the Scriptures written over black and white stills of lonely people refrained with the thought "You're never alone." As he fought back tears, though he didn't believe in Christ, his soul cried, "That's what I'd like to believe."

For the next month, Bryce was last in, first out, last row. Having always associated churches as places that prey on the weak, Bryce's guard was up. He was waiting for the hammer of judgment to fall, and knowing what a weak emotional state he was in, he wanted to make sure he wasn't being brainwashed or manipulated.

Over the next few months, Bryce began to let his guard down, feeling free to be himself—in process. "These two pastors are sharing intimate parts of their lives," Bryce reflected. "They readily admit they don't have all the answers and it's okay that I don't have all the answers. I feel my defenses falling, but I think it's okay. I don't need to be defensive . . . I'm not being attacked. In fact, I'm feeling encouraged to be myself, even to question."

For the first time, Christ started looking intriguing to Bryce as he began seeing Jesus as loving and forgiving rather than as a political ideologue. Over the months, as he heard his questions voiced and addressed in the teaching, he found himself thinking, Perhaps . . . just perhaps . . . there's truth to be found here.

He took the risk to ask questions of people he met. He learned why God is not the author of evil in this fallen world, and why free-willed people need what Christ did for them, and how a restored relationship with God gets lived out. The Scriptures seemed relevant to his life for the first time, so he began reading the Gospels, Christian books, and praying nightly. Looking for false-hoods and historical incongruities in the text of the Bible soon faded into genuine intrigue and discovery. He began feeling a supernatural guidance. He would be struggling or questioning, and the next week, he would discover a book or hear a message that seemed to speak directly to his concerns.

One rainy day in November four months later, while walking his dog, Bryce found himself saying, "Jesus, thanks for this day." He realized he wasn't depressed, and he was willfully having a conversation with Jesus. That night Bryce opened his heart to Christ fully.

Two years later, Bryce has grown immensely. Now, as a growing Christ-follower, he leads Gateway's Compassion ministries, clothing the homeless, building houses for the poor, mentoring kids-at-risk, serving the elderly. Continuing his humanitarian service—in the name of Christ.

Creating Dialogue in Culture

What are some practical ways for church leaders or small group leaders to create a culture where dialogue can happen? How do you build trust where skepticism abounds?

First, if you create the habit of listening and interacting with those who don't believe, asking questions as much as giving answers, you will begin to understand their concerns. People usually love to be heard. How often as a leader do you simply ask questions and listen compassionately so that you truly understand why skeptics doubt?

Voicing Real Questions

It is important not only to listen and let people know it's okay to question, but in messages Gateway teachers will often voice the concerns we hear from skeptics. If it's not clear that leaders have wrestled with skeptics' issues, it becomes hard to trust them for answers. But hearing leaders voicing real questions lends credibility. Consider this email that represents the trust issues so many have embedded in their psyches:

> Historically, there seems to be nothing with more capacity for evil than a so called "righteous man" hell-bent on doing God's will. From the Crusades to the Inquisition to the Salem witch trials to the wholesale slaughter of Native Americans to slavery on up into the 20th century when black men were lynched with impunity, people have performed acts of evil with a sense of self-righteousness. With so much evil done in the name of God and religion, there are times when I just wish I could make God and religion disappear completely. This is the religious crossroad that I have been staring at for a long time now. Thanks for making Gateway the kind of place where someone with the doubts and "religious scars" that I have can feel welcome.   —Darrin

Knowing that these issues often cause seekers to throw up their hands and say, "Religion is evil," we can dialogue even in sermons and messages with them. We can state their concerns publicly, giving voice to their resistance to help them find answers as real as their questions. We have often brought these issues into the light to help Christ-followers and seekers biblically process the tough questions and the reality of human deception and depravity—yours, theirs, and mine included! Knowing and acknowledging the tough issues that we all wrestle with creates trust and helps people strengthen their faith as they wrestle.

Modeling Unity in Diversity

We stress unity and certainty in the core essentials of Christian faith, but we also readily admit there are many non-core points of theology and belief where Christ-followers differ. And we make it clear that we should be able to differ on the nonessentials and remain unified in love and mission as one local church.

In fact, Ted Beasley, also a pastor-teacher of Gateway from the beginning, differs with me on such issues as the number of days of creation being twenty-four-hour days or long periods of time. We differ on our end-times theology. And we have publicly explained that we differ and why we differ when we have taught on these divisive issues, demonstrating for all that a healthy church can be diverse on disputable issues while maintaining unity in Christ on the essentials.

Leading Small Group Dialogue

How we equip small group leaders plays an important role in culture creation. Our goal is to connect every seeker in a small group or serving group, knowing this community environment best helps them sort through doubts and struggles. If a spiritual seeker comes into the group, and the leader has not created a culture of dialogue, the group often turns into a free-for-all of trying to "help" the seeker. This usually backfires.

Koby[††] started our Big Brothers Big Sisters ministry after finding faith. She recalls what a turn-off it was to be "targeted": "Growing up I wasn't given the opportunity to go to church," Koby recalls, "because my dad didn't and still doesn't believe in God. On a few occasions, I would go to church with a friend, but I felt uncomfortable because Scripture was above my head and I was 'honed in on' as a guest."

We tell leaders to try to see all people as a work in process. God is seeking to do his work in all of our lives, and none of us are fully compliant. Those who don't know Christ as Lord have not responded to the first decision of trust—to trust him for forgiveness and relationship. But this learning to trust does not end with one decision of trust, it just begins. To assume that we are all on a spiritual journey, seeking to take next steps of trust, helps level the playing field. A leader need not hide the fact that until that first prayerful decision of trust is made, we all stand alienated from God, but she can do this without giving the feeling that one prayer is the sole goal. It's not. The goal is a lifelong process of deeper acts of trust. "Without faith [trust] it is impossible to please God."[17]

We must also equip leaders to recognize and acknowledge God's work in the lives of seekers. As those who don't know Christ dialogue with us, I find it is important to interpret for them what the Lord is doing in their lives. Affirm them and point out how God is working to draw them to himself. I'm confident of this; God is at work behind the scenes, drawing people homeward, before we ever come into the picture.[18] But often they don't recognize his mysterious whispering in their hearts and minds and in the twists and turns of the events of life, so we must cautiously interpret for them.[19] This is what Rachel and I are trying to do for Kyle. Listen to the way these aspects of dialogue opened the door for him to begin seeking.

Dialogue in the Key of Goth

"Christians are hateful, condemning, nasty, and mean. They like to torture people who don't fit their stereotype. They treat people in any subculture like dirt," Kyle ranted to his friend Rachel as they drove home from Elysium—a Goth club where they had met six months earlier. "See Rachel, you don't know what Christians are like. You're very different than most Christians I've

†† This symbol denotes that the person has requested that his real name be used.

known." Kyle, a twenty-one-year-old 3-D graphic design artist, grew up feeling judged and condemned by Christians.

"Come to Gateway, just once, and you'll meet others. If you don't like it, at least you were open," Rachel contended. Rachel was a believer against all odds. Physically beaten black and blue for a decade, sexually molested as a teen—all by her father who was a professor, pastor, and traveling evangelist. Yet Rachel had discovered the healing grace of a God who despises the horrendous evil her father perpetrated. She had won Kyle's trust because she was a survivor.

"Rachel, I work Sundays and Wednesdays. I would if I could," Kyle said, being polite.

"Okay, next time you're off—you're coming with me." Rachel began praying consistently that night. One month later, Kyle happened to call her on a Wednesday. "Come on over," Rachel said, "We're going to Gateway since you're off work."

"#$%&," Kyle cussed forgetting his vow. "I'm going black—wearing my Skinny Puppy shirt with the crucified dog on it then. If they can't take it, I'm not going. And I'll probably sleep through it too—just to warn you."

Kyle not only stayed awake, he listened to every word as I taught through 1 Corinthians 12 about the unity of the church as Christ's Body. It especially caught his attention that we were not threatened by a diversity of views on trivial, divisive issues. He came up to talk to me afterwards, dressed in black, with long, sandy-blonde hair, dark sideburns, pierced ears, and a goatee. What I noticed most was the crucified dog on his shirt.

"Skinny Puppy? Is that a band?" I asked.

"Yeah—it's an industrial band." With that, Kyle launched in . . . making sure I knew religion was manipulative and mean. I talked with Kyle for about forty minutes, agreeing with him where I could about the evils of some religious people, telling him my story of discovering that all people are messed up—including Christians; but also discovering a loving God really exists—and our only hope for change is one life at a time, humbly letting God do his will in me. He talked more than I did as I asked questions, interjecting personal discovery along the way.

When they walked out that night, Kyle turned to Rachel and said, "I was a real ass to your pastor."

"Great," she said.

"But he took it, and he was really cool. Didn't even react to my shirt either. I think I want to talk to him again."

Ironically, Kyle only comes to the Gathering, our midweek service, where we do thirty minutes of worship and teach straight through books of the Bible. About six months after his first visit, he came up to me to tell me he now considers himself a theist. "It just makes more sense than being atheistic," he admitted.

"Kyle, I can see God is doing something in your life," I told him. "He really does love you, and he wants you to know that he's not like you imagined from watching messed up Christians."

Rachel told me Kyle now argues with Goth friends when they bash Christians saying, "Not all Christians are like that. You should check out this one church before judging all Christians. I've gone in decked out in black vinyl and no one stared me down. At Gateway they don't judge people by appearance, and they don't judge people's opinions—they listen. The pastor doesn't have a loudspeaker on his head."

Recently he told Rachel, "When I become a Christian," then caught himself, "*If* I become a Christian, I'm not singing the songs." Rachel keeps pointing out little evidences that God is trying to get Kyle's attention. This Christmas Kyle made a deal with me. He said he would read *Mere Christianity* if I would watch the movie *Bowling for Columbine*.

■ ■ ■

Jesus would often look at the trajectory of a person's heart and either confront or congratulate him. He would say things like, "You are not far from the kingdom of God."[20] In other words, you're heading in the right direction. We need to affirm and validate those who are truly seeking and making progress, pointing out to them the behind-the-scenes work of the Spirit as we recognize his workings in their lives. This bridges the gap of trust.

A Time To Challenge

Creating a culture of dialogue does not mean you never confront wrongdoing or challenge people with truth. It means you respect the will and opinions of the other person, you seek to listen as much as you speak, and you encourage where you see the work of God's Spirit. And at times, when you sense the promptings of God's Spirit, he will nudge you to confront or challenge. When he does, it is your responsibility to not hold back speaking truth, but to speak it in love.

I was hanging out enjoying the beautiful Austin Hill Country views after an outdoor wedding one Saturday when I spotted Chase talking to Tracy near the bar. Tracy had recently given her life to Christ and had invited Chase to Gateway. I knew Chase had been hanging out at church for about six months, and I knew he considered himself an agnostic. Chase busied himself with extreme sports whenever he wasn't working. It was the height of the high-tech revolution in Austin, and he was extremely intelligent, doing very well at a young age in a start-up tech firm.

I asked Kenny, one of our future staff standing next to me, "Where's Chase spiritually? Is he seeking or stuck?"

"I think he's pretty closed," Kenny replied. "My impression is that Gateway for Chase is more about seeking women than seeking God. I think we missed our chance with him anyway," my friend casually mentioned. "He got a promotion that's moving him to New York soon."

When Kenny said that, something struck me in the gut. I had this strong sense of compassion for Chase. Here was a young guy who was tearing up the world in business, living to the extreme of where his adrenaline rush could take him, thinking he had success in the bag. And in the world's eyes, he did. But as I stood there watching him, I was reminded of the rich young ruler whom Jesus confronted, and I had this nudging that I needed to go get in Chase's face before my opportunity evaporated.

Expecting the response Jesus got from the rich young ruler when Jesus told him to sell all and follow him (the rich young ruler turned and walked), I approached Chase. "Hey Chase, congratulations, I hear you have a new job offer in New York; sounds like a huge promotion."

"Thanks! I'll miss the outdoors of Austin, but the pay and opportunity are too much to resist." Chase filled me in on the details of this new high-tech venture and the stock options he would amass as a signing bonus. Less than a decade ago, he was a pimple-faced latchkey kid, entertaining himself by passionately exploring the emerging world of cyberspace. Now his passion was his power.

"Chase, you've been hanging out at Gateway for a while now, where are you at with God? Are you any closer to belief?" I decided on the direct approach.

Chase nonchalantly shrugged out his answer, "I respect what you all are doing, but it's just not for me."

This was not my first spiritual conversation with Chase, so I decided to bet all my chips on a thought forming in my head. "Chase, you're an incredibly intelligent person. I know you love to learn and it's paying off for you. But think about this. You succeed wildly, make tons of money, and prove to the world how smart you are. Then you die and find out there really is a God who loved you and had a bigger purpose for your life than just living for Chase. Imagine how you'll feel if you missed it because you were too busy doing what Chase thought was best for Chase—that wouldn't be too smart would it? To be so smart and yet miss the whole purpose for your existence?" Since I was going for the spiritual jugular anyway, I asked, "Do you agree?"

To my surprise, he agreed. So I challenged him to take the next two months before he moved and truly seek heart, mind, and soul, to allow himself to be open like never before, asking God to reveal himself. I suggested several books and told him after reading them, we could meet to dialogue about his issues and questions. I was blown away when he said he'd be up for that.

Chase's move was postponed indefinitely, but over the following four months Chase worked through his issues, reading, talking with others, meeting with me. He opened his heart to Christ, joined a small group and experienced significant spiritual growth. The following Christmas he wrote me a Christmas card from the East Coast: "Thanks for spending so much time with me so I can know Jesus! Merry Christmas."

■ ■ ■

As you can see from the variety of stories, reaching emerging generations requires relating not only to a broader distrusting culture but also to people from very diverse subcultures within the dominant cultural influences. These range from purely postmodern, nonlinear relativistic—to darkly nihilistic Goth—to young, highly educated techies who require logical rationality, though contextualized in relationship. Leaders must challenge the assumption that all emerging post-Christian seekers are the same in how they look, act, or think—they're probably the most diverse generation ever. Nevertheless, many seem to struggle with issues of trust.

Creating a culture for dialogue is really about *trust*. It's not only about creating a climate where skeptical, cynical generations can trust. It's first about you as a leader trusting God's Spirit to lead and guide you as you interact with people—valuing, listening, encouraging positive trajectories, at times challenging boldly, but respecting and loving all people as the Father does, despite their response. And remembering that in the end, their response is God's business. This is the only way to reach such a diverse, distrustful generation—Spirit-led dialogue. But dialogue cannot bridge the trust gap for this generation unless a culture of authenticity has firmly been established.

STUDY GUIDE

Culture Check

1. When was the last time you really had a dialogue with a non-Christian person to try to understand why he or she held those beliefs?
2. If a spiritual seeker came into your church, would the average person he/she interacts with try to convince him/her in one conversation to change, or be willing to dialogue and listen as much as speak?
3. Do you feel comfortable creating a culture where people could hang out, question, and doubt for months or years as they wrestle to find faith? What fears or concerns does it raise for you?
4. What personal mindset shift, vision-casting, story-telling, or organizational changes could be made to better create a culture of dialogue?

Small Group Questions

1. Just imagine if you were exploring a foreign religion, what fears or concerns would you have? What environment would most help you be open to new ideas? Discuss how you could create this same environment for a spiritual seeker coming into your group.
2. Read Luke 7:18–23. John the Baptist had seen and heard of Jesus' miracles, yet when he gets thrown in prison, he falls into doubt. In your opinion, what room is there for doubts as people seek an authentic faith?
3. What struggles do Christians face that are pretty much the same struggles that non-Christians face? Discuss what deep-seated needs, wants, and desires are common for all people. How might these commonalities provide an opportunity for dialogue about Christian faith?
4. Ask your group, "When was the last time you had an open dialogue of exchange between someone who differed with your Christian beliefs?" What did you learn? Make it an assignment to have an exchange this week with one person who differs from you in essential beliefs.

chapter 4

Losing My Need to Pretend: Creating a Culture of Authenticity

If we say we have no sin, we are only fooling ourselves.

1 John 1:8 NLT

When my wife, Kathy, was in preschool she fell in love with a comic strip character, Zelda. Kathy wanted to be like Zelda. She wanted to do everything Zelda did. Then Kathy decided she *was* Zelda. Her teachers came to her mom concerned because Kathy would no longer answer to the name Kathy, she wanted to be called Zelda. She would not even turn around or respond to questions unless the teacher called her Zelda.

We've all pretended to be someone we're not. It's fairly common for kids to pretend they are someone else—to pretend to be a great basketball player or an Olympic gymnast or the president of the United States. And it's acceptable if kids pretend because they are still forming their identities. But the goal is to learn to be yourself by the time you are an adult.

Unfortunately, few adults seem to be comfortable enough with themselves *not* to pretend. The fear of disapproval, rejection, and condemnation often causes adults to pretend, including spiritual leaders—not always living on the outside congruent with who we are on the inside, always feeling the need to look a little better or more together than pure honesty would reveal.

Our generation longs for something authentic. They are searching for "the real thing," though they don't really know what "the real thing" is. Because this generation has endured so much "me-ism" and letdown from those they were supposed to follow and trust, they want to see a genuine faith that works for less-than-perfect people before they are willing to trust. They want to know this God-thing is more than talk, talk, talk. They desperately want permission to be who they are with the hope of becoming more. They aren't willing to pretend, because hypocrisy repulses them. But most have yet to realize that every person is a hypocrite to some degree—the only question is whether we realize it and are honest about it.

It Starts with Authenticity

When we launched Gateway Community Church in September 1998, the first service was entitled "Losing My Need to Pretend." Everything we did that morning contrasted the inauthentic ways of the religious leaders whom Jesus deemed hypocrites with an authentic spirituality of the heart. The religious leaders of Jesus' day were focused on religious rule-keeping. Jesus reserved his harshest words for the pretenders, the mask-wearers: "Woe to you Pharisees, because you give God a tenth of your mint, rue and all other kinds of garden herbs, but you neglect justice and the love of God. You should have practiced the latter without leaving the former undone."[1]

The religious leaders of Jesus' day were so focused on the traditions they had formed around the heart of God's message that they were neglecting the things most on God's heart. In Matthew 22:36–39, these religious leaders try to test Jesus by asking him what the greatest commandment is. Here Jesus gets to the heart of the matter: Love God and love people, he says. All of the commandments hang on these two. And these two are inseparable; you can't truly love if you don't love God heart, soul, and mind.

This part of the equation most seekers miss when they say, "Isn't it enough to be a loving person?" How can you be a loving person without loving the God who created you?

On the other hand, you can't say you love God if you don't live it out experientially with others. This part of the equation Christians may miss. A spiritual leader who claims great love for God but has little love for messy, imperfect people is far from the heart of God.

That September morning in the delivery room of our new church, I told our newborn congregation that these stories are a warning against inauthentic, incongruent living. Jesus is basically saying, *Lose the religious pretense; it's destructive to authentic faith. Shed the mask of hypocrisy you hide behind. I want honest, authentic people—not hypocrites who pretend to be something they're not.*

I asked the congregation a question at the end of the message: "Can we be this kind of a church? The kind where people don't have to pretend?

Where we can be ourselves and stop pretending we're more or less than what we are right now? That's the only way we can help each other grow to be all God intended us to be. If we can't do this, we're just playing church!"

So You Want to Be Authentic?

I got an email that first Sunday afternoon from a woman who attended our first service:

> Today for the first time ever I felt like I had found a place to explore spirituality where I would be accepted. Thank you! I hope to be able to talk my husband into trying our church. We both have tattoos and piercings and have always felt uncomfortable in traditional churches. You are just what I've been asking for. P.S. I almost used my work email to send this, but then I thought, why use a mask? This is me. ☺

I hadn't noticed her email address, so I glanced at it: *browneyedbi*. Tia was bisexual! And she had taken me seriously—she wasn't going to hide it from her new church that valued authenticity! Later that month, she invited my wife, Kathy, and me over for dinner. I thought, *Okay Lord, lead us to represent you.* They were a young family, in their late twenties with three children, living in a nice neighborhood. Tia had been a single mom before marrying Jim, the father of the youngest boy.

Over dinner I found out that Jim had grown up in the wealthy part of town but had pretty much been disowned by his family when he kept getting busted for drugs. He now worked as a valet in a strip club because it paid better than any other job he could get. Jim and Tia had both been into spirituality but not into God. They dabbled in the occult and even got married in a "haunted house."

After dinner, we all went into the living room and after small talk about their salt-water aquarium and alternative music collection, Kathy and Jim began conversing about Jim's occultic past and the hypocrisy of Christians. Tia began to tell me how much she was growing since coming to Gateway. I sat in the overstuffed chair, and she made herself comfortable on the adjacent couch.

"I loved the series, 'If You Really Knew Me,'" Tia said. "I know that's exactly why we've been scared of churches—fear that we'd be judged if they really knew us. That's why I love Gateway. I feel so welcome. I wish Jim would come."

"Maybe he will now that he knows us," I ventured.

"The message you did two weeks ago has really helped me already," Tia interjected with eager excitement. "I've patched things up with my best friend as a result of it."

"You mean the week we talked about conflict resolution?" I asked. "If You Really Knew My Feelings" had been a message straight from Jesus' teachings in Matthew 18.

"Yeah! I hadn't talked to Shelly in over a year, and that Sunday I went home and called her, and we were able to patch things up. And I never thought that would happen," Tia replied shaking her head.

"Why? What happened between the two of you?" I asked, wondering what put such a crimp in their friendship.

"Jim got Shelly pregnant when the three of us were having sex together," Tia said as if telling me the weather forecast. I thought she was going to laugh and say, "Just messing with you," but as she continued to expound, I realized she was completely serious. "When Shelly found out, she was furious with me because she felt like I talked her into it—but it wasn't like it was against her will! Still, ever since that nasty fight we had afterwards, we hadn't talked at all in over a year. And now I've apologized, she forgave me, and we're friends again! I really feel like I'm growing spiritually!"

Woe, hang on there a minute—my mind was spinning.

What was it they taught me in seminary about how to handle a situation like this? Nothing came to mind. So I prayed. "Lord, how do I respond? She's being authentic, and I don't know what to say. You knew all this already, so show me how to re-present you."

As we continued talking, my heart started to break for this woman. At an earlier time she had told me that she knew bisexuality was wrong for her, and she wanted to stop for her kids' sake. There had to be something very painful that led her into such a destructive lifestyle. I sensed I needed not to react but to listen. So I asked questions.

"Tia, you said you felt like bisexuality was unhealthy, and you knew you needed to make a change. What made you start down that road in the first place?" I hesitantly inquired.

"Well, I haven't exactly had a pristine sexual past. But I had some really bad experiences with men early on. My parents divorced when I was a baby, and my mother remarried a wonderful man who was like a dad to me since I was three. But I would spend every summer with my biological father, who started sexually molesting me when I was nine."

"Did your mom know?" I said, imagining the horrible confusion this little girl must have felt as her own father preyed upon her.

"Once I turned thirteen, I refused to see my biological father anymore, but I didn't tell Mom why until I was in my twenties. That wasn't the end of it, though," Tia recalled, as I noticed a sadness bleeding through an otherwise hardened exterior. "I was later gang raped by some of the football team in high school. That probably had some effect."

I could imagine the pain of an unprotected little girl cast into the clutches of so much evil. God's heart broke for Tia, who learned from an evil world her value is purely sexual. All of her self-worth centered on her ability to attract others sexually, male or female . . . it was the closest substitute for real love she could find.

"Tia, where are you at spiritually?" I asked later in the evening.

"I'm good with God, but I don't know about the whole Jesus thing. It kind of makes me feel creepy for some reason," Tia confided. "I don't see why it's so important to believe in Jesus."

"The whole reason God sent Jesus was so we could know God in a personal way. So we can know why he will forgive us and make us clean no matter what's happened in the past. He wants a relationship with you, Tia, because he loves you. Do you know that?" I asked.

"That hasn't really been my impression, especially from Christians," Tia quipped.

"Well, Tia, you're on the right path," I took a leap of faith to encouragingly say. "I think God is trying to draw you close so that he can begin a healing process in your life. He's already working in your life, Tia. And I really believe, if you'll stay open and start seeking to understand who he is, you'll find the love you've been seeking."

Tia managed an uncomfortably soft smile as her eyes wandered off to some distant place. "You think so?" she semi-sarcastically ventured after a moment of silence.

"I'm sure of it."

Authenticity Starts with Me

The longer I walk with Christ, the more I see the Pharisee in me. I'm convinced the most important work of spiritual leadership is leading a spiritually authentic life. But to do this, I must break through the deception that I am somehow better than others. That I am somehow a little less in need of God's mercy and grace than the Tias and Jims of the world.

A culture of authenticity starts with me. I must first recognize that I'm no less capable of being deceived than were the religious leaders of Jesus' day. I must constantly remind myself that the apostle Peter was deceived in his zealousness and called down the rebuke of Jesus. I must realize that Paul was deceived in his zeal for God's righteousness to the point of condoning the murder of Christ-followers. I must recount the corrupt yearning for power and self-aggrandizement that stalked the sons of Zebedee, James, and

John, as they fantasized and plotted a path to greatness as Jesus' disciples.[2] Who am I to think I am somehow incapable of being deceived by my own brand of cultural religious piety? I try to read daily from a one-year Bible for this reason. It usually takes me two years to get through it, but that's okay. My goal is not to read through it but let it read through me, knowing I can be deceived if I'm not ruthlessly taking inventory before God. And I must always remember that if I am deceived, I'll be the last to know about it.

Authenticity is hard work. It always works from the inside out. It begins with the inner life of the leader, being authentic with God. It manifests itself in personal vulnerability before others as an intimate connection with God displaces the fear of transparency. This opens for others a view into an authentic spiritual life of a real human—not a religious salesperson. Finally, it becomes embedded in a culture so that authentic, growing communities of people can be formed and transformed.

When I first became a Christ-follower, I came out of years of partying with my peers. I found faith through a Wednesday small group study and decided to commit to growing with that group, reading the Bible regularly, and praying nightly. But I still struggled. I found that Wednesdays were spiritual high-points, but many Saturday nights were like the first drop on a world-class rollercoaster.

This up and down spiritual experience continued for months, until one night I had a breakthrough. It was a post-party Saturday night when I plopped down in bed and, as promised, began my nightly prayer. "God, thanks for the day, be with my mom and sister and Aunt Frieda. . . ." I prayed in my head, all the while trying not to acknowledge that the room was spinning. I had successfully pulled this off before—keeping the truth undercover while praying to God—but that night, something broke through my pretense. In a sober moment, I realized I wasn't fooling God. He knew!

I stopped my prayer of pretense and got honest with God like never before. "You know I'm buzzing, don't you? I know it's wrong, I drank too much, and I'm sorry I did it again." Then I realized why I was hiding, "Lord, I don't want to talk to you about it because I know it's not your will, and I already know there's a party in two weeks, and I want to do it again! So if you want me to stop, I need your help somehow."

For me, that was a watershed moment in my spiritual journey. Where I realized all God needed was honesty and willingness to see his power do what I couldn't do for myself. As I've told my story of struggle openly at our church, I can almost hear the "aha moments" bursting forth in the minds of Christ-followers and spiritual strugglers alike. Authenticity must start with me not hiding anything from God.

The Isolation Trap

As a leader, I need to be transparent not just with God but with others as well. When we first started Gateway, the first two years were a constant struggle. Having to move between six locations, I did not understand what God was doing. During the first year, I found myself feeling beaten down, alone, and isolated like never before. If I shared my doubts and struggles with our staff, I could feel their hope deflating. That discouraged me even more. So I stopped talking about my own struggles with them.

My wife, Kathy, had been neck deep in it with me from the beginning, having started our children's ministry and women's ministry; she was still running both with two young kids. Although Kathy and I had always been equal partners in every ministry endeavor, and I had always been open about everything with her, my fear of failure, coupled with concern that I'd bring her down, caused me to stop sharing my struggles even with her. Inside, I knew pretense was the path to destruction. Old patterns and thoughts began to creep back in as a means of coping with my emotional isolation and internal insecurities.

Knowing what I needed, I cried out to the Lord daily. Two months later, Trey Kent called. "We're starting a pastor's covenant group; we heard you were starting a church; would you like to come?" It was divine timing.

At the first meeting I ripped it open. I decided to let them see it all, and if they couldn't handle it, this wasn't the group for me. Amazingly, this eclectic small group of pastors—Presbyterian, nondenominational, Methodist, charismatic, Pentecostal—got gut-wrenchingly honest that day as we all confessed our sins and struggles and prayed for one another. That group saved me. Experiencing the love and acceptance they demonstrated reminded me that God loves me and I have worth even if I fail *and* this church fails.

As leaders, we must be honest with God and others about who we are, what we want, and how desperately we struggle just to put God at the center of life. This is the authentic spiritual life, isn't it? We must keep asking ourselves the fundamental questions: Am I experiencing a life of growing connection with God? Am I growing in my love for God and people? Do I believe more and more that he is what I'm desperately searching for, or is there something else I think I need? Do I believe he is the source of the kind of life I really want? Am I living a life others would want to live? Have I truly found the experience of life in Christ so fulfilling that I can't contain it—I have to give it away?

I already know of three young pastors of thriving churches who had to leave ministry because of moral failures. Leaders can't afford to pretend we're something we're not. We must be in community where it is safe to be real before it's too late. Where we can be reminded that our value and worth comes from who we are in Christ, not what we do as Christians. Only then can we lead toward a culture of authenticity.

I Feel So Naked

Trust lurks, skitters in shadows, watching
His hands His face His love in you.
Trust peers, aches, tip-toes closer (sometimes farther).
Patient you trust His love in me.
Andrea, with Jim[††]

A culture of authenticity is so liberating! You can hear it in email after email. It's like breaking free of being chained to the expectations of all the sub-cultures we live in. And it's possible to be free since God already knows, and his opinion is the only one that counts. But to create this culture where "the truth will set you free" requires public vulnerability of the leader.

Lee Iacocca had a maxim that rings true in culture creation, "Speed of the leader, speed of the team." In other words, people always want to fit and belong, so they walk into every new setting (new culture) subconsciously asking, "What are the rules?" With authenticity, the leader sets the pace with his or her willingness to be vulnerable, and usually everyone else runs a few steps behind that level of vulnerability. This is true of personal friendships, small groups, and church cultures.

Spiritual leadership requires vulnerability. And vulnerability requires security. And security ultimately comes only from God. As those of us who lead shift the weight of our security onto God, we can freely be vulnerable. But this too is messy. How vulnerable? What's appropriate, or is everything appropriate? What if it makes others uncomfortable? What if they hear what I'm really like and don't want to follow my leadership? How can we be appropriately vulnerable without sinking into spiritual voyeurism—revealing ourselves for our sake more than theirs? There are no easy answers, but there is a Spirit who guides.

Those who teach at Gateway publicly talk about struggles and weaknesses. We get emails like this one, from a Christian stretching in new ways, saying, "I am always amazed at the authenticity of the messages. It strikes at the core of who we are in relating to God at a heart level rather than just a head level." After being vulnerable, I have to confess that sometimes I leave our Sunday service feeling exposed. I drive away feeling like I just stood up there and flashed everybody—they've seen it all! And I feel horribly naked.

I spoke on Jesus' message about judging others. How our insecurities drive us to label and discount and judge all the time in order to feel better about ourselves (Phariseeism 101). And how Jesus says when we judge others, we judge ourselves. I had learned of a local preacher in town who had publicly ridiculed churches like Gateway, saying we compromised the Word of God to get spiritual seekers in the door. I was livid. If we are the Body of Christ, and Christ came to seek and save that which was lost, what church shouldn't be working to restore everyone and all things to right relationship with God? He was discounting what God was doing through us and didn't really have a clue. This attitude is so antithetical to Jesus' final prayer that "all of them may be one, Father, just as you are in me and I am in you."[3]

That same week, I was driving through the wealthiest part of town where they are building all kinds of new, luxury neighborhoods. I noticed how a new church building was springing up in about every other neighborhood, and I had a despising thought, "Why do so many church leaders feel called to the wealthiest parts of town?" I even voiced my cynical disapproval with some joking remark to a friend in the car. Later that night, the Lord turned the mirror around on me. I realized that for some dark reason, without effort, I automatically labeled, grouped, judged, and discounted local, important expressions of the Body of Christ. I did exactly what I hated that preacher doing to our church.

Why did I do it? Because I'm an insecure, struggling, judgmental Christ-follower, and if it weren't for the grace of God, mercifully confronting my shallow, unloving heart, I would just stay blind and stuck.

I shared that with our congregation, and I'll be honest (only because to pretend sure wouldn't read well in a chapter on authenticity!), I felt ashamed, naked, and exposed after I left. I had a running conversation in my head on the drive home, "Now people are gonna think I'm just an egomaniac who thinks I'm better than those other Christian leaders." "Yeah, and so what?" "So what? They'll judge me and use it to discount what they don't want to hear. I should have kept this to myself." And then the thought took over, "This is not about you, John; this is about Jesus."

Be real and fear not!

We've talked openly about struggles with selfishness, ego, doubts, and temptation in the messages, not sharing every detail or thought, but enough for people to see our fallen humanity. Teachers must be vulnerable yet protect privacy of family members. I let my small group in on my victories and my defeats, even when some in my group were not yet Christ-followers.

I've shared with our congregation of standing at the crossroads of faith when my father died. As a new Christian, wanting to curse God for letting this gut-wrenching pain come to me, for his deafening silence to my prayers, for the suffering my father endured as his muscles atrophied to the point of needing help rolling over in his bed. I let them see the internal struggle we all face when God disappoints us—the authentic struggle to turn away in hurt or to trust his words as truth—to trust that he does still love me even when I don't feel it.

But it's a very real struggle to be vulnerable. It's much more powerful and immediately gratifying to play the Pharisee (I've done both). To have people look up to you, tell you how in awe they are of how mature and spiritual you are. To be right all the time and to have an answer for everything and everyone. To never feel the insecurity of being vulnerable to the judgments of others because you never let them see your faults or struggles. There's a real powerful reason to play the Pharisee. Security! Pharisees don't have to rely on God for security—they never feel insecure.

No Perfect People Allowed

From the very first service at Gateway, we've had a motto: No perfect people allowed.[4] We find ways to say "No perfect people allowed" over and over and over again. Culture obeys the law of entropy—without ongoing vision providing energy, it deteriorates. Vision statements like these define a preferred way of acting—a culture. We tell people, "This is not a place to put on your churchy-face to mask your problems. When we pretend we're perfect—we're stuck. But when we allow each other to be works-in-progress, we all find the support we need to authentically change."

These picture-painting visions of a preferred culture become self-fulfilling. If a leader models this vision and reminds people enough, "This is who we are," they begin taking risks to act this way. Even if your current culture dreads transparency, in time people can begin to act their way into becoming the vision of vulnerability if the leader leads and paints a compelling picture.

In the book *Tipping Point*, Malcolm Gladwell chronicles the epidemic spread of sociological trends from the rebirth of Hush Puppy shoes, to fast-falling crime rates, to the rise of teen smoking. A key factor in the "spreading" of the message among groups has to do with what he calls the "stickiness factor." If you can find a simple way to package information so that it sticks—so that it connects emotionally to motivate action and is easily remembered—the message spreads like a virus.

Without realizing this was happening, the vision of "No perfect people allowed" became similarly sticky in our church's culture. Trent came to Gateway because he heard the sticky vision for authenticity from Craig (a seeker who found faith) who had heard it from his friend, Nate, before attending Gateway. Listen to Trent describe how it spread to him:

Gateway is a huge reason that I am not only alive today, but I am blessed with a peace I never imagined would be possible on this planet. It was a Saturday afternoon in 2001 that I desperately called Craig, an acquaintance that I had met in AA a few weeks earlier. He was sober and told me to call him if I ever needed help. Boy, did I ever need help. I had just finished a horrible two-day binge of alcohol and cocaine. It felt that if I continued the way I was going, I would soon kill myself. You see, I couldn't live with alcohol and drugs and I couldn't live without them. So I called and told him I would do whatever was required of me to stop this way of life. I could no longer do it my way.

He told me that he had been going to this church that had really helped him connect with God for the first time in a practical way. I had been trying to connect with God ever since praying a prayer to become a Christian in the eighth grade. But I had resigned that I would have to "endure" this hell on earth until I died, then I would be at peace in heaven. The more I failed, the more I felt uncomfortable in church. But Craig told me that Gateway's policies were "Come as you are" and "No perfect people allowed." That immediately put me at ease, because I definitely qualified: I had lost my car to a drug dealer, I had lost my fiancée, and I was about to lose my freedom to a possession charge. Most importantly, I had just about lost hope that I wanted to live.

Fast forward to today. Two years later, I have been sober since the first weekend I walked into Gateway (absolutely no coincidence). I realized that drugs and alcohol were just symptoms of my real dilemma . . . separation from God. And I have realized that I can enjoy this life rather than simply endure it. I thought that I needed to get well and then come to church. I had it backwards. I needed to come to church to get well.

Trent and his wife now lead our Recovery ministry, all because the vision stuck with Nate, then spread from Craig to Trent.

As leaders drop word pictures, stories, and "sticky statements" of authentic culture into the group, it acts as dye that ultimately colors what everyone sees. But some leaders may fear creating such a messy, imperfect culture. Maybe you're asking whether we should have lowered the bar by saying "No perfect people allowed." After all, didn't Jesus say we are to be perfect, just as our Father in heaven is perfect?[5] But what did he mean by that? Was he implying that some people *could* reach perfection this side of heaven? It hardly seems possible since he immediately follows in his discourse with our need to ask forgiveness for our sins whenever we pray.[6] And doesn't John, the disciple he loved, tell us, "If we claim to be without sin, we deceive ourselves and the truth is not in us."[7]

The word, "perfect," *telios* in Greek, conveys the idea of being "complete" or "whole." God is One. He is complete, perfect, lacking nothing. We are to *be* perfect—complete. It refers to who we become primarily, not just what we do—but it affects everything we do. We are to seek wholeness, completeness, where we increasingly experience the God-infused life filling our souls, until we feel no need to make up for our spiritual deprivation by pretending or exaggerating or hiding. This is authentic spirituality; one that comes only from intimate connection to the Father who injects us with his whole life. We can't manufacture it. We can only receive it—which requires humble honesty. I believe this is how we are to "be perfect" just as the Father is perfect.

■ ■ ■

Jesus' half-brother, James, tells us the path to healing is authenticity—not only with God but also with each other. "Therefore confess your sins to each other and pray for each other so that you may be healed."[8] John tells us that when we live in the light, not denying our sins or struggles but letting the light of Christ illuminate them and cleanse us of them, the result is that we have deep community and connection with one another. Spiritual growth only happens as honesty before God and others draws us into the light. There we can face our imperfections and sins with the vision of who God sees we can become. In the light of community with God and others, we find healing.

Into the Light

Confident she didn't need to pretend, Tia continued to come to Gateway and explore. Feeling safe, Tia ventured out and decided to get into a small group with seven other women meeting in a nearby home. My wife led them through a study of who we were meant to be in Christ, called *The Search for Significance*.

Every meeting, Tia would curl up in the same chair quietly observing, listening, and taking it all in as other women opened their hearts about personal struggles with dark lies, exposing them in the light of God's truth. She listened as Lisa, not yet a Christian, shared of the pain of rejection caused by her ex-husband's affair. She listened as Christy, a young lawyer, who had walked with Christ for years, shared how God's truth in Christ led her to a liberating freedom from approval addiction. Tia's mind slowly began to wrap around God's grace offered in Christ, as she experienced other women sharing real struggles but finding acceptance and love and support from each other to become who God intended them to be. Tia never missed a meeting, did her homework, and over the next six months began to read the story of Jesus for herself in the book of John. She cut off her bisexual relationships as she found increasing hope for healing.

One night, as Tia sipped a Diet Coke from her usual comfortable chair, Jaime told for the first time of the painful memories she'd locked away of being sexually molested by a trusted relative. Through tears, Jaime revealed the shame and guilt she had carried her whole life, feeling dirty, slutty, unworthy of the purity of God's love. Yet now she understood how that event had so distorted her view of herself as she learned what was true of her in Christ. As the words cascaded out of Jaime's mouth in a wash of relief, Tia could feel the cleansing flood of tears welling up in her own heart. As she listened to Jaime recount the release from shame she experienced, knowing God had not rejected her, Tia yearned for the embrace of the same Savior.

Pushing down the rising lump in her own throat, Tia began to tell her story. Not just recalling the facts but, for the first time, feeling the pains of the wounds that had festered so long, locked behind the hard-callused memories of her past. That night began a healing work in her heart as she experienced Jesus himself loving her, comforting her, grieving the evil perpetrated upon her, speaking words of worth and affirmation he intended her to hear long ago—now voiced through his Body, the church.

I'll never forget our second baptism service when Tia and I waded into the river together nine months after our first meeting. A Texas-sized storm had suddenly rolled in, overshadowing our usual pristine hill-country setting. Rain pelted the river. Lightning cracked the sky. Tia and two others were the last of thirty-five getting baptized that day. I looked at her and asked if she wanted to wait.

"I've waited long enough," she said, "nothing's going to stop me now."

■ ■ ■

Creating a culture where people are free to be themselves, warts and all, is the soil in which God's Spirit causes growth. We've seen it in seekers' lives, we've seen it in believers' lives, and I have seen it in my life. Authenticity breaks down the trust barriers keeping our generation from pursuing faith.

This kind of realness may threaten some leaders. If you value "fixed-up" or "put-together" people, don't risk allowing people to be authentic. You'll hear things that frustrate you, disappoint you, hurt you, cause you to doubt your efficacy, and make you wonder if people take your teaching seriously. I've had leaders admit to me of falling back into sexual sin or going back to smoking pot to relax or frequenting porn sites on the web, and we've had to walk with them toward restoration before they could lead again—it's painful. But I've decided authenticity is the only way past it.

Just because you don't know about something doesn't mean it's not there! When we allow people to bring their struggles into the light, we can walk together toward healing and wholeness. And more times than I can count, this authentic messiness has led to authentic growth and greater spiritual maturity. I can think of dozens of people from Gateway who went from major foul-ups to wholeheartedly following Christ and ministering to others, some in a full-time capacity. All because they refused to pretend and hide, and in the light of authentic community they found healing and growth.

But authenticity can be dangerous if left alone. If you create a culture where people will rip it open and let others see the dirt and grime of life, but you have not created a culture of acceptance, where grace abounds, you're setting people up for a great letdown.

In the next chapter, let's look at why it's essential to marry authenticity with acceptance if we want to create churches and groups where postmodern seekers and believers can take steps forward in faith.

STUDY GUIDE

Culture Check

1. "Speed of the leader, speed of the team," said Lee Iacocca. People will only be as authentic and vulnerable as the most vulnerable among them—usually that means the leader. How willing are you to model authenticity and vulnerability? What fears must you face?

2. Are you tempted to believe the lies that tell us, "I can't tell them that, they wouldn't follow my leadership"? This leads us to isolation. Are you willing to find at least one safe person and commit to opening up to them about everything? This is the only path to authentic leadership.

3. What could you do to create a culture where authenticity becomes expected and passed on throughout the culture?

Small Group Questions

1. When you were growing up, was it okay to doubt and question faith, or was it forbidden? How did this affect your faith? Did it strengthen it or create greater doubt? Why?

2. Read Luke 11:42–46. If you read the Gospels, Jesus' harshest words were reserved not for the blatant "sinners" of his day, but for the religious leaders who were inauthentic. Why do you think authenticity is so important to the Lord?

3. Read 1 John 1:8–9. Why is it so difficult for us to admit our sins and shortcomings to God? Why is practicing regular, immediate confession such a critical step on the path to spiritual growth?

4. Read James 5:16. The recovery movement understood the power of taking a fearless moral inventory and fully telling all to at least one other person (Steps 4 and 5, see page 245). What fears do you have in doing this? Why do you think Scripture says it's so important?

5. What could we do as a group to become more authentic with one another? How could we better live out James 5:16?

The Struggle
with Tolerance

Artist: David Reed

Come as You Are: Creating a Culture of Acceptance

Accept one another, then, just as Christ accepted you.

Romans 15:7

Jerry? Jerry, are you in there?" Christy knocked on the locked bathroom door. "Jerry, if you're in there, open the door." Her rapid pounding on the white door escalated as the anxiety in her tone increased. Fighting back tears she screamed, "Jerry, say something to me, I know you're in there . . . answer me!" Christy rushed to the hall closet, her heart beating wildly, as her mind imagined the worst. She grabbed a coat hanger, bending it straight.

Why did I leave him alone? She had gone shopping partially just to get out of the depressing environment, but she returned home early, feeling uneasy about leaving Jerry by himself. Her hands were trembling as she tried to thread the wire hanger into the tiny hole in the center of the doorknob, a trick to release the antique locking mechanism. "Come on . . . come on," her mind was racing as she frantically poked to unlock the door.

"Click," the door swung open. Christy stood frozen for a second as she took in the scene. Jerry lay sprawled out on the bathroom floor, pills littered the tile around him. The worst of her fears were confirmed. Rushing back to the phone, she dialed 911.

■ ■ ■

It was a Friday morning, and I had just put the finishing touches on the weekend's message. Searching through my desk for a phone number, my eyes locked on the heading of an email I had printed, *jerrymanning@austinrr.com* "Growing through Loss."

"I wonder what happened to Jerry," I thought to myself, glancing over his old email. I recalled meeting with Jerry and his girlfriend, Christy, a year before. I had never heard such a "Job" story before. Jerry had lost his entire family of four, one by one, in a matter of years. When the last member of his family, his twin brother, died of leukemia, Jerry sank into despair. The day Jerry came to talk he was struggling for a reason to live.

An agnostic most of his life, I assumed that without God the tragedies had left him hopeless. But little did I know it was guilt from a seared conscience after his brother's death that caused him not to want to live. That never came out in our first meeting. Christy had convinced Jerry to come to Gateway, hearing you could "come as you are." She didn't feel like they belonged in church, but she also knew they desperately needed help from somewhere. She didn't know where else to turn.

"Lord, I don't know what happened to Jerry," I prayed that day, compelled to reread the email. "I don't feel like I helped him very much, and I haven't seen them in a year. Please help him come to know your grace and redeem all the loss he's felt." After praying for Jerry, I went back to my work. But for some reason, I couldn't get Jerry off my mind. It kept bugging me thinking that the Lord is the only one who can redeem such tragedy, and yet, I felt like I failed to help Jerry see it. Finally, unable to get Jerry out of my head, I took it as a prompting and sent him an email.

■ ■ ■

Tuesday morning, Christy drove Jerry home from the hospital in silence. Christy wondered how much more of this she could take. After a weekend in intensive care, Jerry had survived his near-fatal suicide attempt, but he didn't seem any better. She loved Jerry, but they weren't married, just living together, and he was destroying both their lives. She felt so unworthy of God's help, but for a season, going to Gateway, she started to believe that maybe God really cared. Maybe God was for her, not against her. Either way, now she had reached the point of desperation. She silently cried out, "God, please help Jerry, and help me know what to do. We need your help."

That morning, as Christy checked their email, she noticed my email address. As she read the email, she couldn't help but feel like God had answered her prayer. She printed it out and handed it to Jerry, who sat comatose on the couch.

Jerry glanced down without a word and read:

> Jerry, I ran across an old email of yours this morning and felt like God
> wanted me to pray for you. I don't know where you are or what's going on,
> but I just wanted you to know I am praying for you and would love to talk if
> you ever need a listening ear.
> —John

Jerry noticed the date—it had been sent the morning he was pondering taking his life. With unprecedented energy, Jerry got up and dialed the church office.

Jerry walked into the office that afternoon looking like the living dead. Risé, our administrator, had briefed me about his condition. I had assumed it was despair over his loss that drove him to want to end his life, but I was wrong.

"I just can't get rid of this guilt I feel," Jerry confided, explaining why he nearly took his own life. "I miss my family terribly, but what haunts me is what I did to my brother. I loved my twin brother and looked up to him my whole life. But he resented me for years after I got involved with a girl he really loved. He felt betrayed and told me, 'You're no longer my brother.' For years we didn't talk because he refused to see me. I wanted to try to resolve it, but before I could, he passed away. I feel so horrible for what I did to my brother, I just don't want to live."

I couldn't believe it. What Jerry needed most was not an explanation of why tragedy happens, what he needed was simply to understand God's grace. I told Jerry the story of David, who had wronged his neighbor Uriah by sleeping with his wife, then conveniently had Uriah abandoned on the battlefield to cover it up. I read the words of David, in agony as the guilt ate into his soul, realizing that his sin was against God and God alone. I read passage after passage to Jerry about God's grace offered in Christ, to remove our guilt. As I read the Scriptures, I noticed tears of relief pooling in Jerry's eyes. He prayed with me accepting God's grace. I suggested he go home and write a letter to God about all the things he'd like to tell his deceased brother, then read it out loud to God. Jerry later recalled in an email what happened after that night.

> As I read the letter out loud to God that night, it felt like a huge weight
> lifted off my shoulders. I wept tears of release as I felt the guilt finally leave.
> Not long after, I got involved in Gateway's Depression Support group, where
> I made some wonderful friends who taught me how to grieve and experience
> laughter and joy again. After years of therapy, pills, medical bills, and an
> attempted suicide, to think I could have found this relief by accepting the
> grace of God offered in Jesus Christ. It would have saved me years of guilt
> and wouldn't have cost me a dime.

Beyond Tolerant

Jerry's story reminds us—God's grace is amazing! What our world needs more than anything else is grace. Not more talk about grace—but grace that seeks out lost people like God does. Grace with skin on it—because people are born to run from God without it.

> Due to a bad childhood experience, I hated church so much that I would nearly vomit before I stepped foot in the door. When I agreed to go to Gateway with my husband, two things hit me coming through the door: a wave of nausea, and the sight of people my age, in jeans, drinking coffee. The message was on patience. The next week you spoke on generosity. Again, a message I needed. I realized then this church is filled with God-seeking adults like me, who get lost, frustrated, confused and irritated. You showed me I don't have to be cute, well dressed, politically correct, or always wear a smile. I just have to be "me." "Me" is not great by any stretch of the imagination, but it is good enough for your church. Thanks for making my nausea go away!
>
> —Deanna

We all know deep down that something's wrong with this world. It is not hard for people to comprehend Paul's words in Romans 7, "I really want to do what is right, but I don't do it. Instead, I do the very thing I hate."[1] Yet like Jerry, instead of turning to God for help, naturally we run from God, the only one who can heal us, change us, and give us life. We automatically feel unacceptable to God.

Until we believe that God is truly *for* us, not *against* us, we will keep running and hiding (Christians included!). For this reason grace forms the foundation for all significant spiritual growth. A come-as-you-are culture brings this grace to life, so that people can truly become all God intended them to be.

Gordon MacDonald said it well, "The world can do almost anything as well as or better than the church. You need not be a Christian to build houses, feed the hungry, or heal the sick. There is only one thing the world cannot do. It cannot offer grace."[2] The uniqueness of Christianity boils down to this one word: Grace. Philip Yancey notes, "The Buddhist eight-fold path, the Hindu doctrine of *karma*, the Jewish covenant, and Muslim code of law—each of these offers a way to earn approval."[3] Grace says God accepts you and loves you unconditionally—"as is."

But if you interview people on the street, few, if any, associate Christianity or church with anything closely resembling grace. What they feel is law—zero tolerance, judgment, and condemnation. Why doesn't the church utilize its greatest asset? Though the world cannot offer grace, in its absence, it found an inexpensive substitute: tolerance.

The very idea of toleration implies enduring or putting up with something you don't like or value. Our culture diets on the candy of tolerance, but what it really craves is the meat of grace. Tolerance does not value people but simply puts up with their behavior or beliefs. Tolerance alone cannot accommodate both justice and mercy—it can only look the other way. Tolerance might deal with differences, but it can't embrace us in full knowledge of sin and remove our guilt.

If you think about it, God tolerates rejection of him and his ways more patiently than any being in the universe. Who else puts up with so many beliefs and practices contrary to his own? He's been watching us destroy ourselves and each other, yet has held off his righteous judgment for millennia!* Paul points this out in Romans 2, addressing those who judge others as unworthy yet fail to see their own sin: "Do you show contempt for the riches of his kingdom, tolerance and patience, not realizing that God's kindness leads you toward repentance?"[4] God far exceeds the requirements of mere tolerance; he restrains his judgment and even showers unworthy people with grace. If we are to represent God through the church, we must not just occasionally tolerate people we don't like; we too must show grace.

■ ■ ■

Grace is the most liberating truth of the Bible, yet it is so counterintuitive, so otherworldly, so much the antithesis of the three-strikes-you're-out way of the world that it requires painstaking efforts to help people "get it." People do not naturally understand what Romans 8 goes on to say, that even though we fail to live up to God's standards, or even our own: "There is now no condemnation for those who are in Christ Jesus."[5] Not only are we set free from the fear of judgment and condemnation through Christ, but God accepts us and pulls us into the closest of relationships: "We are God's children."[6] And God is for us. He's not mad at us! In fact, it says, "If God is for us, who can be against us?"[7] Nobody! God makes the unacceptable acceptable. But how

---

* Human tolerance is an end in itself, the virtue of suspending one's judgment of another in the midst of disagreement. God's tolerance is somewhat different in that he is patient but always has a future judgment in view. He, unlike us, does have authority to judge humanity, and most assuredly will (despite his temporarily choosing not to do so, see Psalm 50:21). God sees every evil act perpetrated and tolerates it for a time so that all willing people can receive his grace—forgiveness and a restored relationship with God, even for the worst offender. He is tolerant so that we will repent (turn from our evil ways to follow God's ways) and let him change us. The stark reminder is that those unwilling to receive his grace for evils done in this life will receive his just judgment in the next life when God's toleration of sin comes to an end.

can we put skin on this kind of grace? As Philip Yancey noted, you only learn grace by being graced.[8]

Acceptance is the most tangible out-working of grace—drawing near in relationship without condemnation. How accepted do you think people feel coming to your church or small group? Can you tangibly show people different than you how much they are worth to God by accepting them? Scripture reminds us of the costly price of acceptance: "Christ also suffered when he died for our sins once for all time . . . that he might bring us safely home to God."[9] There is no cheap grace—if we offer acceptance based on grace, it is only because it was freely given to us at the greatest cost.

God accepts us into relationship. He lets us live at home with himself despite the fact that we continually try to play God in our own lives or others' lives—usurping his authority and following our will rather than his. (Still, we all sin, believers and unbelievers alike.) Yet despite that, he draws us close in love, accepting us "as is," if we are willing. Scripture admonishes us to "accept one another, then, just as Christ accepted you, in order to bring praise to God."[10] This passage goes on to say that those thought to be far away from God will discover his mercies and find hope in him. Acceptance puts skin on the idea of grace. The soil of acceptance allows God's grace to take root in hard hearts. Without this, no one changes.

No Prerequisites Needed

But most people assume they will not be accepted *until* they change, not by God and definitely not by church people. So we must tell them the truth over and over. That's why we have said "Come as you are" since the beginning of Gateway. We try to clear out the confusing messages in order to make one thing clear: God says, "Come as you are," and so do we. Every week in our program newcomers read:

> Come as you are. . . .
>
> You don't have to dress up. You don't have to be any particular age. We couldn't care less who you voted for in the last election. And please, don't feel the need to pretend about anything. Gateway Community Church is a place where God meets seeking people who are far from perfect. That means anyone is welcome, no matter where you are on your spiritual journey. So learn at your own pace. Ask questions. Seek. We believe you'll find what you're looking for. You'll learn how to relate to God. You'll experience Christian community. And here's the big thing—you will change. Join us as we seek God together. Just come as you are.[11]

This vision-casting statement sets people at ease. They read it and think, Maybe this is a place that will accept me. Church must re-present to others the Body of the One who is willing to accept rather than condemn—who draws near in relationship—who is *for* them, not *against* them. Everybody longs to know this—that despite everything, they can be accepted and forgiven. But words alone won't do. Theological statements like "Christ died for your sins" and "God so loved the world" have been leached of all meaning for seekers today by what they have experienced. Many people can't believe God will accept them and love them until those who claim to know God start to show them.

Us Versus Them?

Instead of acceptance that draws them into relationship and says "I'm for you," seekers pick up an "us versus them" mentality from many Christians. It is subtle but deadly.

We had to work hard to root out lobby conversations or attitudes that portrayed to seekers, "We are right and you are wrong" or "I have it all together, and you have nothing without Christ." While some of this may be true, the attitude conveys a message that stinks of ungrace—as if we did something for ourselves apart from God's grace. This attitude gets interpreted as looking-down-the-nose in judgment. As Mark Twain so appropriately put it, some people are "good in the worst sense of the word." This attitude sends the message, "We know the law and live it, and you don't." Nothing could be more patently false.

Paul says the law makes things worse, not better, because no one can live up to it.[12] It makes people run and hide. The Old Testament law shows us when we've done wrong and points out how we need to change, but it will never help us get better. It leaves us hopeless. This is why Paul said in Romans 7:4–6 we had to die to the law in order to become who God intended.

Only by giving up trying to live up to law and surrendering to the leading of God's Spirit do we get any better—we can't do it apart from grace.[13] Yet for some reason, seekers hear the hopelessness of law more than the life-giving message of God's Spirit. Unfortunately, many who desperately need God run from God and run from his church because they fear judgment and condemnation for the way they are. Instead of "come as you are" what they have heard most clearly is "you're unacceptable as is."

■ ■ ■

When Kylie Kent came to Gateway, her defenses were up. Kylie worked for the attorney general's office overseeing programs for domestic violence and sexual assault. As a feminist, all she had seen or heard gave her the impression that faith in Jesus was a very oppressive, intolerant, unloving, manmade religion. Listen to how the experience of acceptance and grace changed her mind:

> As an adult, I was never involved with church at all, except occasionally on holidays. I felt that religion was just a manmade belief system created by desperate people to fill some sort of void within. When I thought of Christianity, I thought of bigots and gay-bashers. My hometown of Topeka, Kansas, is also the home of a nationally known street preacher. On every major intersection, he and his congregation held high their signs proclaiming, "God hates fags" in the name of Christianity. I knew I would never align myself with people like these.
>
> My husband, Tucker, was raised in the church and wanted to look for one to attend when we moved to Austin. When friends invited us to Gateway, I figured this church would be like all the rest; I'd be uninspired and unimpressed. The first thing I always looked for when we visited a new church was what that church did for the community. I figured if I had to go to church, I might as well go to one that understood their responsibility to address social injustice. Right away, I noticed Gateway had an impressive Compassion Ministry. I needed to see that they cared about other people to give the church consideration.

Kylie needed to physically see the grace of God extended in love to others. For her, our compassion efforts opened the door. Even before becoming a Christian, Kylie decided she wanted to be a part of the "good" that was happening at Gateway, got involved with Compassion, and started talking to us about a new ministry for survivors of sexual assault or domestic violence. If our staff had acted like Kylie had nothing to offer or teach us about sexual abuse since she wasn't a believer, I'm convinced it would have closed the door for her. But those conversations affirmed Kylie as a person of value who demonstrated a heart of compassion like Jesus portrayed. Even though some of her beliefs seemed at odds with ours, Kylie felt accepted and valued as a person who mattered to God and had something to offer. This sparked intense biblical study for Kylie that ultimately turned her view of Jesus upside down. As she tells it:

> After attending Gateway for over a year, asking questions openly, researching, and soul-searching my current beliefs, I was able to see Jesus and Christianity in a whole new light. Studying Jesus' life and teachings at Gate-

way also helped me realize that Jesus modeled something totally different than what I saw modeled growing up. Jesus loved and served others. He is the ultimate servant. He is not judgmental; he is the greatest advocate for social justice! All people are welcome to come to Christ, no matter who they are or where they have been. I couldn't believe the truth about Jesus had been so obscured. When I came to understand the nature and character of Jesus, I gave my heart to Christ and was baptized. I am so glad Gateway strives to be a safe place for people to discover the true Jesus, who is compassionate, serving, and loving, and who longs to bring even feminists and liberals into his love!

Kylie now leads our Comfort and Hope ministry she helped start, showing grace to survivors of sexual abuse and domestic violence. But as you can see, she had to soak in grace to believe it. For Kylie, seeing Christ-followers show love and compassion to those outside the church helped kickstart the process. Feeling accepted, respected, and valued when she wanted to help meet a need, even before she was a believer, helped her reconsider Christian faith. But notice how she had to completely redefine her whole view of the God of Jesus.

It wasn't a tragic event or longing that brought me back, but a wonderful chain of events that started with my girlfriend and continued through the openness and acceptance of Gateway. Reading books, hearing messages answering my long-held questions, all these things brought me to a point that I realized I needed and wanted God in my life. Since asking Jesus in, I've seen a huge change. I'm able to take more risks, and I do things that challenge me and take me out of my comfort zone knowing God is there. —Chad

You Ought to Fire That God!

When Christians wrongly assume their job is to help make others acceptable—even though we could never make ourselves acceptable—this tells people God will not accept them "as is." Consequently many people reject the God of Christianity not realizing the god they associate with Christ is a false god! We must constantly teach to clearly define the true God of grace.

Keith Miller, author of *A Hunger for Healing*, talks about being a Christian in a recovery group, overhearing a new guy talk to this old-timer about taking Step 3—the step of surrendering your life and will to God.

The new guy said, "No way I'm going to turn my life over to God! He'd ruin me—and I'd deserve it!"

The old-timer listened patiently to the young guy's description of God and then said, "You ought to fire that God; you ought to fire him! You've got the wrong God for this program, friend. The God who operates here is loving, 95 forgiving, and gives you all the chances you need to get the program; he is honest and will always be there for you. I had a God like yours when I first came here, but I had to fire him and get me a new God."

"What can I do about a God if I fire mine?" the new man asked.

The old-timer thought for a minute and said, "You can use mine till you get on your feet."

As he listened to this, Miller thought, "I'm quitting this program! Making up their own gods to fit their needs—we're talking about Ultimate Reality, friends, you can't just *fire* God and get a new one!"

But on his way home, he started thinking about what the old-timer meant, rather than what he said. He realized we all have misconceptions of God—often masked with the face of parents, authority figures, or others. And even though he had been a Christian in ministry for decades, even on the staff of a seminary, he too needed to fire his god. Not the God of Jesus, but the imposter god in his head that kept him from becoming a more loving, joyful, peaceful, patient, kind, self-controlled person. Though his theology claimed one thing, his heart followed the dictates of a lesser god.[14]

One of the main tasks of teaching must be to continually paint pictures of the God of grace until the lesser gods are overthrown. Many people come into church needing to fire the god in their head that they've associated with the God of Jesus. To create a culture of grace, a leader must first experience grace—then give it out liberally. I'm afraid many leaders theologically understand grace yet do not really experience the liberating reality of it.

I'm convinced this constitutes the central problem for Christians as well as seekers—we don't trust God. We still feel the need to "do" or "succeed" or "prove" somehow we are acceptable. We might not say this in words, but the absence of feeling deeply loved, or truly at peace, or regularly feeling ambushed by joy betrays our true beliefs. We live stressed, worried, anxious, controlling, joyless lives because we do not yet trust that we are fully accepted "as is" and God is "for us not against us." When we truly live in grace, we find freedom.

Isn't this why Jesus taught in so many parables? He knew just talking about God's grace and acceptance was not enough, he had to paint graphic pictures to illustrate it. He says God is like a shepherd risking his ninety-nine sheep and his own safety to go after the one lost stray. God is like a father whose son rejects him, moves out, and squanders half the family fortune, yet when he returns, his father humiliates himself by running to meet his lost son with open arms. God is like a housewife jumping up and down with excitement after finding one seemingly worthless coin she thought she'd lost.

God is like a man who throws a party for his son and tells his servants to go into the streets to invite the good and bad, all who will come are welcome![15]

Over and over again, in a thousand different ways, we try to let people know that God is not their enemy. He is the one who has been searching for them, longing to draw them near in relationship to help them become all they were intended to be. As I read Scripture, I see a God who truly values relationship with his children much more than perfect behavior. He wants us to do right and avoid wrong, but not to be acceptable. He wants obedience because he loves us. We yield our hearts and minds to follow his will because we trust the God of grace. Only then do we grow.

Grace Gifts

But to truly believe the good news about God's grace, we must often experience grace mediated through other people. At Gateway, we teach our leaders and congregation to give up trying to fix people—it's not our job—that's God's job. Instead, seek to accept and love people in order to reconnect them with God. That is what Paul said sums up our job with others: "If you love your neighbor, you will fulfill all the requirements of God's law."[16] This doesn't mean you never point out sinful or destructive behavior, but you don't focus on it.

If you saw a Rembrandt covered in mud, you wouldn't focus on the mud or treat it like mud. Your primary concern would not be the mud at all—though it would need to be removed. You'd be ecstatic to have something so valuable in your care. But if you tried to clean it up by yourself, you might damage it. So you would carefully bring this work of art to a master who could guide you and help you restore it to the condition originally intended. When people begin treating one another as God's masterpiece waiting to be revealed, God's grace grows in their lives and cleanses them.

Can your church or small group welcome a gay couple or a radical feminist or an atheist or a homeless crack-addict with open arms? Stop and picture it for yourself. Can you? When you consider these people entering your group, what are the first thoughts that come to mind? Thoughts that focus on what you think needs to change? Or thoughts that focus on their worth as people? Do you see the mud or the masterpiece? The priority of thinking reveals your priority of law or grace. But don't think that outwardly messy people are the only ones who need acceptance. "Perfect" people do too!

The Pains of Perfection

I wrongly assumed Cassidy knew the grace of God. Knowing she grew up in a predominately black Baptist church, I figured she knew about God's forgiveness. She understood it in her head but not in her heart. Though she was baptized in Christ at age seven, Cassidy somehow got the idea her salvation depended upon her perfection. As she grew up, she was the "perfect" girl: good grades, respectful, role model at church, voted "most likely to succeed" in school. But inside Cassidy felt immense guilt, shame, and anger because she knew she was far from perfect, and she wasn't sure that was acceptable.

The day Cassidy sat on stage at Gateway and told her story, you could hear a pin drop. "This inner shame haunted me all the way through college," Cassidy revealed through the fountain of beautiful braids framing her face. "I eventually hid myself, my true self, from family, friends, and especially God. My sophomore year in college, I got into a relationship and soon felt pressured to have sex. I had determined to remain a virgin and save myself for my husband, but in one night of horror, my boyfriend raped me. I soon found out I was pregnant. I was nineteen, terrified and living alone in my house full of shame. I aborted the baby just before Christmas break," Cassidy choked out her confession with eyes turned down. The room fell as silent as a winter snow.

Regaining composure, she continued. "For the next thirteen years I hid from God and people, and my depression grew. I felt I had completely ruined all my chances with God, and I would have to be punished tenfold for what I did. I stayed with the guy who raped me for two more years, suffering through his verbal, physical, and emotional abuse because I thought I deserved it. I believed God had a tote board he was pointing to saying, 'You haven't paid enough for that sin yet.' At times, I wanted to die. When friends or family tried to hug me, I would flinch. The touching actually hurt."

As Cassidy told her story, I could tell many were feeling the same pain of isolation by the sniffles across the room. Cassidy started seeing a therapist for her depression. Her therapist was not a Christian but recommended Cassidy find a church. After opening up to a coworker at the University of Texas, he suggested she check out Gateway.

Cassidy opened up that day about the healing discovery of grace mediated through others. "Gateway helped me understand little by little God's grace, forgiveness, and mercy. Every service encouraged me in some way, to not live in fear and punishment but to receive God's grace and mercy. I took a huge risk and opened up about my past to others in a small group I had joined. When I felt loved and accepted despite my ugly sin, a new freedom dawned. This healing process was a slow journey, but I finally came to realize completely that God was truly merciful, and I didn't have to crucify myself—Jesus had already paid my penalty. I know he loves me and accepts me unconditionally as his wonderful child, imperfect and all."

Cassidy hid all this from Gateway friends for over a year. You would never have known her secret burden. People all around you shoulder burdens that only grace mediated through an accepting group can unload. Cassidy now uses every opportunity to help others experience the freedom in Christ she found as she leads a small group of her own, because she knows the power of acceptance and love from Christ's Body, the church.

The Art of Grace

We have found the arts can sneak behind the walls of defense so many of us put up against grace. One of our all-time favorite worship songs, "Just the Way I Am," was written by our music director, J. J. Plasencio, to remind people of God's open arms:

> When I feel I'm all alone,
>   you take me just the way I am
> You hold my hand, don't let go,
>   you take me just the way I am.
> I need your peace to know your will,
>   you take me just the way I am.
> Though I fall, yet you still,
>   you take me just the way I am.[17]

Often at Gateway, we will do a multimedia that puts into words the ungrace so many feel, so that the teaching on God's grace connects with the heartfelt need. Last weekend our programming team created a multimedia of powerful images set to a popular song that the band played. The words echoed the questions so many under the weight of guilt and shame experience. By asking publicly the questions no one seems to voice, it created a yearning to hear there's an answer. It connected the abstract concept of grace with a sometimes-painful felt need. Then in turn, the multimedia infused the deep longing and hope for God's grace everybody desires. Our goal is that every time they hear this song they will feel that longing for grace and healing, and hopefully recall the message from that day. Just as music videos infuse songs with visual meaning, we utilize the power of media to help people get in touch with often suppressed longings for grace.

Sometimes the very fact that our band would play a song that seekers are familiar with communicates acceptance in a strangely roundabout way. We avoid doing songs just to be "cool" but willingly take songs expressing a spiritual longing in the culture and use them to show God's provision. We utilize the words of modern poets in today's culture, just like Paul did in Acts 17 to communicate the message to a Greek culture.

The architect who is designing our new facility came to faith at Gateway from a totally agnostic background. He considered himself a "good person" and a humanist. His first day at Gateway, back when we were meeting in a movie theater, our band played "Pride (In the Name of Love)" by U2 while images of Martin Luther King followed by images of Jesus filled the screen. Ironically, he and the woman he lived with thought, "Well, if they'd play that, maybe they'd accept us." Both became growing Christ-followers, were married, and serve in numerous ways four years later—but it started with acceptance. It has surprised me how many people feel they might be accepted simply because we use art forms or songs they recognize or relate to in everyday life.

> About two years ago, I finally realized what was missing in my life was a relationship with the Lord. So I went looking for a church. Most were too churchy for me. I don't like to dress up, especially on the weekends and I can't stand organ music! Then I heard an ad on the radio for Gateway Community Church. It talked about the great music they had, and that you could "come as you are." I couldn't believe my ears! I knew this was the place for me when I looked at the guy sitting next to me who was wearing shorts and Fred Flintstone slippers. Then the band started to play a Michelle Branch song! Immediately I knew this was my new church home. God knew I needed this kind of church to be part of a church family. —Reilly

Acceptance but Not Agreement

Of course, the big argument against taking the risk of accepting everyone with open arms—they might not change! They may misunderstand our acceptance as agreement with beliefs or behaviors God would not agree with.

If we accept others, are we accepting wrong behavior and therefore condoning things God clearly says are against his will—sinful? And if you've been fighting these thoughts, you're not the first. In Romans 6 Paul heads this fear off at the pass by saying, "So since God's grace has set us free from the law, does this mean we can go on sinning? Of course not!"[18] But what he proceeds to show is that grace-based relationship is the only hope for authentic growth—there's no other option.

We grow through relationship, as we all learn to offer our very selves to God to obey his Spirit's leading. And this happens best in communities of acceptance. A come-as-you-are culture forms the grace-based foundation on which God builds his church. Sure, people may misunderstand, they may take it as license, and they may never change. But changing people is God's job, not ours!

Acceptance of people is not the same as agreement with their choices, beliefs, or behaviors. I received a letter from a woman who tried out for our vocal team and decided to leave the church because "we weren't really accepting like we claimed." As it turned out, she was living and sleeping with her boyfriend and was not really intent on following Christ. Our music director gently explained that in order to lead others in worship of God, it required the hearts of vocal leaders willingly following God. After pointing out that God tells us to save sex for marriage for our benefit, he asked her if she was willing to follow God in this area. She wasn't. Though he encouraged her to keep coming and wrestle with what they talked about, in the end, she felt rejected. She did not understand why leadership required a step beyond "come as you are." She obviously had not heard the next phrase we often tag with it—"But don't stay that way."

People will misunderstand acceptance as agreement. But it's still worth the risk. If God's willing to take that risk, shouldn't we be willing?

Determining Trajectory

One of the most challenging tasks of leading a culture of acceptance is determining how to provide acceptance yet also confront unloving or destructive behaviors. Part of the solution is taking a "process" view of growth. All people are in process, and if they are willing, God is going to be gently cleaning the mud off his Rembrandt until their final day. So we must be patient like God.

Clearly, when you have a relationship established and the other person knows you are for them, not against them, it's easier for them to hear you speak truth in love. But if the relationship is not established, we must be sensitive to God's Spirit, asking him to help us determine the trajectory of the person. The question we ask in counseling is, "Which way forward from here?" In other words, which way is this person moving—closer to God or farther away—and how can we best help them move forward? Sometimes we stop the spiritual momentum of seekers or new followers because we try to play God and "fix" something we don't like before the time is right. If a person is not committed to following Christ in community, we can't expect them to act like it.

Jesus used a parable in Matthew 13 of a farmer (God) who sows good seed, but his enemy plants weeds at night that sprout up among the good wheat. His servants come and ask him, "'Shall we pull out the weeds?' they asked. He replied, 'No, you'll hurt the wheat if you do. Let both grow together until the harvest. Then I will tell the harvesters to sort out the weeds and burn them and to put the wheat in the barn.'"[19]

How often do leaders try to get weeds out of the church but inadvertently yank up good plants that were just so tiny that they looked like weeds? I think about Natalie and Chad, who came into our church while living together. We don't condone living together, but Natalie and Chad were on the right trajectory. If their small group and others had focused first on weeding out their living situation rather than watering the soil with acceptance—conveying how much they mattered to the God who was for them—it would have uprooted their spiritual growth. But soaking in grace, they both started following Christ after six months. Nine months later they came to see me for premarital counseling. I asked them about living together and their views on sex before marriage. They told me they had stopped having sex six months prior, after hearing a message on the subject and realizing God was trying to protect them. Chad and Natalie stayed on that growth trajectory, and they now lead a couples' small group four years later. This story has been repeated over and over again in our church.

Two gay men came and sat in our church for a year before coming to faith in Christ. They got connected in a small group, they started growing spiritually—finding an increasing sense of worth and value rooted in Christ. On their own initiative, they decided the Lord wanted them to stop their sexual relationship. They have put support systems in place to follow the Lord's leading (we will talk more about this in a later chapter). But only in the soil of acceptance can people find the love and security and value to allow God to do his work in their lives.

I have seen so many seekers soak in grace, begin to grow, and truly change over the years because God's Spirit is alive and working in their hearts, through his Body, the community of grace. But it takes time for those tiny shoots of faith to grow fruit. How many leaders get impatient and yank up good wheat because it looked like a weed to them? Jesus says, "Don't do it!" No, it will not be a pretty, tidy garden, but if the Lord of the Harvest is okay with letting it all grow together in a tangled mess and sorting it out later, can we be okay with it too?

Grace is the soil where people best grow, and creating a culture of acceptance defines the work we can do to prepare the soil of grace. But how do we provide the water and fertilizer and support structures to keep people growing? That's the subject of the next chapter. Come as you are . . .

But don't stay that way!

STUDY GUIDE

Culture Check

1. What most prevents you from personally experiencing grace—from feeling perfectly acceptable to God and pulled in close, no matter what?

2. When you hear of a person's sin, do you naturally focus on the mud that needs removing, or do you yearn to see the valuable Masterpiece revealed? How might this affect the way you treat them?

3. What ways could you story-tell, vision-cast, or equip people to better create a grace-filled environment of acceptance? What scares you about creating a culture of acceptance?

Small Group Questions

1. Why do people long to feel accepted?

2. Read Romans 7:15. Have you ever felt this cycle Paul describes? How did that feel? What do you think caused it?

3. Read Romans 8:1–6. How does God's promise (v. 1) to not condemn help us grow? Verses 5 and 6 indicate that God's non-condemning acceptance frees us to set our minds on what the Spirit desires. Why do you think this is so important for growth?

4. Read Romans 15:7. If we could truly feel accepted by each other, how might it help us grow?

5. What fears or concerns do you have about creating a culture of acceptance? What can we do to help create this environment?

chapter

6

But Don't Stay
That Way:
Creating a Culture
of Growth

*And love is not the easy thing . . .
the only baggage you can bring
Is all that you can't leave behind.*

U2, "Walk On"

planted the seed, Apollos watered it, *but God made it grow*."[1] Stop and ask
yourself whether you really believe the words of Scripture you just read—
that God alone makes people grow. That no amount of teaching, Bible
study, prayer, classes, or disciplines can change people—only God can! Sure,
he powerfully uses his church community in the process, as Paul indicates,
but God alone changes people, and only when they are willing.

If this is true, what implications does it have on the way you approach
helping people grow spiritually? Have you felt the frustration of trying to
make people change?

I have experienced and tried many different paths, plans, and curriculums designed to grow people toward Christian maturity, but very few
emphasize this radical idea that we can't change ourselves—at least not into
what God intended! Jesus stated this simple notion his last night on earth:
"I am the vine; you are the branches. Those who remain in me, and I in
them, will produce much fruit. For apart from me you can do *nothing*."[2]

The message subtly conveyed in some groups is that you are made right
with God by grace so you can go to heaven one day, but for now, it's up to
you to grow up to an "acceptable" Christian standard. Often, the standard

has more to do with outward conformity than with inward spiritual growth. As long as you *don't do* certain outward things—like smoking, getting drunk, having sex outside of marriage, or cussing—you pass. And as long as you *do* certain outward things—like reading the Bible, attending church, and praying regularly—you're acceptable. Even if on the inside you're still controlled by greed, jealousy, insecurity, impatience, fear, or anxiety; even if you're emotionally shut down, or controlling, or secretly addicted to lust or material possessions—just don't let it show, and you'll still be viewed as an upstanding Christian.

> *I grew up in church, I knew the church speak, the clichés, I had heard enough. I hated the fundamentalist suburban Christian culture I grew up in because of the judgment, legalism, and cookie-cutter mentality. I hated how we were trained to beat people over the head with the gospel.* —Lisa

Paul's whole message to the church in Galatia was a reminder that only God causes growth: "Are you so foolish? After beginning with the Spirit, are you now trying to attain your goal by human effort?"[3] Apparently, this is a common trap churches and groups fall into—starting with grace but backpedaling into trying to make ourselves or others acceptable by our own efforts (recall Paul's rebuke of the Galatian church[4]). The Scriptures make this very clear; people don't grow spiritually that way, they just conform outwardly and stay stuck inwardly. But as leaders create the right culture, God does for us all what we could never do for ourselves. That's Josh's story.

Memoirs from Mexico

It felt like 110 degrees to Josh as he looked out from the roof of the concrete church building over the most poverty-stricken area of Matamoras, Mexico. On his third Gateway mission trip, working alongside the Mexican people, he thought to himself how perfect the moment seemed.

"How ironic," Josh thought to himself, "I feel so alive, so full of life, like the man I was intended to be—but how different this looks than the picture I had of myself five years ago." He thought about his wife and the depth of love and contentment he felt. "I would have destroyed us all, Lord," Josh whispered in a prayer of thanks. "What an amazing thing you've done in my life, Jesus."

In a blur of prayer mixed with daydreaming, Josh reminisced, "Five years ago, my life was all about maintaining this image of 'the man' who had it all: A millionaire by age thirty, getting any woman, in control of my world. It was such an unfulfilling lie I had swallowed. But I didn't realize it."

Josh thought about the man he once was: "I could justify anything if it equated to having and holding more money." He recalled his former bosses at the brokerage firm. "They barely missed jail time. I didn't think twice about my illegal practices if I could count more in my pile of money at the end of the day. I was so greedy, Lord. But that was my life, my hoard—my god. I decorated with free furniture, drove thousand-dollar cars, ate cheap food just to save more—even when I had well over half a million in the bank. The only time I ever parted with a dollar of cash or a minute of time was for my own pleasure: trips to Vegas, Cancun, drinking, and skydiving. I could never have made this marriage last with that attitude. I'm so grateful for what you've done in me, Lord."

He felt a pang of regret as he thought of the many weekends going out with friends, getting buzzed, waking up the next morning in someone else's bed. "The next morning, I'd just want to leave. That's all. How broken was that, Lord? And yet it's like crack cocaine—you know it's messed up but still you want more. I couldn't stop. I was so controlling, so manipulating, so self-centered, yet never satisfied. But somehow you changed me. I'm so in love with my wife, and I'm so different now . . . more content. It's so much better! So much more fulfilling!"

Josh thought back to some of those pivotal spiritual moments. His first men's small group and the friendships that grew out of it—a group of highly motivated twenty-somethings, two with MBAs, two others owned their own businesses already, yet all were seriously broken in the way they saw themselves as men, especially when it came to women. "We admitted it to each other," Josh recalled. "We all had way too many sexual encounters, saw our manhood wrapped up in conquering women and money, and nobody wanted to give it up. It was too much of our identity."

He thought about that pivotal night, studying the book *Man in the Mirror*.[5] They had talked openly about addictions to masturbation, pornography, meaningless sexual encounters, workaholic tendencies, greed—all the guys were just beginning to seriously follow Christ. But that night they talked about the future. What if things never change? And together they realized this "persona" they were living for would never allow them to commit to loving relationships or to become secure men—not without the props. That night Josh decided to ask God to change him.

With other men around him to affirm this new direction, he started to really grow and so did others. The group studied the Scriptures, continued to talk openly about struggles, not trying to fix each other, but pointing out sinful patterns that kept each other from going the way of Christ. Josh recalled a late night conversation, standing in a parking lot with a guy he trusted.

"Josh, look at the pattern in this," John pointed out. "Is this what you want?" Though he had successfully drawn new boundaries with intercourse, he confessed his ongoing sexual struggle with heavy petting. He had four fouled-up relationships in a row with anorexic or bulimic women. "Why do you keep getting in these roller-coaster relationships, going too far with hurting, needy women?" his friend asked.

"I didn't see the pattern until that night," Josh reminded himself. "But as I reflected on it, I realized it was another symptom of the deeper disease—trying to play God of my life. My only criteria were thin, sexy, broken women because I could control them. I realized my deep insecurity was driving everything: my hoarding of money, my effort to be in power over women, my inability to truly connect and love and give to others."

He thought back to those meetings with Tommy, his spiritual "running partner" (accountability partner). At first, every week they confessed their failures—but nothing seemed to change. Accountability wasn't working.

"I'm a terrible person," he heard Tommy say in shame one day. He felt the same way, but as they committed to read Scripture and memorize passages about who they are in Christ, something dawned on Josh.

"You're not a terrible person—you're all these promises in Christ," he one day told Tommy during their weekly breakfast. "We need to help each other believe these promises, and let God take away this other stuff."

They started asking each other, "What do you think God's trying to do in your life?" "What's one thing you can intentionally do to better pursue God's will?" They focused on praying God's will in the areas of struggle. As they encouraged each other to become the picture of the man God intended, change happened.

With friends all around Josh helping to redefine what it meant to be a man, and as he put intentional practices in his life, he grew. He practiced praying in the moment—paying attention to the second and third lustful look and asking God to give him love in place of lust. He took a huge step after learning about tithing and in faith started giving money instead of just hoarding it. Josh soon found himself serving the homeless, taking mission trips, praying with friends, maintaining healthy dating patterns, leading friends to faith, and eventually leading his own small group—God was at work in his life.

"And when my biggest fear in life became reality," Josh recalled, "I was okay." Josh thought back to the stock market crash, losing most of his wealth overnight. "My friends around me loved me and affirmed me—it was the most freeing thing that ever happened to me!" Josh thought. "Lord, it's hard to describe, but I don't feel so oppressed by the money and worry. I found security in you that a pile of money could never bring."

Josh looked down from the roof at his friends helping build this Mexican church. "Lord, I'm amazed at what you've built in my life over the last five years with the help of my friends. I was unprepared for all of those things ... but you have done it in me."

The Way of Christ

Josh's story outlines how authentic spiritual growth happens. How do people grow? What does it really take to grow spiritually? It's very simple—do life with God! Paul explains in Romans 8:1–5 that once we stand in grace where we don't have to hide, we can become who God intended, fulfilling the intent of the law, as we "no longer follow our sinful nature but instead follow the Spirit."[6] Keeping our "minds set on what the Spirit desires."[7] So simple! But how do we help people do this very simple thing that's so difficult to do?

If you study Scripture, you don't find one curriculum or seven easy steps or a program every person can follow toward growth. Why? Because growth is personal to each person. God is always trying to get our attention long enough to lead us down the path of growth, but the worries, the busyness, and the noise of life distract us. This led us to try to discover the common biblical elements of spiritual growth at every stage of the journey, which follows the same pattern God designed for physical growth. We call this spiritual formation path *The Way of Christ*.

Messing Our Spiritual Diapers

Think about the way any growth happens. How do healthy children grow toward maturity? First, there's a clear *Picture of Maturity*—right? We know what a mature adult looks like, so we can see if a child is progressing or getting stunted. As a child matures, eventually she should feed herself, relate with others in healthy ways, take responsibility—adults who still bite and pinch when they don't get their way are not generally considered mature—unless they're pro wrestlers.

But growing up is a very messy process. So there's a *Context of Relationship*: loving, supportive relationships where kids grow best. There are

> Never have I been part of something so wonderful and special in my life. Every day, I hear of another person's life being changed by someone that affected them at Gateway, from the love of someone on staff or a fellow church friend to the grace given them or the learning opportunities through small groups.
> —Sharon

people in her life like Mom and Dad, who ideally love her and support her, encourage her and keep her on the path toward maturity. And there are friends, coaches, teachers, relatives, and mentors who encourage and guide and set examples.

And there's a *Personal Development Path* she's on to learn the skills and wisdom and habits necessary to grow into maturity. She will have to keep intentionally taking steps down this path. At first when she tries things like feeding herself, it's ugly! Ever watch a toddler eat? But with people around her patiently encouraging her to keep trying, she eventually gets half of the food in her mouth—and only a quarter of it on you! She goes through the many falls of learning to walk, then finally starts to get it. Her family will endure the cacophonous noises of learning a musical instrument as she grows up, but with encouragement and support she will start to make music. She will make brainless adolescent decisions and hopefully learn the way of wisdom through the pain. And on and on it goes. It's a messy journey—but that's how people grow.

■ ■ ■

When Jennifer and Ryan met at Gateway it was messy. Jennifer had been divorced at age twenty-seven and was headstrong about where she was going. Having traveled the world, she struggled with the "intolerant view that Jesus is the only way to God." Through asking a thousand questions in her small group, she came to faith in Christ and was baptized. Not long afterwards, she met Ryan at Gateway, and they got engaged and moved in together. I confronted them about how detrimental this was to a lasting marriage. But not fully trusting God's Word, or secular research, they didn't listen to me. But they did keep growing, got married, and learned to truly follow God's Spirit. I'm so glad we didn't treat them like spiritually mature adults and derail God's gentle work. Listen to how Jennifer describes it looking back:

> The past three years have been just incredible. I don't even feel like the same person I was six years ago . . . which is a good thing. In many ways, I feel more in touch with the "me" I knew as a child, before all the junk with my parent's divorce, before so many other things went wrong. I know that I can attribute this growth to allowing God's unconditional love to reach me through knowing him and through opening up to others at church. I have found that when I let God be in charge of my life, things work out so much better. I am constantly amazed that when I pray for guidance, he answers my prayers, by opening doors I didn't know were there or through a message at church or in my Bible reading. I never knew that having a relationship with God could be such an active relationship . . . where we can

both interact so fully with each other. I don't even know if there are words to express how wonderful an experience knowing God in Jesus has been for me.

Spiritual growth is a messy process. Leaders must assess trajectory carefully—is this a hard-hearted "mature" Christ-follower, heading away from God and needing church discipline so he won't do damage to community? Or is this a toddler trying hard to walk the way of Christ but falling and failing as she learns to trust? Different people exhibiting the same outward behavior may actually be heading in opposite directions and need drastically different approaches to help them move forward on the way of Christ. Some need discipline, but some just need patience.

The Way of Christ is a spiritual formation path we encourage at Gateway. We first ask people to make a Decision and Commitment to grow. They need to see a spiritual *Picture of Maturity*, which we spell out for them in a Bible study called *Investigating the Way of Christ.** First they must decide if they are willing to go there. But they also need people who will journey with them—in the *Context of Relationship*. We call this having a spiritual Running Partner or Running Group. But that alone is not enough—they must take steps of Intentionality on a *Personal Development Path* to stay connected to God who causes the growth. Finally, they need to periodically look back to Assess and Celebrate how far they have come down the path of growth. Let's walk through how each of these elements helps create a culture for growth.

Decisions and Commitments

I am convinced that everyone would enjoy the life God intends for them—but until they believe

> *Generation after generation my family has self destructed in an endless cycle of pain, guilt, depression, and helplessness. With agnostic alcoholic parents, I found myself in my early teens looking for joy in all the wrong places. By the age of nineteen, I had become a battered girlfriend of a drug-addicted man and found myself pregnant. Love God–Love People was just the principle I needed to hear to start my journey back to God's loving arms. The process that I've been going through ever since has been painfully hard, and the burden of my past is sometimes too much to take. Gateway has taught me to stick with it because: 1. God's grace in Christ is the only source of security, worth, love, and acceptance. 2. No matter where I've been or what I do he never leaves me, and he always loves me. 3. As I continue to develop my relationship with God, I will let go of the past and find new life.* —Karen

---

* For copies of *Investigating the Way of Christ*, email *WOC@gatewaychurch.com*.

that God's plans for them will fulfill them, and until they commit to becoming all God intended, they will stay stuck. Therefore, the first responsibility of culture creation for growth must be to help people see a clear, compelling picture of life with God—one that motivates them to commit to following him.

What does that life look like?

I'm convinced Christian spirituality is relational to the core. Through the Great Commandment, the Second Commandment, and the New Commandment, Jesus reiterates that the measure of spiritual maturity is love.[8] Every other commandment is really just commentary on what this means.

But people often think of love for God or others as merely interpersonal. There are personal and corporate aspects to living a life of love, which can easily be neglected if not given focus. For this reason, we spell out this personal category of loving God and others through Building Character. And we make explicit our corporate love for God and others by functioning together as members of one Body to Build Christ's Church. This kind of spiritual maturity is not a destination, but a lifelong journey.

Here's a short overview of the *Picture of Maturity* found in our *Investigating the Way of Christ* study:

Loving God

According to Jesus, *The Way of Christ* first means growing in loving God. Honestly, I don't think most people consider loving God a net gain in life. But if you ask them, "How would you like to experience such confidence that you almost never felt insecure? How would you like to have moments of feeling so loved by God you couldn't contain it? How would you like to know God as a loving parent, a friend, an encourager? How would you like the peace of making decisions knowing your Creator cares for you and guides you?" Everyone wants that! Understanding how God loves us, internalizing his love by knowing him, catalyzes our love for him. "We love because he first loved us."[9] But we must creatively help people see this motivating picture.

Loving People

The Way of Christ also means growing in love for people. Everybody wants to be a more loving person. But how do you grow in your ability to resolve conflict? How do you grow to celebrate differences that make up God's mosaic of people? How do you make amends with people from the past? How do you grow in motivating, encouraging, and speaking truth in love to build up others?

People need to see what love really looks like to willingly allow God's Spirit to take them there. Since Christian faith is relational to the core, we can benchmark maturity based on the health of our relationships. Like the apostle John said, "If anyone says, 'I love God,' yet hates his brother, he is a liar. For anyone who does not love his brother, whom he has seen, cannot love God, whom he has not seen."[10]

Building Character

The Way of Christ means growth in character traits, the fruits of God's Spirit. As you help people see that love, joy, peace, patience, kindness, goodness, faithfulness, gentleness, and self-control—which most people long for—are actually what God will produce in us as we yield ourselves to him, people begin to see *The Way of Christ* as the way to get what pleasure, possessions, and people could never give them. But this personal aspect of growth is still all about love. To love God means to trust his Spirit to produce these fruits. But it's not just personal joy or personal peace for me; it's joy and peace I can offer in love toward others.

Building Christ's Church

And finally, *The Way of Christ* means a growing role in building Christ's church—a community of love. Each one of us has been given resources: unique gifts and abilities, finances or possessions, and available time to use under God's direction to love and serve him by uniting together to love and serve one another. Every person has a unique role to play in God's plans for Planet Earth, but never as a Lone Ranger. Rather as a unique part of a unified effort with others, we re-present to the world what Christ is like as one Body. Only together can we demonstrate to the world Christ's sacrificial love.

> I guess what I'm trying to say is that through my experience at Gateway, God has shown me the joy and freedom that comes from dying to my sinful self and pursuing wholehearted obedience to my Lord, whom I love more than anything. I am excited about serving in full-time Christian ministry in New York City precisely because of the lessons I have learned the last five years at Gateway.   —Justin

■ ■ ■

Leaders must creatively find ways to paint compelling pictures of life on *The Way of Christ*. We do that through teaching, through personal stories, drama, or multimedia, or using illustrations from life much as Jesus did. We then encourage people to do a Bible study called *Investigating the Way of Christ* that shows them the Bible's picture of maturity. Then we ask them to commit and affirm that commitment to a church leader so we know who has decided to take this journey with us as one Body.

Jesus challenged the crowd that had caught a glimpse of God's kingdom to decide and commit. "He turned around and said to them, 'If you want to be my follower you must love me more than . . . your own life. Otherwise, you cannot be my disciple. . . . Don't begin until you count the cost.'"[11] The first goal of culture creation for growth is to help people move beyond desire and decide to follow *The Way of Christ*.

But deciding alone is never enough, as Brett and Lindi's story illustrates so well.

Running Away or Running Together

"Brett, I can't live this way. I'm moving out." Lindi's words cut Brett like a butcher's knife. "You criticize and critique and distrust my motives constantly. I feel like I'm a bad little girl," Lindi confided about the voice of shame from her past her new husband constantly triggered.

Brett and Lindi had been friends for over three years before getting married. Before meeting Brett, Lindi had grown very bitter, despairing almost to the point of not wanting to live after her first husband cheated on her. In her early thirties in the wake of divorce, she came to Gateway at the insistence of a friend. Though coldly agnostic at first, over the course of a year Lindi's heart warmed as she understood and received God's grace and started following Christ.

Lindi invited Brett, who had grown up in church. Although great friends before marriage, within a year after getting married, Lindi felt like a turtle closing into a familiar, dark shell of self-protection. Once married, Brett found himself increasingly obsessing on the past. Lindi had dreamed about her ex-husband. Brett immediately thought, *she must still be passionate about him—maybe he was better than I am*. While engaged, Lindi had commented to Brett about an ex-boyfriend who would always have a place in her heart. Brett's insecurity churned the thought in the blender of his mind; *she would go back to him if she had the chance*. Lindi wanted to go shopping with her best friend. *See, she doesn't want to be with me*, he concluded.

Brett's mind would lock on to these comments like a laser-guided missile—once fixed in his thoughts, nothing could detour the emotional explosion sure to come from intense feelings of insecurity and rejection stored up from the past. This was his second failed marriage, and when Lindi moved out that day, all he could think about was getting out—divorce. He felt betrayed, hurt, and vengeful. Yet no one would ever have known the constant struggle inside of Brett. He had friends, a graduate degree, a great career, nice house . . . and he was an all-around "good Christian guy."

Looking back, Brett confesses, "Now I realize I was playing Christian. See, I wanted God's salvation through Jesus Christ, but I still wanted to call the shots. I wanted to run my own life."

Fortunately, Brett had glimpsed snapshots of authentic life on *The Way of Christ*, so instead of running away from the pain of his wife moving out, he decided to allow God to use the pain as a catalyst to learn what it means to love—even those who hurt you. But Brett also knew he couldn't do it alone; he knew he needed relational support, so he found a spiritual Running Partner.

Running Partners

Have you ever desired to get in the best shape of your life? I've had that desire for many, many years. I would love to have "six-pack" abs. So why do I still have a two-pack circling my whole waist? Because I haven't really decided to do intentionally what it takes to help me get there.

The closest I came, though, was when I had a workout partner. Someone to run with, lift with, and share the sometimes painful journey of getting physically in shape. We need the same relational support to get in shape spiritually. So we tell people they need to find a spiritual Running Partner if they want to journey on *The Way of Christ*.

Our main strategy since day one has been to get people into small groups. Small groups (of eight to twelve people) help people cross the line of faith and truly grow. People were not meant to do life alone but in the context of loving, supportive, grace-giving, truth-telling relationships. From Genesis to Revelation, the Scriptures paint pictures of the necessity of doing life in community.[12]

In his book *How People Grow*, Henry Cloud says,

When I came to Gateway I was on a search for something. I believed in God but knew little of Jesus or the Bible. Having done things the other way, I could see pretty readily how Christian principles were meant to give me a better life and draw me closer to God. It didn't take long for me to open my heart to Jesus, and the decision to get baptized was an easy one. A few months later I joined a small group where I began to experience true community. I am amazed to find so many others who, despite whatever pain or anguish they have suffered before in their lives, have opened their hearts to God and to one another. It is now through my relationships with others in the church that I am learning the truth about Jesus. An open heart, growing within myself, and apparent in others, is something I so did not expect to find, but underneath it all was something I was probably longing for all my life. —Joy

People's most basic need in life is relationship. People connected to other people thrive and grow, and those not connected wither and die. It is a medical fact, for example, that from infancy to old age, health depends on the amount of social connection people have. . . . Virtually every emotional and psychological problem, from addictions to depression, has alienation or emotional isolation at its core.[13]

In our connection-starved world, healing comes through relationship with Christ and his Body—people running spiritually alongside each other, demonstrating God's grace and truth tangibly. As in Josh's life, God uses these close friendships to redefine a person's view of himself at the core. Oftentimes, until trusted connections are formed, no growth can occur because relationship is so central to the abundant life Christ promises.

Our small group leaders are encouraged to have one person in the group aspect of *The Way of Christ*: Loving God (usually a learning and prayer component), Loving People (a community component), Building Character (a Running Partner component), and Building Christ's Church (outreach and compassionate service component). We encourage small groups to not only study Scripture and pray for each other, but to pair up into Running Partners or smaller Running Groups. Some do this within the context of a small group meeting. Others meet together weekly for coffee in twos, threes, or fours. But the goal is to get rigorously honest with each other in the context of grace, allowing God to do his work in and through us all just as Scripture talks about: "Each one should use whatever gift he has received to serve others, faithfully administering God's grace in its various forms. If anyone speaks, he should do it as one speaking the very words of God. If anyone serves, he should do it with the strength God provides. . . ."[14]

This is different than classic accountability groups. Cloud points out the flaws of what "accountability" has come to mean for many: asking each other if they are living up to the standard, offering forgiveness if they've fallen short, then encouraging each other to go try harder. Cloud says, "This common evangelical mode of operation is a good picture of the law at work."[15] This style of accountability can expose a problem, but it doesn't fix it.

What the person needs is grace and truth, where he is not condemned, even in failure, and where he hears the truth that he's unable to become what God intends just by trying harder. This kind of ministry directs him to depend on God's Spirit, by pointing him to places where he can be given what he cannot provide for himself, like support, structure, healing, and help with the appetites driving the behavior.[16]

For this reason, we have established "Rules of Running" for Running Partners to help create the right environment for growth:

1. *Accept and encourage as often as possible* (as we covered in the last chapter).

2. *Ask questions often, and give advice only with permission.*

We ask Running Partners to ask each other a few simple questions—but the power of slowing down and reflecting on these questions is spectacular:

Running Partner Questions

- "What do you think God is trying to do in your life right now?"

- "If there's one area in loving God, loving people, building character, or building Christ's church you need to focus on right now, what would it be?"

- "What's one thing you will intentionally do this week to allow God to grow you up in this area?"

It always struck me how Jesus asked the blind man, "What do you want me to do for you?" Seems obvious, doesn't it? Yet Jesus knew something we don't often realize—sometimes people don't want to get better! People become dependent on a broken way of life. Consequently, several times Jesus asked people questions to get them to a place of willingness. It's amazing how people know most of what they need to do once they simply learn to listen and set their minds on responding to God's will.

3. *Give reproof only when absolutely necessary* (Proverbs 27:5–6).

For people to really grow, they have to take responsibility for their growth before God. You can't take responsibility for them! Nothing kills good groups or Running Partner friendships faster than "Mr. Fix It"—the person who wants to quickly give the fix-it answers to everyone's issues. Sometimes, however, reproof is necessary. When people keep walking in the same hole again and again and don't see it coming, true friends speak the truth in love, but then let the other person take responsibility for what he does with the truth.

4. *Give condemnation—never. Protect confidentiality—always* (Romans 2:1).

In this kind of supportive spiritual Running Partner relationship, people can look honestly at their shortcomings because they don't fear judgment or condemnation. They know their Running Partners are for them, so they can begin to address stuck places where God wants them to grow. And they can get the support to figure out what intentional steps they can take to allow God to do his growth-work in their lives.

Facing Ourselves

God used this supportive context to reveal a pattern that was destroying the people Brett loved most. Brett had several trusted friends from his small group, but he also asked Dan to be a Running Partner with him, knowing he would understand. Dan and Debra had come to Gateway during divorce proceedings, yet as they both experienced grace, it allowed them to let down their guard, and God changed them both. They sought counseling, community, and intentional growth, and finally reconciled. They now lead our marriage ministry four years later.

Dan spoke truth in love to Brett that first night, "You have no grounds for divorce, Brett—she is still willing to work on it." A series of questions revealed to Brett he wanted a divorce to feel in control. He was feeling out of control in the face of his greatest fear—rejection. Instead, Dan and others helped him get marriage counseling and start putting intentional practices in place to allow God to grow him up in his ability to love. Brett talks openly now about what he realized as a result.

"Through these supportive friends, I gained the confidence to face a very negative cycle that God revealed to me. It affected all my relationships: with God, marriage, family, friends, even work," Brett admitted. "Fear of rejection spurred a barrage of negative thoughts, which in turn spawned jealousy, distrust, hurt, anger, or resentment. When my wife or others triggered this fear with something they said, I would react in harsh judgment or criticism to protect myself. Yet that just produced more isolation, leading to more insecurity, and greater fear of rejection, and deeper into the whirlpool I would go, drowning in my emotions."

Allowing pain is God's crowbar to open us up to change, and in the midst of his greatest pain, Brett had a breakthrough. One day, driving in his car listening to a tape, he was graced! As Brett describes it, "I had heard Gateway talk about God primarily wanting relationship. I had heard many times that we must die to ourselves to let God be God in our lives. Dan had told me this over and over, but until that day I didn't get it. Like scales falling off my eyes, I realized God wanted me! I didn't have to prove to God or the world I was acceptable. I was wanted . . . 'as is.' Up until that moment, I tried to prove I was a 'good, moral Christian' but the truth is, I was a judgmental, angry, insecure hypocrite—that had to die for me to live."

As Brett's small group surrounded him with grace and truth—affirming him as he humbled himself before God—for the first time, rather than blaming others, he was able to take responsibility for his hurtful tendencies. But Brett could not change himself. With the support of Running Partners, he put Intentional Practices in his life to help him yield his mind to God when the insecure feelings overpowered him.

Intentionality

Spiritual Growth is something God does in us. Most of us get stuck in habits and patterns that we want to be rid of—if we could just wave a magic wand and make them go away, we would. But we try and try and nothing seems to happen. Why? It's because we are not intentional about making ourselves available to God when the pressure is on.

I used to race sailboats for the University of Texas. Sailboats have no power of their own. They depend completely on the power of the wind. So the key to sailing fast comes down to constantly adjusting the position of your sails to utilize the power of the wind. You move forward by staying in tune with the wind.

To live in the kingdom of God here on earth, we must intentionally adjust the sails of our mind to move with the wind of God's Spirit. But to do this, we must interrupt habits and patterns we have established during a lifelong training program for living in the "kingdom of this world." Dallas Willard points out in *The Divine Conspiracy* that we all establish "automatic" patterns of response that govern most of our behavior.[17] We don't think to ourselves, "I'm going to act selfishly and manipulate him to get my way." It flows out effortlessly. We don't think about getting impatient in traffic, it automatically happens. We don't purposefully lust, with one look the habit takes over naturally. Most of these self-centered patterns formed over years, as a result of lies we believed about how we would find love, security, and freedom.

> *Perhaps the greatest gift Gateway has given me is to see how God is at work in my life. He always has been, I just didn't see it. Through Gateway, I have learned how to develop a relationship with God. For the first time, I understand what grace is . . . my husband and I have found friendships and programs (First Steps, Gateway Encounter Marriage weekend, parenting-with-intimacy and financial seminars) that are so essential to our success as a couple, as parents, and as Christ-followers. God has truly changed my life!*
>
> *—Kasey*

So in Romans 6 Paul says to "not let sin control the way you live. . . . Instead, give yourselves completely to God."[18] But to do this, he explains in Romans 8, we must disrupt "automatic" habits that set our minds on what our old nature desires, with intentional practices that help us set our minds on the Spirit, who leads us to life and peace. You can see why grace leads to growth. Knowing that God doesn't condemn us, we can turn our minds to receive his help even as we lust or rage or pout or spew. And as we learn to automatically do this, he really does help us to fully live![19]

We teach people that the epicenter of spiritual growth is giving up playing God and letting God *be* God in your life. But naturally, we do just the opposite. Naturally, we play God! Proof of this is how often we get stressed, frustrated, and angry when life and even God will not obey our will. So we must practice making ourselves available to doing God's will if we are ever to move in his direction for us. It requires intentionality to move down this path.

Down the Path of Personal Development

I am convinced God knows the personal development path for each of us. As we listen and reflect in Running Partner relationships, we get a sense of what God wants to do. At Gateway, we are working to develop a resource database to help people locate tapes, seminars, books, practices, experiences, and spiritual disciplines to help them intentionally do something different than what comes naturally. These serve as tools that Running Partners can point each other toward to keep the sails of the mind set, harnessing the power of God's Spirit who works mightily within them.

> I simply and painfully had to realize that I wasn't capable of doing what I wanted to do under my own power. If someone would have told me four months ago that only through the most painful experience of my life would I be capable of becoming whole, then I can't say that I would have jumped on board. But now, I wouldn't trade this life for anything. —Aaron[tt]

Oftentimes, pain or crisis provides the greatest catalyst for spiritual growth. But how do you program pain? You can't, not legally! But when you create a culture of growth and educate people about the role of trials,[20] then organize in such a way to bring relational support and tools of intentionality to the person—it's amazing what God does. Brett used this pain to motivate greater intentionality.

■ ■ ■

Brett made it a practice to start each day asking God to help him think positive thoughts instead of believing the twisted lies that spun tales in his mind. He started reading Scripture, though inconsistently. So he listened to Christian radio and tapes Dan and others suggested as he drove across town every day—trying to soak his mind in positive, true thoughts. At first, nothing seemed to really help. Every time he talked to Lindi, defenses would go up and everything in Brett screamed, "Divorce her fast." But he made it a habit to call Dan or one of three other Running Partners he confided in for affirmation and counsel.

"Brett, you do what God wants you to do regardless of what Lindi does—this isn't about her, it's about you letting God teach you to love," Dan would reiterate.

Knowing Brett was a concrete thinker, Brett's counselor suggested he imagine his unforgiven hurts like a stringer of fish he had attached to him. Brett would meditate on these visual images—asking God to help him see "truth that would set him free." "You've got to let them go Brett—watch them swim away," his counselor advised, "give them back into God's care." Brett admitted he had a long stringer of unforgiven hurts. He meditated on Scripture about forgiveness and pictured himself releasing those fish into God's care. Yet even months later, he would still slip into old habits.

"Well, Lindi, you're the one who left this marriage," Brett's indignation was mounting on the phone that night three months into their separation.

"Brett, I don't want our marriage to end, I want it to succeed. I still love you." Lindi fought hard to overcome her own hurt, trying her best to reassure Brett.

She doesn't mean that, Brett thought. His hurt and insecurity had taken over on the other end of the phone line. I don't think she ever loved me, I think she loved my money. For a split second he wrestled, Capture every thought and give it to Jesus—ask him what to do—too late.

"Yeah, well, Lindi," Brett reached for the fish of abandonment on the stringer and sarcastically quipped, "Leaving the marriage bed doesn't exactly say 'I love you.' Sometimes I wonder if what you really loved was the lifestyle I gave you." Oh ... he regretted it as it came out.

Silence!

"See, Brett," angry tears could be heard in each of Lindi's words. "You can't even hear me say 'I love you' because you're so busy judging me and defending yourself. And I can't live with that. I can't live with every word twisted back on me."

"Fine, you don't have to." (Click)—Brett hung up. "Divorce," his pride felt comforted as he embraced the word. Yet he knew he needed to call someone. He promised in these moments he would call a Running Partner. He picked up the phone, "Dan, I'm done with all this."

"Die to self" were the first words out of Dan's mouth.

"It was exactly what I needed to hear," Brett recalls. He finished with Dan, called Lindi back, and simply apologized for not accepting her gesture of love. As Brett talked it over with others, he realized his first inclination had always been to assume an underlying motive. "What does that person really mean?" He wanted to take every thought captive, die to insecurity, and live to do God's will, but he needed help changing this automatic response.

He took a journal and for one month wrote down every positive thought he could, asking God to help him see the truth, and he would review it with a friend each week.

Over the months, Brett began feeling a new freedom, a release. Instead of "Brett . . . you're so bad" crashing him on the head constantly, he began to experience words of Scripture he had memorized saying, "I am for you, Brett! Who can be against you, Brett?" "Nothing can separate you from my love, Brett." Lindi began to see a change. Over the months they began going to church together again. When Lindi's year-long lease ended, Brett had changed so much, she asked him if she could move back in.

Assess and Celebrate

As Brett and Lindi and many other couples at Gateway have seen, authentic spiritual growth helps you become a more loving person. But it takes a Decision to grow, Running Partners to keep us motivated, and Intentionality to help us stay connected to God who causes the growth. We are continually working to vision-cast, organize, and resource people in order to create this culture for growth. But creating a culture of growth also requires regularly taking Assessment and Celebrating progress.

People need encouragement and celebration for the work God is doing in them because we tend to quickly forget God's works.[21] We ask Running Partners on *The Way of Christ* to use an assessment we developed to yearly evaluate spiritual growth in the areas of Loving God, Loving People, Building Character, and Building Christ's Church. The main purpose is to celebrate God's work. Without this recognition of progress, people easily become discouraged and give up being intentional. But this assessment also helps them to pinpoint areas for future growth and development.

This kind of culture really helps people grow. As you paint a compelling picture of life on *The Way of Christ*, they Decide and Commit to the journey. In the context of supportive Running Partners, they find encouragement to face patterns they've denied for years. With the right resources, they can put Intentional Practices in their lives. As they set the sails of their mind to follow God's Spirit, soon they will automatically start to respond to God. Then, just as Brett discovered, the God who is love will make us more and more like himself.

■ ■ ■

"How do you feel about giving me the key to the house?" Lindi asked as Brett handed her the key and garage door opener. "What were you thinking when you were getting this ready?" she asked.

"Part of me didn't want to tell her," Brett recalls, "because I didn't want to blow something up. But I was learning to respond to God, to do his will, and to make amends when I didn't. I thought, I can do this without screwing it up." Brett confided out loud, "On the one hand, I was so excited because I loved you as a friend, wanted the best for you, and then fell in love romantically. I realized how much God has blessed me to have you back. On the other hand, I was very scared because I don't want to go through the pain of you leaving ever again. But if you hadn't left, I would never have learned what God's taught me about love."

"Did you ever think what I might be feeling?" Lindi asked.

Defenses went up . . . but Brett caught it, "Lord, help me," he prayed. As compassion melted his resistance he gently replied, "No, what are you feeling?"

"I love you, Brett, but I'm scared too," Lindi hesitantly admitted. "Though you've really changed, and I want to move back in and make it work, I'm afraid I will go back to always feeling like a bad little girl."

"I'm sure I'll still make mistakes," Brett said. "But Lindi, I'm willing to work on it together. With God's help, we can do it together."

■ ■ ■

This is the Way of Christ—a lifelong journey toward spiritual maturity with Christ's community. It's a challenging expedition, and struggles and detours are inevitable as we walk toward exhibiting Christlike love. But love . . . a solid kind of love that changes us all . . . is what it's all about.

But why do you have to follow Christ to become a loving person? Don't all religions lead us to this same place in their own way? That's the natural question on the minds of many, which we will consider in the next chapter.

STUDY GUIDE

Culture Check

1. There are many different models, curriculums, and paths for spiritual growth. However, to be effective, all must have a Picture of Maturity (or what defines progress). How has your church or group defined spiritual maturity? How do people decide and commit to that goal?

2. Supportive relationships form the context of all significant human development. Where do people you lead find this relational support to grow?

3. How do people you lead find resources, practices, experiences, or disciplines to intentionally put in their lives to better respond to the Spirit?

4. How do you help the people you lead Assess and Celebrate growth?

Small Group Questions

1. What do you think the goal of Christian spiritual growth is? (Refer to Matthew 22:36–39; John 13:34–35). How do you think people grow? Think of one area right now that God wants to help you grow in. What is it?

2. Read John 15:1–5. According to Jesus, what is the secret to spiritual growth? How do you stay connected in a practical way?

3. Without relational honesty and vulnerability with a trusted, supportive group of friends, significant spiritual growth rarely happens. Why do you think this is true? Do you have anyone you are a hundred percent honest and transparent with? Why or why not?

4. What Intentional Practices, experiences, or disciplines have most helped you stay connected to God's Spirit and grow spiritually?

5. Discuss ways you can better help each other grow. What do you need relationally? How can we be more intentional? How can we assess and celebrate growth together?

What about Other Religions? The Tolerance Litmus Test—Q1

For you were killed, and your blood has ransomed people for God from every tribe and language and people and nation.

Revelation 5:9 NLT

Shae and Suzie walked into the co-op living room from the organic garden outside. "You know, Suzie, I just don't even think I can be friends with my old roommate anymore—or any Christian for that matter," Shae's voice betrayed a hint of sadness mixed with anger. "They're just so judgmental and intolerant," she stated emphatically, "so opposite of everything we stand for here."

Shae and Suzie went to Stanford University together where Shae studied human biology and archeology. They lived at the Columbae vegetarian co-op on campus—an enclave of liberal-thinking women and men who were active in social affairs. Shae helped run the Women's Center on campus, campaigning for women's rights and environmental concerns. Her activism grew out of her longing to make the world a better place.

"Why do you say that?" Suzie questioned as they plopped down on the retro couches decorating the living room.

"They're just so narrow-minded and arrogant. I mean, who are we to say one group or culture is right or wrong? To say Native American Indians, for instance, were wrong in all their beliefs because they knew nothing about Jesus? That's ridiculous."

"So what is it you believe?" Suzie asked.

"Every culture has its own customs, beliefs, and values that need to be respected. I see the biggest problem with religion is it divides people—it creates hostility. It seems all religions are basically saying the same thing anyway, so why argue and fight about who is right or wrong? Personally, I'm more of an existentialist—I find peace in the truth of knowing I don't need to stress out about life because there is no higher purpose."

"You know, actually, I consider myself a Christian," Suzie confided.

"You?" Shae was astounded. "But you're not like any of the Christians I've met. How do you feel about other religions? I mean, surely you don't hold the same arrogant views my other Christian friends do—that you're right and everybody else in the world is wrong—do you?"

"I don't think I'm right and everybody else is wrong," Suzie contended, "but I do think Jesus revealed to us what God is like and made a way for us to come back to God."

"Wow, I would never have guessed." Shae was perplexed that her social-activist friend could be a Christian. The two just didn't seem to mesh in Shae's mind. "So, like you think Jesus is the only way to God and all who disagree are going to hell?"

"Well, it's not my place to say who goes to heaven or hell, but I do think Jesus died to forgive all our sins, so that anyone could come back into right relationship with her Creator. And Jesus is the only way I know of that God has provided for that," Suzie explained.

"Okay, how could that possibly be fair?" Shae was obviously bothered. "I've been on archeological digs in Peru, uncovering the Chavin Temple where ancient Peruvians worshiped their gods. They knew nothing of Jesus, never had a chance. Most Christians I know would say all those Peruvians went to hell because they didn't believe in Jesus—of course, they'd never heard of him, but tough luck, huh? That just seems ridiculously ethnocentric to think God would only care about mostly white Europeans who had the chance to hear about Jesus."

"You feel pretty strongly about this, don't you?" Suzie could tell Shae's temperature was rising and now was probably not the time for debate.

"I hope this doesn't offend you Suzie," Shae responded sharply, "'cause like I said—I don't think you're like this—but it just seems like Christians haven't thought too hard about what they believe and how those beliefs could possibly make sense in the world we know today."

"You know, I've got to head to campus in a few minutes," Suzie replied, "but maybe we can talk later, and I'll explain more of why I believe what I believe if you're interested."

"Sure." Shae was polite but less than enthusiastic as she got up. "Sorry if I got a little worked up. I just don't understand why it's so important to think your religion is right and all the rest are wrong."

■ ■ ■

Although Shae didn't find resolution to her questions at Stanford, Shae became a follower of Jesus several years later, resolved those questions, and is now a small group leader at Gateway. Not only did Shae come to see Jesus as the unique provision to forgive her sins but also as the one leading the mission to make our world a better place.

As we have reached into the unchurched culture of our generation, this one question, phrased in many ways, gets asked more than any other: "How do you feel about other religions?" It has become the tolerance litmus-test question for our generation, and we must think carefully about how to remove this challenging barrier to the "good news" of Jesus.

When we did a "Free-For-All-Q&A-Sunday," we asked people to submit their burning questions, and this one came up more than any other. Here is a sampling of the ways this question gets asked:

- If there is no correct religion, why is Christianity the only way?
- What happens to people who have never heard of Jesus?
- Are all Jews, Muslims, and Buddhists doomed to hell?
- What happens to people raised in other religions?
- Do you think God loves those who are not Christians?
- Why just Jesus? What about Buddha, etc.?
- Are all religions the same?
- Isn't it arrogant to believe Christianity is the only path to a full spiritual life?

To reach emerging generations, leaders must understand the questions underneath the question—the real concerns and issues that need addressing to help people understand the amazing tolerance shown in the offer God has made for all people everywhere through Christ. Creating a come-as-you-are culture in a post-Christian society requires us to anticipate and answer these underlying litmus-test questions. As leaders, we can often help them overcome their misunderstandings if we can address their real concerns. Here are the actual questions we have discovered underneath the question.

Isn't This Just Religious Pride?

Over the years, I have found one major concern people have with Christianity is religious pride and arrogance. When they ask, "How do you feel about other religions?" sometimes the question beneath the question is "Do you think you're always right and everyone else is always wrong?" They are sniffing out arrogance they believe has caused so many religious problems. And rightfully so!

Shae grew up in Buffalo, New York, watching TV religious leaders fall like shooting stars due to one moral or ethical scandal after another. Her high school taught her about the pogroms and religious wars fought by the Church in the Middle Ages, slaughtering people in the name of the "right" faith. A doctor in her town who performed abortions was killed, purportedly by pro-life Christians who felt murder acceptable, because they were "right."

Though these all represent extreme sins of those who hold a dubious claim to Christian faith, they had profound effect shaping a generation's views.

Shae formed the opinion early on that religion (especially institutional religion) was often about money and politics and arrogant power plays. She grew up with friends from diverse religious backgrounds and learned to value this diversity of belief. At the core, she decided all religions taught moral codes that were very similar. Word on the street told her "all religions basically say the same thing." The shaping of Shae's worldview mirrors that of many adults today.

Shae and many just like her hear Christians say that Jesus is the only way, and they immediately think we are saying, "We're right and everyone else is wrong because our way is always right." They see it as nothing but pride and arrogance—the same pride and arrogance that would cause Christians in the Middle Ages to slaughter Jews and Muslims.

The way to address these concerns is head-on. I'll say flat-out in a message, "One of the biggest problems people have with Christianity, I find, is this idea that Jesus is *the way* to be made right with God. It feels so narrow, so intolerant, so religiously snobbish—kind of a 'we're-right-because-you're-wrong' kindergarten mentality."

Anticipating and openly voicing this question-beneath-the-question often diffuses people's resistance to even listen. This allows them to relate to you and actually want to hear your answer. When you affirm where tolerance is needed—you can also show its natural limits.

Tolerance is a good thing when it comes to differences in people, tastes, or preferences. We should be tolerant of others' opinions and even beliefs that differ from our own. But this doesn't mean we have to *agree* that everything the other person thinks is *true*. You can be tolerant and disagree. Here's an example I've used to make this point.

Let's say I'm buying a used car. I like black cars, you like red cars. For you to try to convince me that red cars are the right cars for everyone because red is your favorite color, and black cars get too hot in the summer—it's ludicrous. There is no right or wrong color—maybe I like black and don't mind the heat. It's a preference among a variety.

But let's say we're talking about safe, reliable used cars, and I insist that the best car for the money is the Ford Pinto (which Ford discontinued because they blow up!). But I'm a firm believer in the Pinto because I can get a Pinto for $1,000 with less than 20,000 miles. Are you intolerant of my faith in the Pinto if you try to convince me that a Honda is a much better value in reality because it's more safe and reliable than a Pinto? If you said, "Don't entrust your wife and kids to a Pinto, they blow up when rear-ended at 20 mph. It may be cheap, but it's dangerous." Would you be a mean, intolerant person because you didn't agree with my view that Pintos were the best value for a used car? No—you would be caring about me by sharing what you knew to be true. Now, if you attack me or my character or intelligence— then you're not motivated by love but by your need to be right.

We must explain and demonstrate how to be tolerant while disagreeing and respecting the free will of others—just as God does. We can point out that some truths are transcultural. For instance, technology and the truth found in mathematics and science work in a system of Eastern thought and Western thought. If a piston blows in western Europe—it makes the engine worthless. If a piston blows in Tibet, it still makes the engine worthless (it's not an illusion just because it's owned by a person who believes this world is ultimately an illusion—*Maya*). If you want to drive, you need a new engine block—that's the truth, right? So some truths *are* transcultural.

The question is—where does religious thought fit? In the category of preference or truth? Is saying "I believe Muhammed" or "I believe in Jesus" the same as saying "I like red" or "I like black"? Or is it more like saying "I believe Pintos are reliable" or "I believe Hondas are reliable"? That's where the real question lies.

My experience tells me that most people these days think religious belief is more like a preference thing—red or black—whichever makes you happy. And I will acknowledge that they are right—it *is* just preference, *if* God has not revealed himself to our finite, fallible world. But *what if* God took the initiative to show up? That would take away a lot of our subjective opinion.

Today's leader must understand that when asked about other religions, oftentimes the underlying question is, "Do you always think you're right and everyone else is wrong?" It has become a tolerance litmus test for arrogance. We must demonstrate a humility and willingness to learn—remembering all truth is God's truth, and truth has nothing to fear. I have found when leaders humbly acknowledge that we don't know everything, and that religious arrogance *has* caused problems in the past, it helps people drop their first defense. As we acknowledge the good aspects of tolerance, yet differentiate tolerance from agreement, we can better communicate the right heart.

Again, the tone and attitude a leader projects answers the arrogance question as much or more than the verbal message. I have made the mistake of "winning" an argument on this question while losing the person, because she sees my argumentative spirit as religious arrogance to avoid at all costs. Yet if I can help her see that the question is not so much about who is right or wrong, but rather, "Who is God?" and if I show I truly care about her, defenses often come down. Then we can get to the next question, which has really become an assumption: that all religions say the same thing.

Don't All Religions Say the Same Thing?

There is a Jain parable of an elephant and four blind men that I have heard paraphrased in different conversations with seekers. It describes a common view of the world's religions among emerging generations. Four blind men happen upon an elephant one day. One of them felt its trunk and said, "An elephant is like a hose." Another felt its side and said, "No, an elephant is like a wall." The third blind man put his arms around its leg and declared, "An elephant is like a tree." Finally the fourth blind man grabbed its tail and insisted, "No, an elephant is like a snake."

Many people today think this accurately explains the many religions' descriptions of God. Many have learned that all of the world's religions are trying to explain the same God, but in our limited ability to truly comprehend, we all describe God a little differently due to our cultural limitations.

If you know history of religion or philosophy, you know that all cultures for all times have tried to answer several basic questions. The religions of the world all tell us a story of our blind search for meaning and purpose. In all cultures for all time, humanity has searched to explain our relationship to the cosmos and how to best live this life according to this internal moral compass we all have. I have studied the great religions of the world and read many of their sacred writings. And they do all say similar things about right and wrong. It's uncanny how similar the moral code is of every major religion—almost like this innate understanding of right and wrong comes from within. Actually, that's exactly what the Bible teaches.[1] And personally, I think that's why there are so many different religions. I think religion is our attempt to answer questions about God, or human evil, or the way out of suffering. Different cultures and people have answered the questions differently. In fact, there are probably as many religious variations as people.

Whenever I'm asked this question-beneath-the-question, "Don't all religions basically say the same thing?" I can affirm that all religions *do* agree on some things. But the more important question is not whether one religion or another is the right one. The more fundamental question is, "Who is God?" Has God revealed himself clearly so we *can* know what he's really like? You see, the problem with the blind men in that Jain parable is ... *they're all blind*. None of them is right! An elephant is not really like a hose, wall, or tree. What we really need is someone who can see, someone who can see the whole elephant and describe clearly to us blind folks what an elephant is really like.

That's the human dilemma. The problem is that we can't find God on our own. The infinite, eternal Maker exists beyond the limits of time and space. Science and philosophy can demonstrate why God must exist.* But we can't really know much more beyond a blind guess of what the hidden Creator is like, unless he chooses to show up—to reveal himself in a way we can understand in our finite, limited existence. That's the only way out of this dilemma.

Almighty Creator of Flatland

"Just pretend you're the Creator for a minute," I proposed to Alex.

Alex worked for a law firm in town and had come to our church at the invitation of a woman who worked in his office. He believed all religions were basically saying the same things, and struggled with this idea of any religion claiming to know truth about the one, true God.

"Imagine if you as a three-dimensional creator created a two-dimensional world," I suggested. "You are Almighty Creator of Flatland!"[2] I waved my hand across the flat table between us. "If this comes too easy for you, we can talk about that later."

Alex grinned and corrected me, "Actually, we exist in four dimensions. Time being the fourth dimension."

"You're right," I admitted, "but for sake of simplicity let's just say three.† Anyway, these two-dimensional people can move forward and back, left and

---

* Mortimer Adler, editor of the *Encyclopedia Britannica* and Director of the Institute for Philosophical Research, explains why philosophically there must be one, infinite, eternal Creator in his book, *How to Think about God: A Guide for the 20th-Century Pagan*. In *The Case for a Creator*, Lee Strobel outlines scientific discoveries pointing toward the existence of a Creator.

† The four dimensions being: length, width, depth, and time. Most people relate more easily to being 3-dimensional, so I usually refer to us as 3-D creatures.

right, but they have no comprehension of up or down. You can watch their every move from above, but they can't even comprehend you as a 3-D Creator 'above' watching in. You can do miracles in their world—your finger could appear and disappear." I acted like my finger penetrated the plane of the flat tabletop, and then pulled it back up. "They can't imagine where it came from or where it went. Now, you could remain completely hidden, and they couldn't even comprehend your existence in another dimension. But what if you wanted to relate? If you wanted them to understand you—even love you? You would have to take the initiative to reveal yourself in 2-D descriptions, or in a form they could comprehend–because they cannot possibly 'see' you unless you pull them out of their two-dimensional world 'up' into your 3-D world. But you could penetrate their 2-D plane of existence, appearing as a flat, round, two-dimensional slice of your finger. In that form, you could help them see, not all of your 3-D splendor, but as much as is flatly possible for them to understand in two dimensions. Does that make sense?"

"So you're saying that's the point of Jesus? God appearing in a 3-dimensional 'slice' of time and space?" Alex inquired jumping ahead of me.

"Yeah!" I was hoping something was clicking. "Not that Jesus revealed everything about the God who is Spirit, who exists beyond time and space. But he revealed all that limited, finite, 3-D creatures can comprehend. In fact, this analogy helps me understand this mystery of God as Father, Son, and Spirit—three persons yet one God.

"I grew up in a very liturgical church," Alex said, "It wasn't even legal to ask my questions about how God could be Father, Son, and Spirit. It always seemed like the same kind of mythology that produced Zeus, Apollos, and Aphrodite to me. Christians just stopped at three for some reason. That's part of why I see all religions as an evolutionary attempt to explain life, and maybe all of them have parts of truth about God, but they all have myths that have crept in as well—like the paradoxical idea of the Trinity."

"This analogy actually helped me understand why the paradox of the Trinity makes sense. The Trinity of God is describing a being not bound by time and space in 3-D language. Think about it, if you as God of Flatland, tried to explain yourself in words, you would say, 'I'm not just one slice, but a plurality of slices—but I'm only one person.' That would be paradoxical to them—why? Because many slices in a 2-D world can never be 'stacked up' into one being (there is no 'up')! They'd picture you as many round circles or slices side by side. But I'm getting off track. Did I confuse you?"*

---

* All analogies of the nature of God fall short, as we can only describe an infinite Being in finite terms.

"I think I'm following—but how do you know Jesus is the 3-D 'slice' of God?" Alex asked.

"As you scan the horizon of human history," I continued, "and read the sacred texts of the world's religions, asking the all-important questions, 'Who is God, and has God revealed himself clearly?' one name stands out above the rest. Only one man has ever made such a claim and done anything by which history would even consider its viability: Jesus."

As we continued to talk that day, Alex found himself willing to explore the identity of Jesus. Our conversation framed the discussion in a new light. Rather than debating whether Christianity is right and others are wrong, he found it easier to focus on the more primary question: "Who is God, and has God revealed himself?"

Truth in the World's Religions?

Leaders of the emerging church in a hypertolerant age must be able to educate people about the world's religions because most everyone assumes they all say the same thing. And we have found it very important to diffuse the accusation of narrow-minded intolerance by giving credence to the similarities they do have and explaining the key differences. Some Christians act as if there is no trace of truth in the world's religions because they do not proclaim Christ, but this view is not biblical. As Paul realized in trying to reach out to a polytheistic Greek culture, *God has been at work behind the scenes in all cultures, and we can find remains of truth everywhere to build bridges of faith in Christ.*

In Acts 17, Paul was waiting in Athens and became terribly bothered by the hundreds and hundreds of idols set up to Zeus and Aphrodite and all the Greek gods. In his zeal, Paul could have rightly said, "You're all wrong for worshiping idols." But years earlier, Jesus had given him the command, "I am sending you to them to open their eyes and turn them from darkness to light."[3] Paul knew that if their eyes were to be opened, they needed to see the light of the true God already at work among them. So he first "walked around and observed" all the dark idols until he found a trace of light. Showing incredible tolerance and restraint, he then encouraged the Athenians saying, "Men of Athens! I see that in every way you are very religious. For as I walked around and looked carefully at your objects of worship, I even found an altar with this inscription: TO AN UNKNOWN GOD. Now what you worship as something unknown I am going to proclaim to you."[4]

Paul affirmed them in every way possible, recognizing that God has always been at work behind the scenes in all cultures and that buried in their misguided mythological religion were traces of light illuminating the one true God. Paul then quotes their own poets (just like we can use spiritual reference points in songs, movies, or art of our day) as a bridge to explain God's revelation: "The God who made the world and everything in it is the Lord of heaven and earth and does not live in temples built by hands . . . he himself gives all men life and breath and everything else . . . so that [people] would seek him and perhaps reach out for him and find him, though he is not far from each one of us. 'For in him we live and move and have our being.' *As some of your own poets have said,* 'We are his offspring.'"[5]

Paul affirms truth that points to the one true God in their own poets' words! He assumes that all their religious pursuits were partly in ignorance, but now they can know this unknown God who has clearly revealed himself in Jesus (Paul uses the Greek name for God, *Theos,* which would be like a Christian referring to God as "Allah," which means "God" in Arabic)—and the God of Jesus, Paul is saying, *is the Unknown God you've ignorantly worshiped in the past!* As we have applied this missiological principle by acknowledging the traces of truth in a seeker's religious pursuits, it serves as a bridge to understanding Jesus. Sometimes though, we must educate people about the limited claims of the world's religions in order for them to see Christ's uniqueness. That was the case with Matt. Matt needed this third underlying question answered in order to consider the unique claims of Jesus.

What *Do* All Religions Say?

Matt grew up in Seattle, Washington, in a nonreligious family. "Most of my teachers at Washington State were of the counterculture Baby Boomer movement," Matt recalls. "They were out to rebuild traditional institutions, so a common theme was that anything pre-sixties was old and evil—most of all religion. That pretty much summed up my view as well. Most of my friends studied philosophy or history, so nothing was absolutely true for us. We all kind of saw the religions of the world as different viewpoints of corrupt institutions. I didn't see any difference or relevance in any of them."

After moving to Austin, Matt and his wife started attending Gateway after hearing our radio ad on secular radio—it made them laugh . . . and made them curious. Feeling like they gained helpful insights into everyday life issues (even if it was from the Bible), they kept coming. Then one Sunday as we taught about the world's religions, the need for Christ hit Matt between the eyes. Here's my actual message text from that morning, so you can get a feel for what he heard that day:

> Without a doubt, there are common moral truths taught in all the great religions of the world. Mortimer Adler, editor of the Encyclopedia Britannica, who was not a Christian, wrote a book called *Truth in Religion.*

In it he states, "In spite of the possibility that all religious faiths in the world may be factually false, or that only one may be factually true, nevertheless . . . there is a common core of sound morality and prescriptive truth in all or most of the major religions."[6] And many Christians don't realize this even though it is revealed in the Bible. When people say, "Aren't they all basically saying the same thing?" I think this is what people mean. Scripture tells us that God has written his moral law in our hearts: "Even when Gentiles, who do not have God's written law, instinctively follow what the law says, they show that in their hearts they know right from wrong. They demonstrate that God's law is written within them, for their own consciences either accuse them or tell them they are doing what is right."[7] If this is true and there's a Moral Law Giver—that's the most reasonable explanation of the similarities we see throughout every culture and religion. And so, in most all of the major world religions, we see evidence of this similar moral law that God has written in our hearts, which comes out in our religions. So in this aspect of declaring moral law, they appear to be saying the same truths. In fact, here's a summary of what they all basically say morally—taken from moral laws given in ancient China, Babylon, Anglo Saxon culture, American Indian culture, Judaism, Christianity, ancient Egyptian, Greek, and Hindu culture:

> Don't do harm to another human by what you do or say (the
> Golden Rule)
> Honor your father and mother
> Be kind toward brothers and sisters, children, and
> the elderly
> Do not have sex with another's spouse
> Be honest in all your dealings (don't steal)
> Do not lie
> Care for those weaker or less fortunate
> Dying to self is the path to life[8]

Now, let's take a time-out and see what this teaches us. In just about every culture and major world religion since antiquity, we see this common moral law—stated in various ways, but basically saying these things. So we all basically agree on what's right and wrong—it's within us, and always has been. God's written it in our hearts. So let's look at how we've done. How well have we kept this common moral law of humanity? Let's make this participatory—you just give me a thumbs-up if you think humanity has pretty much kept that one. Thumbs-down if there's evidence we haven't done so well.

"Don't do harm in word or deed." What do you think? People have been pretty darn nice, haven't they? We don't pick on each other on the playground. We don't gossip about others or think hateful thoughts or say hurtful words. We don't fight or do mean things or hold grudges or murder or start wars—do we? What do you think—thumbs up? . . . No? Watch the news—we're still not doing so well. . . .

"As I sat listening that Sunday morning," Matt recalls, "something clicked. As John walked through each moral law the religions of the world teach us, it hit me like a ton of bricks . . . we know what is right and wrong! We always have! And yet, we fail, over and over again. It is said the definition of insanity is to expect a different result from the same input. I was tired of fighting and failing. For the first time, I had the thought, 'I want to know God.' As John continued on, I found myself wanting to understand more."

So what do the world's religions teach all of us? We're all royal screw-ups—myself included, Jews and Christians, Muslims and Buddhists! The world's a mess! We all know the right things to do, they've been in our culture or religious tradition, they're in our hearts—and yet, the history of humanity shows that we fall short! We can't live up to what we know to be right. So in this sense, there is universal truth communicated through all the major world's religions. Here it is: people have a problem—you have a problem, I have a problem, and it's affecting all of us. We need God's help! We cannot become who we know we were intended to be without God!

The Bible claims that the problem is that all people, in all religions, know enough about the one, true Creator God and what is morally right or wrong, but we've all turned away from him, thinking we know better at some point—in every religious tradition. Scripture says, "For since the creation of the world God's invisible qualities—his eternal power and divine nature—have been clearly seen, being understood from what has been made, so that [people] are without excuse. For although they knew God, they neither glorified him as God nor gave thanks to him, but their thinking became futile and their foolish hearts were darkened."[9]

So does the Bible teach that all other religions are wholly wrong and Christians are right? *No!* It teaches that every single person is wrong, and God is right, and our problem is we all tend to turn from God and go our own way rather than humbly seeking God and his will. So all the religions may basically say the same thing about people and what's right and wrong. But they definitely do not say the same thing about God or the solution to the human problem. And if you think they are all saying the same thing about God, you just haven't read or studied the claims of the original founders of the world's religions. They don't say the same thing.

So the real problem is that we need God! We need his forgiveness and his help. And here's something that very few people realize. Not all the world's religions claim to be revealed from God. And you would think that if God exists and loves us, he'd care about our plight. And he would give us a solution—a way out of our predicament. But because God is infinite, beyond our discovery—our only hope is if God has chosen to reveal himself. In other words, God had to take the initiative to communicate. And if God has, the natural place to start looking would be the claims of the world's religions—right? But if you read the sacred texts of the major world's religions and just take them at face value—most do not claim that God has revealed a solution to the human dilemma.

Mortimer Adler says, "Only three religions claim to have a supernatural foundation to be found in a sacred scripture that [claims] to be a divine revelation . . . among the other religions . . . only some claim to have logical and factual truth, but the truth they claim to have is of human, not divine, origin."[10]

What Adler, who was not a Christian, discovered is that if you just read the sacred texts of all the world religions, only three even claim that the one, unique, Creator God has revealed himself or his will directly: Judaism, Christianity, and Islam.[11] Interestingly, all three speak of a Messiah. The other religions claim to be wise human solutions to the problems mankind faces, or they are devotional poems and songs and stories, but do not factually claim God has revealed himself. Now, if this upsets you and feels narrow or judgmental toward other religions—take it up with the founders of the religions—but don't assume they say more than they really do.*

Matt wrote me the next week saying, "As I am opening my heart to God and learning of Jesus, I found my skeptical mind throwing up arguments against the prophecies of Jesus you mentioned several weeks ago. But last week, when you stated that we, mankind, fail because we willfully reject God, my mind reeled. I'm tired of fighting and failing, and I want to know God." Matt and I met for lunch and worked through one more underlying

---

* I always try hard not to attack or put down other religious beliefs when I speak on this as I find people just shut down from listening if they feel I'm attacking or judging other religions. One misunderstanding I've had to correct from this message is to explain that although the Buddha claimed to reveal nothing about God, many modern Buddhists profess belief in God. This is indicative of religious expression originating from other faiths as well. Syncretism always creeps in.

question before he crossed the line of faith, "So if Jesus really is the way back to God, what about those who never hear?"

How Can It Be Fair That Jesus Is the Only Way?

I believe this question of God's fairness is the motherload question underneath all questions about tolerance toward other religions. This constitutes a formidable barrier for postmodern people.

Every quarter or so in our weekend service, we draw the line in the sand, explaining the decision of faith in Christ we must willfully make to know we are right with God. After one of these Sundays, Jared came to talk to me about this question of fairness.

"How can you say Jesus is the only way to God?" Jared questioned. Jared was our postmodern engineer. Though trained in linear, rational thought academically, he easily held all moral truth as relative and all religious claims as equally valid, even if they claimed contradictory things. We had been in discussion about this before, but as we talked more about his concerns, this time something dawned on me.

"Jared, I think I just understood your real concern. Is your real concern that it doesn't sound *fair* that Jesus is the only way?"

"Exactly!" Jared exclaimed. "How could it be fair that God would send a little Chinese kid to hell even though he never had the chance to hear? Or what about some holy man who devoted his whole life to doing good and serving God as he understood him, but had always been taught that Jesus was nothing more than a prophet?"

■ ■ ■

I have found this to be a huge barrier for our generation. If the fairness question does not get addressed, seekers will often jump to the conclusion that Christians are just arrogant, and they will miss the truth that through Christ, God has been more than fair. Often, if we get caught up in arguing that Jesus is the only way when the real question is with fairness, we can *win the argument* but *lose the person*. What I have found helpful is to acknowledge what we *do know*, and what we really *do not know* about God's offer of salvation in Christ. This helps people respond to what they can know—and allows them to suspend judgment on what they cannot know.

We know Jesus said, "I am the way and the truth and the life. No one comes to the Father except through me. If you really knew me, you would know my Father as well."[12] So according to Jesus, everyone made right with God must pass through him. But we do not totally know how this works except that it is by faith only.

This still does not specifically tell us how God deals with those who have never heard about Jesus. Joy's story illustrates God's sometimes unconventional ways of drawing people to himself. Since she came to Gateway as a Buddhist with Buddhist friends, I'll let you see her response to our usual way of answering the question of fairness underneath the question of other religions.

Finding Joy

Joy went to the University of Texas in search mode. Raised by an atheist mom and a distant dad, she lacked the moral direction needed to spare her from many adolescent mistakes and pains. She took classes called "God and Man" hoping to learn about God. She studied philosophy, sociology, and psychology trying to understand the metaquestions of life. One day, while sitting in a sophomore literature class listening to the professor pound into her head how difficult it is to be open-minded, Joy had the strangest thought, "If I'm going to be open, then I need to be open to Christianity."

"No sooner did I have that thought," Joy recalls, "than people started coming out of the woodwork. Within a six-month period, I came in contact with six or seven Christians who had very pointed messages about believing in Jesus."

Unfortunately, no one seemed to understand how to walk with Joy in this new search.

"I was on a serious search for God that year," Joy says, "and it seemed like Christians kept coming my way, but I felt more pushed than pulled by them. Near the end of my search, a girl in my accounting class told me she was a Christian. When I showed interest, she gave me a fifteen-minute presentation of what it meant to be a Christian. I was very receptive to the explanation, but it felt very simplistic. She wanted me to say a prayer and get baptized. I had no history at all with Jesus, and this was opposed to everything I had been led to believe. I wasn't ready to accept it and get baptized after fifteen minutes—the pressure scared me! I just couldn't believe this very superficial story that all I needed to do was say a prayer and accept Jesus as the only way to God. I said to myself, 'I just can't believe it.' For two days everything felt lifeless. For six months, I had thought about nothing but the question of God. Finally I resolved that I don't know, but it's okay that I don't know, and I moved on."

After college, Joy's company offered a counseling benefit, and she started seeing a therapist to help her through a quarter-life crisis. "Forrest and his partner, Mary, really helped me," Joy recounted. "It was group counseling, but there was something very spiritual about the way they worked. At times, I felt as if God were in the room. In that group, I experienced a love and acceptance I didn't really know growing up. I let myself be known because it felt safe—I was finding emotional freedom. They encouraged me to do things in faith, not faith in God, but faith in the process of letting go of my tightly wound fears—I learned to trust and found a new peace emerging."

"One afternoon," Joy recalled, "Forrest let us know about meditation classes he was holding. I found out Forrest was getting ordained as a Buddhist priest. That explained the shaved head. I thought he was just trying to be hip! I began to search again, but this time, in a more relaxed way. For several years, I explored Buddhism through meditation and yoga. I studied Tai Chi Chuan and karate, would go see psychics, and read many New Age–style books on spirituality. Forrest and Mary became my mentors as I pursued my masters degree in psychology.

"One weekend, Forrest sponsored a conference in Austin with a Buddhist Lama from New York who had studied in India. The moment I walked into the room, I could feel a very peaceful, loving presence. It made a strong impression on me. He seemed very open, authentic, and loving, with a great sense of humor. Forrest and Mary had helped me see so much truth about myself, and I loved them dearly, but I was still trying to figure out if this was the path for me. As I talked to the Lama that day, I just couldn't find the solid foundation for denying all desires [a tenet of Buddhism], and I didn't feel like totally losing my self-identity to become one with everything. I desired to be married and be a mother one day, and I didn't see why these desires were wrong. There were traces of truth that attracted me, but something was missing. I kept making the same mistakes in life and didn't know how to deal with the condemning feelings I had carried for so long.

"Not long after the conference, I was in meditation class and the leader directed us to focus our minds by picturing a Buddha. I tried, but couldn't. Only a half-image would appear in my mind. Then suddenly and uninvited, an image of Jesus appeared in my conscience. I wasn't a Christian and still knew almost nothing about Jesus, yet there he was! That day I decided I really needed to understand more about Jesus.

"Not knowing how to begin, I attended the Church of Conscious Harmony and several Unitarian churches, but they didn't do it for me. A gal I knew to be Christian said she had heard great things about Gateway, though she had never been.

"From the minute I walked into Gateway, I could feel that it was different. I sensed it was okay to be in process, and that I could be accepted for who I was while I was learning. They were doing a series on the world's religions and the uniqueness of Jesus. The speaker said that all religions reveal mankind's search for truth, and there are traces of God's truth found in most all of them, but not all religions answer the 'Who is God' question. He explained that God is the God of all people regardless of religious or cultural background—he created us all and shows no favoritism, and God wants all people to know him intimately. This resonated with me. If he had talked about other religions in an arrogant or condescending way, I think I might have shut down, but what I sensed was a genuine concern and love from him, combined with a hope for knowing God. It jibed with my experience—there was a love and peace in the people I knew as Buddhists, but there was no bottom to it—no solid foundation I could find to answer the God question.

"I heard the speaker say God doesn't care about religion but about your heart. When he said that, it dawned on me, maybe God had led me here and actually was helping me know him. When he talked about a God who wouldn't condemn us because of what Jesus did, I wanted to know more," Joy remembers. "I needed to hear that God could unload the weight of condemnation I had shouldered so long. He read passages where Jesus claimed to be equal with God and the unique way back to God.

"I remember thinking, if Jesus was the way and the truth, what about the truth I felt I had been learning from these Buddhist mentors I loved dearly? Were they wrong? I really loved them, and what did this mean about what they believed? And what about people across the globe who never heard about Jesus? How can that be fair? When the speaker acknowledged these questions and the mystery of God's work, it set me at ease to keep exploring."

God Will Be Fair

Here is the transcript of the message that helped Joy understand the "How can it be fair?" question. After going through several verses where Jesus clearly claims to be the only way to the Father, I stated the question of fairness I knew some were asking:

> But if Jesus is the only way, what will God do with those who never hear about Jesus? I often find that some people aren't even open to considering Jesus' claims because this seems unfair, so let me tackle it. And let me say, ultimately, my answer is—I don't know! I don't know how God will judge others because I don't know their hearts. But here's what I do know and what I don't know from the Scriptures:
>
> 1. First, I do know God is the God of all people. The Scriptures say, "The eyes of the LORD search the whole earth in order to strengthen those whose hearts are fully committed to him."[13] Scripture also claims that all people know about God just through nature. And we also all know when

we do right and wrong—our consciences tell us.[14] So no one has an excuse for outright ignoring or rejecting God. And God looks at the heart, not religion, of every person.

2. Secondly, I do know there will be people in heaven, made right with God, who never heard the name of Jesus! All of the people of faith in the Old Testament, like Abraham, Noah, Rahab the prostitute, were all made right with God by their faith.[15] Jesus acknowledged this.[16] So clearly, if Jesus is the only way, then God took the faith they placed in the light and knowledge revealed to them (recognizing their need for God's forgiveness and leadership), and God looked ahead to Jesus' death on their behalf, applying Jesus' substitutionary sacrifice to them. Scripture tells us people from every tribe, tongue, and ethnic group will be in heaven.[17] But nobody will be in heaven because they lived a good life or because they were sincere, but only because of God's gift of forgiveness and relationship made possible through Christ—accessed by faith. In Acts 10 God saw a Roman soldier seeking God humbly, and God sent Peter so Cornelius could find faith in Christ. That day Peter proclaimed, "I see very clearly that God doesn't show partiality. In every nation he accepts those who fear him and do what is right."[18] So I do not know exactly how God deals with those who have never heard of Jesus but are humbly seeking God, but I'm confident that everyone has an opportunity to choose life with God.*

3. Third, I do know God cannot be unfair. God looks at the heart, as we've said all along, and God will not unfairly judge a person because of a lack of knowledge or cultural or religious conditioning. I'm confident God will not send anybody to hell for lack of knowledge or place of birth or ethnicity—it will only be because they truly did not want God's leadership and relationship—and in the end, I believe God sadly will say, "Okay, your will be done."[19] But really, we shouldn't worry about God's fairness,

---

* Though not all will believe, God's provision appears to be for all people: Genesis 12:1–3; John 1:7–12; Acts 14:16–17, 17:30–31. Even in Romans 10:12–18 where Paul asks, "How can they believe if they never hear?" Paul makes the argument if you follow it closely that all *have* heard "the message." In verses 17–18 he says, "Consequently, faith comes from hearing the message, and the message is heard through the word of Christ. But I ask: Did they not hear? Of course they did: 'Their voice has gone out into all the earth, their words to the ends of the world.'" Paul quotes Psalm 19 suggesting nature itself voices "the message" to the ends of the world, apparently enough for faith or rejection. Paul's obvious point though is that this message of righteousness by faith not by works, made obvious through nature and the "good news" of the Old Testament prophets like Isaiah, Moses, etc., is the same message of Christ—made complete so that anyone who calls on the name of the Lord will be saved.

since we cannot accurately judge the heart of another or play judge of the fairness of God. Especially when Jesus continually talked about how surprised people will be when it's all said and done.[20]

4. Finally, I do know that God wants people to find confident assurance that they are right with him, so he sent Christ. John says in Scripture, "I write these things to you who believe in the name of the Son of God so that you may know that you have eternal life."[21] God wants everyone to know with confidence that they can approach him without fear of condemnation because of what he's done through Christ. And Scripture is clear—Jesus is the only provision God has made to justly forgive us for doing our will rather than God's will—so if God sees the heart of a person who never heard about Jesus but is seeking to be forgiven and made right with God by faith, and God somehow does for her what he did for Abraham, it is only through what Jesus did on the cross.*

Finally, the important question for you and me is not, "What about other religions?" or "How will God judge people who have never heard?" We don't really know. But I promise this, he cares more about them than you do. Christ gave his life for them; I doubt any of us care for those people that much, so rest assured God will be more than fair if he didn't spare his own son for their sake. The better question for us is, "What will I do with the claims of Jesus now that I've heard?"

The religious leaders who ultimately crucified Jesus kept saying, "'The only Father we have is God himself.' Jesus said to them, 'If God were your Father, you would love me, for I came from God and now am here. . . . Why is my language not clear to you? Because you are unable to hear what I say.'"[22]

Jesus is saying that the person who is truly a seeker of God, when they hear and really understand what God has lovingly done for them through Christ, they respond in love and gratitude. Why wouldn't they at least seek to check it out? After all, Jesus claims he's done what we all demand—"Just show yourself, God!" But Jesus says, some people will not even consider his claims—they're closed-minded to God in reality. So the pertinent questions for us today are really these: "Is my heart truly seeking to know God?" "Am I open to honestly considering Jesus' claim to be God revealed?"[23]

"When I heard that," Joy said, "I wanted to know more. The speaker said he didn't know how God deals with people who never hear. That made sense to me and it felt honest," she recalls. "There must be mystery to God, so we don't know everything about how God works, but the thought that we could be confident and reassured through Jesus intrigued me. That invited me to look at the

---

* C. S. Lewis sets forth this idea in *The Last Battle*, 164–65.

Scriptures for myself. I heard it mentioned that Buddhism does not answer the question of 'who is God.' It was interesting to note that most religions do not claim to be directly from God. But I thought of those I loved who were Buddhists—what did it mean for them? At the same time, I was receiving so much that it was like a wave of love and information, and I was riding that wave.

"Over the next three months," Joy continued, "I set aside my concerns for my Buddhist friends and 'those others' and learned about Jesus for myself. Christmas Eve I spoke with John along with Janet, who became my small group leader. They clarified my understanding of God's grace. When Janet asked if I felt like I understood enough to pray and open my heart to Christ, I said yes. Now I was truly ready."

■ ■ ■

Joy now leads her own small group, and she has helped others wrestle with the question, "How can this be fair?" Her analysis as a spiritual traveler and psychotherapist is insightful. "I think the concern for God being fair to others has more to do with ourselves. I don't think most people are honestly that concerned for others. The pains of our own lives are underneath these questions—pain that makes us wonder about all fairness and hope. But at least now I know there is hope for us all!"

In every person's life I have mentioned in this chapter, God has had his hand in their lives in mysterious ways, drawing them toward the light. Some found it, some never did. But gone are the days when Christian leaders can make assumptions that we are a Christian nation. We must honestly and humbly address the tolerance questions emerging generations will continue to ask about the world's religions. But never forget, God is the Creator and lover of all people, even if they've yet to realize it.

Does this include gay people? That's the second big litmus test question of tolerance our culture asks the church.

STUDY GUIDE

Culture Check

1. In an increasingly global village, the question of the world's religions will be one of the most asked by seekers. How can you better prepare yourself and your leaders to interact on this question?

2. In Acts 17:22–28, Paul gives principles that can help you lead people from diverse religious perspectives toward Christ. How do these principles apply to your context?
3. How would you answer the questions underneath the question of the world's religions?

Small Group Questions

1. People often say, "With so many religions, how can Jesus be the only way?" What are the main struggles you hear people voice regarding Jesus?
2. What new realizations did you discover about Jesus or the world's religions while reading this chapter?
3. Read Romans 2:14–15. When people say, "All religions basically say the same thing," in what areas does Scripture agree with them? Where would Christianity differ?
4. How are the claims of Jesus unique among the world's religions?
5. Read Acts 17:22–28. What cultural bridges does Paul build to lead people to faith in Christ? Do you think Paul is saying that Jesus is the fulfillment of their pagan religious pursuits (v. 23)? Why or why not? How might we apply Paul's principles today?

How Do You Feel about Gays? The Tolerance Litmus Test—Q2

I tell you the truth ... the prostitutes are entering
the kingdom of God ahead of you.

Jesus, Matthew 21:31

don't know this for certain, but I have a sneaking suspicion that if Jesus retold the parable of the Good Samaritan today, it might go like this:

> On one occasion a Christian religious leader stood up to test Jesus. "Teacher," he asked, "what must I do to inherit eternal life?"
>
> "What is written in the Law?" Jesus replied. "How do you read it?"
>
> He answered: "'Love the Lord your God with all your heart and with all your soul and with all your strength and with all your mind'; and, 'Love your neighbor as yourself.'"
>
> "You have answered correctly," Jesus replied. "Do this and you will live."
>
> But the religious leader wanted to justify his actions (for if the truth be known, he despised some people who safely weren't his neighbors), so he asked Jesus, "And who is my neighbor?"
>
> In reply Jesus said: "A man was going down from Jerusalem to Jericho, when he fell into the hands of robbers. They stripped him of his clothes, beat him and went away, leaving him half dead. A priest happened to be going down the same road, and when he saw the man, he passed by on the other side. So too, an evangelical Christian, when he came to the place and

saw him, passed by on the other side. But a gay man, as he traveled, came where the man was; and when he saw him, he took pity on him. He went to him and bandaged his wound. Then he put the man in his own car, took him to a hospital and stayed to care for him. The next day he paid the hospital saying, 'Look after this man, and when I return, I will reimburse you for any extra expense you may have.'

"Which of these three do you think was a neighbor to the man who fell into the hands of robbers?"

The religious leader replied, "The one who had mercy on him."

Jesus told him, "Go and do likewise."[1]

When Jesus told this story of a "good" Samaritan, it shocked his Jewish listeners. He confronted the self-defined limits religious leaders of his day put on God's commandment to love. The *Expositor's Bible Commentary* notes that Jesus picked the most hated of all persons in that religious culture, the Samaritans, in order to make his point.

> The Jewish "expert" would have thought of the Jewish victim as a good person and the Samaritan [gay man in my paraphrase] as an evil one. To a Jew there was no such person as a "good" Samaritan ... [this religious leader] needed to learn that God does not bestow the life of the kingdom on those who reject the command to love. Such rejection shows that they have not truly recognized how much they need the love of God themselves.[2]

Maybe the same could be said of some Christians and their treatment of gay people. As mentioned before, one of the top two most asked questions I get from unchurched people is "What do you think about gays?" Not just from people who are gay or have a close friend who is gay, but all kinds of people want an answer. Why has this become a watershed issue in our culture? Maybe because of the lack of mercy—no, downright hatred—our culture perceives from the Christian community toward gay people. So how should the emerging church answer this question?

Before I try, let me first admit I didn't want to write this chapter. As I struggled with why I didn't want to write it, I realized it's because I don't have all the answers, and our church has not cracked the code on ministering to the gay community. I feel a tension over this subject that I don't like, and if it were simply up to me, I'd choose not to live in the tension. I'd choose something more personally comfortable. But I'm convinced that's not what God calls me to do; Scripture forces me to live in the tension if I take it seriously. There's a tension in Scripture that says every person matters to God, has the hope of God's grace and forgiveness, eternal adoption into God's family, and should be treated with love as my neighbor, which includes gay people. Pulling against this truth are the Scriptures that indicate homosexual sex is wrong.* So what are the questions and answers that create this tension, and how should the church respond?

Should the Church Open Its Doors to Gays?

Actually, the real question is not whether to let gays into the church, they're already among us. The real question is whether to let them talk about it, so they can find hope and support to grow spiritually, and allow God to do his will fully in them.

In a weekend service, Ted read a letter from a gay person hiding among us. Before you jump to conclusions about this person, let me tell you what's most important to him. He spent a good part of his life trying to change his sexual orientation. He has loved Jesus and sought to follow him wholeheartedly from an early age. He believes homosexual sex is wrong, and for years begged God to change his sexual orientation. Teased, called a "fag," he concealed his struggle on the outside. But the pain of his secret, the guilt of his thoughts, ripped apart his insides.

Finally one night in despair from being alone, hating himself, living a secret lie at a Christian college, he tried to take his life. A friend found him in a bathtub of blood. He survived physically, but the emotional trauma still remains. He writes to Gateway:

Dear Church,

I have a secret to tell you. I'm gay. I'm truly sorry I never told you before, but I was afraid of how you might react. I've seen it happen before. I have been the subject of arguments between people I considered close friends. And some of those friends I've lost because of it. Some cried hearing the news, embraced me, and have since been a source of support and unconditional love. Others cried and walked away, not knowing what to say to me, at least not to my face. Three small words ... "I am gay," and

---

* Although I will not go into various interpretations of these passages, here are the relevant ones for study: Genesis 1:27–28; 2:18–24; 19:4–9, Leviticus 18:22; 20:13, Romans 1:26–27, 1 Corinthians 6:9–10, 1 Timothy 1:9–10. For further study of various positions, I would recommend these books by two biblical scholars: *Scripture and Homosexuality*, by Marion L. Soards (Westminster John Knox, 1995), and *Straight and Narrow?* by Thomas Schmidt (InterVarsity, 1995), and for an alternative interpretation, *Christianity, Social Tolerance and Homosexuality*, by John Boswell (Chicago: University of Chicago, 1980).

suddenly people I've known for years—that I talked to almost daily, laughed and cried with, shouldered through rough times—turned away from me. So I learned to adapt. I embraced the Army's philosophy, "Don't ask, don't tell." Can you forgive my lack of genuineness?

I've been with Gateway from the beginning, sitting next to you, sharing your meals and stories and laughing with you (usually a lot). For the most part I've been at peace with being silent . . . Even while some of you (usually guys, but not always) told jokes about homosexuals, not realizing that one was sitting right next to you. I endured listening to morons, with wrists bent and lisps perfectly placed, just so I could be around other believers in Christ. Others who believe like me, that God is the creator of the universe and that his Son is the salvation of mankind, that the Bible is his Word and his message is for all people for all times . . . and above all else, that we must all love God and likewise, love his people . . . ALL OF THEM.

It's probably important to note that I don't revel in being gay. I don't wear my sexuality like a giant "rainbow" badge of honor . . . it's just a part of me, a facet of my life, but certainly not the whole or sum of my being. I'm also not "in the closet"—a term I hate! The people at my work know I'm gay (and my closest friends), but most of them don't go to church. The world doesn't care what kind of label you slap on yourself, as long as it's in fashion. So, what's the problem then? Fear. Where there is fear, love can't abide. I can't seem to connect with the people at Gateway, or most churches for that matter. I've been in small groups and the people in them were great, but then they would use words like honesty, openness, accountability, and trust, and I knew that I wouldn't be able to fulfill my end of the deal.

How can I trust you to love me? All of me? Can you look past that and see me like God does, like he sees you? Sometimes, when I'm really weak, I wonder if it would just be better to leave the church and make my way in the world. But the truth is, I need God in my life, and I know I wouldn't make it without him. Better than that, though, God called me out of the world and I heard him, and I just can't go back to "nothing" and pretend that he doesn't exist. But it's so hard sometimes and the world can be so lonely . . . that's why we need each other, to lean on and to hold each other up. I will do what I have to, with or without you, to carry on. God just won't seem to let me alone (and I love him all the more for it, though I might kick and scream). But I'm tired of hiding . . . of being afraid of your rejection . . . from the people who are most supposedly the ambassadors of God's love and grace. Jesus came for the lost, the sinners, for the kinds of people that most "upstanding citizens" would rather cross the street to avoid than walk next to. I am a sinner . . . what I do (or don't do but think about a lot) to earn that moniker shouldn't be more important than the fact that regardless . . . I need Jesus and it's only through him that I might have life.

Sean

What I find most amazing is that Sean is celibate. In fact, because of his love for God and his commitment to living out God's words, Sean is not sexually active at all and never has been! In terms of a hero of the faith, willingly following Jesus despite the cost, there are few people with his commitment to Christ, which currently costs him acceptance in all camps. I've watched him grow as a Christ-follower, seen him humbly serve the church with his gifts. And yet, he still doesn't feel safe in Christ's community. What is he doing wrong? What are *we* doing wrong?

The church in Corinth opened its doors to people like Sean. "Do not be deceived," Paul says. "Neither the sexually immoral nor idolaters nor adulterers nor male prostitutes nor *homosexual offenders* nor thieves nor the greedy nor drunkards nor slanderers nor swindlers will inherit the kingdom of God. And that is what some of you *were*. But you were washed, you were sanctified, you were justified in the name of the Lord Jesus Christ and by the Spirit of our God."[3]

Notice the list . . . not just homosexual offenders, but greedy people and alcoholics, sexually immoral heterosexuals, and modern-day corporate creative accountants all make the list together. So what does this mean? It means just what it says, "We all need to be washed, sanctified, justified" to experience God's kingdom life, and we can't do it for ourselves. In the original Greek, the passive construction—"were washed . . . were sanctified . . . were justified"—indicates this is something done for us *by* the Spirit of our God.

So who are we to deny the Seans of the world a place at the family table if God is able to make him clean just like he did the materialistic struggler, the heterosexual struggler, or me? But what if Sean's sexual attraction doesn't change? Can he still be welcomed as a struggler? That brings up another question.

Is Being Gay a Sin?

I got this email not too long ago. What would you say to Samantha if she wrote you this email?

Hello. I met you last Sunday. A friend of mine invited me to Gateway. I have to confess, church was the last place I ever wanted to go, but I have to be honest that your approach, the entire church's approach, has me hooked! Hooked on Christ! I really never thought I'd say that. I'm trying to do things to learn, to bring me closer to Christ and to be more open and less judgmental towards organized religion. But now I'm afraid. I want Gateway to be my church home, where I come for comfort, for guidance with my hopes and dreams, failures, everything. What initially got me to attend was the philosophy "Come as you are." But you see, I'm a lesbian. I am in love with another woman and we will spend the rest of our lives together. This may not seem like a big deal, but I have Christian family who oppose our relationship to the nth degree. So my question is: Are we welcome and supported within Gateway? I guess what I need is some assurance from you or Ted that I'm not going to hell because I'm in love with a woman. Lost sheep trying to find my way.

So what do you tell Samantha? Here she was far away from God, wanted nothing to do with Christ or Christians, yet after sitting and learning about the love and grace God demonstrated in Christ, and after being around a community of Christ-followers, she's hooked—on Jesus! Do you tell her she's uniquely unable to receive the grace of God? That even though Christ died on the cross to wash, sanctify, and justify people who struggle with everything from materialistic greed to lustful heterosexual thoughts; and even though they may still fight the temptation to hoard or look at pornography even after accepting Christ's forgiveness, she's somehow uniquely different? Her struggle is unique in the list? It alone is unforgivable and irredeemable in God's eyes?

That's not the gospel of Jesus Christ, the one who said the prostitutes were getting into the kingdom of God ahead of the religious leaders of his day![4]

And yet, here's the tension. God shows no partiality, and Christ died to forgive her and make her a child of God just as much as he did for me, yet the Scripture indicates that homosexual sex is not God's will. So what do you tell her? I invited Samantha and Susan to come meet and talk. We met for three hours, shared a meal together, laughed a lot (Samantha's a riot), but also tackled the real tension head on.

Living in the Tension

"Okay, so just tell me," Samantha smashed through the get-to-know-ya talk, restating her question to me, "Am I going to hell because I love Susan?"

"Well, I'm not the one to judge who goes to hell, but I can tell you certainly it wouldn't be because you *love* Susan," I said. "But let me back up.

First of all, I don't think 'gay' is who you are in God's eyes. He created you for a purpose, and that's more than the sum total of your sexual attraction. I think our culture polarizes the issue."

"Good, I agree," Samantha pitched in.

"The Scriptures are abundantly clear," I continued, "that being made right with God is a gift that's free to all who receive it, and I don't see anybody excluded who wants it." I pulled out a Bible to show them Ephesians 2:8–9: "For it is by grace you have been saved, through faith," I read out loud, explaining that grace just means "something you don't deserve." "And what are you saved from?" I asked rhetorically. "From life apart from God, now and on into eternity. The only people who spend life and eternity apart from God, which defines hell in my opinion, are people who reject his free gift of restored relationship offered through Christ—who really don't want God to be God of their lives. See, God won't force us back into a relationship with him as God, but that's what he wants.

> Most people would agree that the church should be a place of refuge, a place of solace from a hating, nonloving world. That is not necessarily true for many gay men and women. In the very place where they are seeking peace, seeking community, they are instead given a cold shoulder at best, a hell-and-brimstone boot out the door at worst.
> —Mark

I believe he created each of you for that very purpose, for a love relationship with himself; and out of that relationship, he wants to help you better love others as he desires—including each other. And it goes on saying, 'it is the gift of God—not by works, so that no one can boast.' So if it's a gift you can't earn, what do you have to do? What do you do when someone offers a gift?" I asked.

"I guess receive it in gratitude," Susan piped in.

"Exactly," I said. "Just like you can't force another person to love you, God won't force you to love him. He could force you to obey him, but obviously, he doesn't, does he? What he wants is your trust, your heart, your willingness. That's all he needs to enter into life with you and help you become all he intended you to be. So let me ask, where are each of you as far as opening your heart to Christ and receiving this gift of relationship? Ever just told him "That's what I want"?

Susan said she had. Growing up in a Hispanic culture, she had always believed in Jesus as God's Son, but she had only recently really understood grace and opened her heart to him.

"I'm close," Samantha admitted. "I have to admit, I'm falling more and more in love with Jesus as I listen and read the Scriptures with fresh eyes. Which I never thought I'd say! But I'm also scared. I haven't fully surrendered yet."

"What's holding you back?" I asked.

"Well for one, my family has been telling me God hates homosexuals and that I'm doomed to hell. Doesn't exactly sound like God would want me if they're right. So are you saying they're wrong?" Samantha pushed for clarity.

"Well, let me be totally upfront with you about what I do think the Scriptures say. They don't say homosexual sex is the unforgivable sin, but they do seem clear that homosexual sex is wrong. It's not what God intended." I could see the blood draining from Samantha's face, but Susan maintained her composure.

"So then you do think it is wrong to be gay?" Samantha pushed.

"Here's what I understand so far and how I make sense of the tension I see. I know lots of studies have been done indicating that homosexual orientation is not a choice. I've read about the genetic studies, but honestly, they seem inconclusive. Other research demonstrates disruption of certain hormones in the fetal development of rats, which significantly alters sexual orientation. This indicates that possibly a pregnant mother's intense nervous tension or trauma can interfere with the later stages of fetal development, disrupting the normal 'imprinting' of the brain with testosterone. This might offer a cause for male homosexuality, but not lesbianism. And some researchers think lesbianism comes from more psychosocial influences while male homosexuality stems from more biophysical influences. Others see evidence of lack of nurture of males by fathers as a source of some homosexuality; same-sex abuse clearly has some tie in many cases. But all evidence points away from a simple, single cause as far as I can tell.[5] I think we don't know the cause. But from talking with many gay people, I've come to believe most would not choose same-sex attraction if they could choose."

"It's good to hear you say that," Samantha confessed as I continued.

"Many people have told me horror stories of the agony of wanting and trying to change often to the point of self-hatred so intense it led to suicidal thoughts. I know others who drifted into it and are really more bisexual. Here's the point: God does not condemn us for being in a state we didn't choose, even though it may not be the way he intended originally, but he does hold us accountable for our choices. For instance, there are many unfair things about this life that are not as God says he originally intended. A friend who is one of the most faithful, loving Christ-followers I know has had terribly unfair things happen with his children. After having two kids, they discovered surprise triplets; two were born with Cerebral Palsy due to a lack of oxygen in later fetal development. After all that, his oldest son had something 'click' in his mind during puberty and became extremely uncontrollable and even violent. I don't believe these were God's ultimate intentions, but that he allows the effects of an evil messed up world to affect the 'good' and 'bad' indiscriminately for a time. Look at the propensity for children of alcoholics or addicts or abusers to fall into these same traps. Clearly this world is messed up, and no, it is not fair at all.

"Still, all people as they grow up will have choices to make according to unique challenges they face. They are different choices than ones I will have to make. But our choices will either honor God in faith and allow him to move us back toward what he intended or out of self-will move us further away from God's intent. We are all responsible for our choices—not compared to everyone else—but before God. My friend's son will still need to overcome his violent behavior. An adult child of an alcoholic will need to overcome the tendency toward addictive behaviors."

"So are you saying being gay is an abnormality?" Samantha asked.

"Well, yeah! But in the same sense that we're all abnormal. None of us are as God originally intended, that's why this world's so messed up. Look, I don't think every gay person just wakes up one day and says, 'I think I'll choose same-sex attraction.' From all of the pain and isolation and social stigma attached, I can't imagine anyone willfully choosing it, and I know many gays who would choose the opposite if offered a switch that would just 'turn it off.' So no, I don't think a person is forever condemned because of a predisposition—if that's the case. But we are responsible for our choices. So there is a distinction between a predisposition and what we choose to do with it."

"Someone told us we could never be leaders in church because we're gay, is that true?" Susan asked. "That's what's hard—to feel like a second-class Christian."

"The only reason we would say you can't lead is the same reason we would say a heterosexual person could not lead, because you were not willingly following Christ. If a heterosexual is involved in premarital sex, or some ongoing pattern of disobedience to God's revealed will in the Scriptures, she can't lead others effectively by his Spirit because she's not really fully willing to follow him. The same would be true of you. If you are willing to follow Christ with your sexual expression, which according to the Scriptures would mean not having homosexual sex, and assuming you were spiritually qualified and had no other ongoing patterns of willful disobedience to God, then you could lead."

"Oh, wow," Samantha had a hopeful look on her face to my surprise. "So there's no glass ceiling of participation in the church because I'm gay?"

"Again, I don't think God sees you as gay, but as a person. You're made right with him by faith, not by what you do. Even if you didn't choose same-sex attraction, you do have a choice as to whether you act on it or not."

Samantha looked at Susan with a sly smile, "Sorry, no more sex . . . It didn't happen enough anyway."

"Very funny," Susan said. She looked at me more seriously, "The sex really is not the main part of our relationship, you know. It's not the most important thing."

"Well then," I said, venturing out into uncharted territory, "let me make a suggestion." I decided to risk a thought that had been forming in my mind. Here's the thought: *I can never change another person, and even though God can, he doesn't usually zap away all temptation. Instead, he changes the heart and strengthens the will as a person is willing. The only way forward, the only way for God's will to be done in these women's lives, is if they're willing. And unless they grow to love and trust Christ, they won't be willing. How God does or doesn't change people is up to him, not me.* So I continued with a risky proposition.

"Let me suggest this," I proposed. "I think there's something right about the love you have for each other. It may ruffle some people's feathers for me to say this, but you obviously really do have a genuine concern and love for each other or you wouldn't have stuck by each other for six years. Scripture says David and Jonathan loved each other with a deep love that wasn't sexual (though I know gays love to put that on them). But real love comes from God . . . always! There's a pure part of the love you have for each other, but I also think there's a sexualized part that wasn't as God intended."

"It's good to hear you admit that. My family could never admit that, they think it's all about sex," Samantha said, then turning to Susan with a smile she joked, "If it were all about sex, it would never have lasted this long."

"Okay, Samantha, enough of trying to push the pastor's buttons," Susan smirked.

I continued to explain my proposal for a way forward from here: "I imagine when gay people hear that God's will is against homosexual sex, you probably feel like God just wants to rip away from you one of the most important things in your life and leave you empty. But I'm convinced that's not true. Whatever God wants to do in your lives will not leave you unfulfilled and empty. It may be difficult, or at times painful, but it will leave you more fulfilled than before in the long run. That I know is God's promise.

"So here's what I want to ask. Can you pursue Christ, and keep learning about how much he loves you and wants the best for you, and keep seeking to trust him with everything? Willingness is all he needs. So if you can trust that he won't leave you abandoned with a hole in your heart, begin to pray for his will. And pray for his will in your relationship too. See if you can hold each other up to God like this—" I opened my hands, palms up, gesturing a sign of letting go and holding the relationship in open hands "—and ask him to help you love this other person as he desires. If you do that and follow him willingly, I think you'll find it's the path to a deeper, more fulfilling life than you imagined."

Susan nodded her head in agreement, and Samantha said, "I think I can do that. But . . . I'll do that if you'll re-look at those passages of Scripture about homosexuality. I'm still not convinced it's not just a cultural prohibition rather than a moral one."

I told her I'd study it again with her, but having already waded deep into the Metropolitan Community Church teaching as well as reading opinions of scholars and sociologists on both sides, then studying the critical passages in the original languages, I felt pretty confident. I told her we could talk more in depth about the passages I showed them at another time.

Two weeks later, Samantha stopped me in the hall. "We're talking," was all she said.

"You're talking?" I questioned.

"Not just 'Now-I-lay-me-down-to-sleep,' we're really talking—me and Jesus, and it's really amazing what's happening!" Then she whispered, "I think he's really there!"

"He is really there," I laughed. "Keep listening and talking with an open heart . . . and open hands!" I encouraged.

■ ■ ■

I have no idea what God will or won't do with Samantha and Susan. Will they both truly follow Christ wholeheartedly? Will they end their sexual relationship? Can they express a love for each other without being sexual? Will they find their desires changing over time? Some do, but others don't. All I know is that we've got to find a way forward, helping all people who are willing to fully trust Christ. The only way for people to become what God intends is through his power working through their willingness. Apart from that, there is no other way. We can make people conform but not *become*. So the better path is to help people trust God, and that's a struggle for all of us! Even for religious leaders who often struggle trying to control people's behavior, because it feels like a reflection on us. We must all let go and trust God to lead and guide us into wholeness and healing.

Is There an Alternative Alternative-Lifestyle?

One thing I do know: not all gays want to be sexually active and promiscuous as they are sometimes stereotyped. Many want to follow Christ, and they

157

want a supportive community that encourages their spiritual growth as people who are much more than their sexual orientation. If the emerging church is not willing to live in the tension, many of these people will be forced to choose between being loved, accepted, and celebrated in the gay community versus being forced to stay isolated and alone in the church, without the love and acceptance and support needed to truly follow Christ. The church must at least be an alternative to the promiscuously unfulfilling, alternative lifestyle.

I recently did a funeral service for a bar owner here in town named Sue. She had contracted liver disease and emphysema, sold the bar, and came to Gateway two years ago at the invitation of her sister, where they both opened their hearts to follow Christ. Sue had moved away, but listened weekly to Gateway messages on the web and studied the Scriptures daily the last two years of her life. Because Gateway helped her turn to Christ, she wanted me to do her funeral. What I didn't know until the day before the funeral is that the bar was a gay bar. Though Sue was not gay, she treated the regular customers like family. Though she had been out of the bar business for years, the funeral was packed with past employees and patrons.

I noticed two things during the funeral. First, it was the loudest, most raucous funeral I've ever conducted. Second, as they told stories about Sue and bar life, it reminded me of what God intends the church to be like (minus tequila shots and drag-queen comedy shows).

One person stood and said, "When Sue hired me she told me, 'I can't pay you as much as you're making bartending now, but trust me, we will more than make up for it—we're like family here.' What you all gave me in acceptance, love, and friendship," he said choking up, "was worth far more than a few bucks an hour. Sue was right when she said, 'we take care of each other here.'"

A woman stood up and said, "I remember when I was feeling at the end of my rope, you all took me in, Sue believed in me, and you all even helped me financially get back on my feet. Sue was like a mother to me and created a family for us all."

The bar had even taken up a collection totaling thousands of dollars to pay off all of Sue's medical debts after her death. As I listened to them tell stories, it reminded me of Christ's vision for his community, and I realized, *that's what we're all longing for! It's not the sex or the buzz or the bar—it's love and acceptance and hope for becoming more in the context of community!* Something we were intended to find through Christ.

People long for Christ's community of grace, and when they don't get it from church, they find alternative, broken ways to get a cheap substitute.

The church must be the hope of the whole world, including the hope for those who want an alternative to the alternative lifestyle, which often hides the painful cost that comes with pseudocommunity.

Derek's story illustrates a path many more gays desire to take—and some lessons for Christians wanting to help.

God Hates You

"God hates fags," the man yelled in Derek's face as he walked especially close to the sign-toting group, screaming at the gay-pride marchers as they paraded down Congress Avenue. The pain from years of hurtful comments swelled like a giant, powerful wave rolling his anger to the surface.

"I'm gonna get closer to them, just to infuriate them even more," Derek thought to himself. "Who do these Christians think they are? Who are they to judge when they have so much hatred toward me? They don't even know me."

As a gay-rights activist, Derek loved to antagonize Christians, to do all he could to provoke their repulsion and anger. Deeply entrenched in the gay community, Derek had gained a stronger self-identity and assurance than he had ever had . . . and a deeper anger toward church and Christians. But it hadn't always been that way.

Derek grew up in a military family. His father, an African-American stationed in Japan, married a Japanese woman. Derek, their fourth born, was the only child put up for adoption. Derek's adoptive dad, also in the military, was physically abusive to his only child.

"Man, how I longed for my father to just compliment me, just encourage me, while I was growing up," Derek told me. "But what I heard most was, 'You worthless little $%#@,' 'You're the a&#hole of the world.' That's who I was to my father, so I grew up very unsure of myself."

When Derek was twelve, he went on a scout campout. "Before that event, I had never had a homosexual thought once," Derek recalls. "I was actually a really naive kid, when this bully at camp coerced me into my first sexual experience. He both bullied me and scared me, but also took me under his arm and let me into his world of pornography and taught me about sex, which I knew nothing about. Looking back, it was a twisted way of meeting a deep need I had. He was abusive like my father, but he complimented me and encouraged me, and though I felt terrified and ashamed, it felt good to be appreciated for the first time."

Not being able to talk to his father or mother about it, and with the family violence escalating, Derek continued to give in to this bully's coercive threats that he'd tell everyone if Derek didn't comply.

One night, after seeing a movie alone, the incessant feelings of worthlessness unrelenting, Derek decided to end it all. "I was headed across the base, intent on jumping from the highest building, when I spotted a light on in the chapel. Something mysteriously drew me toward that light. As I talked that night with the chaplain, he explained the love and grace of God who would forgive me of all my sin through Christ. I believed it with all my heart . . . it was all I had to hang on to."

Shortly after that night, relief came to Derek in the form of a military transfer to Fort Hood, Texas. "During eighth grade, I found myself increasingly attracted to men, especially my teachers who were nice to me. I idolized authority figures like my gym teacher who encouraged me. I wanted to be strong and masculine, just like him. Then I noticed it shifted from wanting to be like him, to wanting to serve him, to almost wanting to mesh with him. I realize now, I was searching for masculine connection, identity, affirmation. This realization hit me one Christmas.

"I had gone to the base chaplain's home. We were all singing Christmas carols. As I sat there, watching the chaplain sitting next to his teenage son, turning the pages of music as his son played piano, I had an epiphany. It hit me so hard, it felt like a brick in the face. That's what I'm missing, I thought, fighting back tears as I watched this father and son. Since then, I've realized this is common. I can only think of a few gay men I've known who had good relationships with their fathers, and they are definitely the exception."

Never feeling at home in church, feeling ashamed of his thoughts, Derek fled from God as a teen, feeding his pain with pornography. After a tour in the Air Force, Derek ended up in the Castro district of San Francisco, where he was exposed to gay culture, history, and the full lifestyle.

"It felt freeing to start to come to the conclusion, 'This is who I am,'" Derek admits. "It felt good to get all these affirming hopes for a future and a community where I could belong." Submerged in the gay lifestyle for years, Derek moved to Austin. He dove deep into the gay community immediately. He became an activist for gay rights, fighting against the hate-filled Christians he had come to despise. At the gym where he worked out, there was a group of Christians who knew Derek was gay.

"They would look at me in a snarling kind of way," Derek recalls. "Once in a while, one would say something in a disdainful tone like, 'The way you live . . . you need Jesus.' I would try to provoke their comments, just to upset them. They did anything but convince me Jesus was what I needed."

Jesus Loves Me, This I Know?

"Then one day, Jay asked if I'd spot him while lifting," Derek remembers. "As we talked, it became clear to me that he too was a Christian. I immediately put my guard up. But each week, he continued to be friendly to me, even though he realized I was gay. Sometimes I'd try to provoke him to say hateful things, but he remained consistently kind. The fact that I could tell he didn't judge me, but for some reason seemed to care about me—that really made an impact. He worked out with me often and invited me out for coffee afterwards. He didn't preach at me but shared his life and faith openly as if it were something I too could have and would want.

"I had no attraction toward him," Derek revealed. "Straight guys always fear that, but it's not like that. What I saw in Jay was Christ. I saw a person I wanted to be like. Just his kindness reminded me of Jesus with the woman in John 8, whom the religious people wanted to condemn to death. Jay showed me a possibility beyond condemnation. I started thinking, maybe God does love me."

Derek emphasized to me that just "being Jesus" to people in the gay community can make a huge difference. Looking past their sexual orientation and fear-based comments, and treating them as people created by God, offers a hope that many are searching desperately to find.

"At that point in my life," Derek continued, "I had recently been through three painful relationships. I was going to bars, activities, swims, events, doing the whole gay-social life, but inside, I was starting to unravel. I found much of the gay world very narcissistic. I had become accustomed to being used and using others. I felt like I didn't know myself, and the promises I thought the gay life would fulfill left me unfulfilled and losing hope."

Jay kept encouraging his new friend to find a church and turn his life over to the God who loved him. Derek started going to church but, not long after, fell into another painful sexual relationship. Feeling like a failure all around, he tried to hang himself from a tree one night.

"I jumped out into the darkness to kill myself—and the branch broke!" Derek recalls. "As I lay there on the ground in the dark, I thought, 'God if this is not what you intended, then how in the h#$@ am I supposed to find my way out of this life?' I thought about Jay and his life, and I said, 'Okay God, you showed me Jay, show me how to become more like that.'"

Shortly after that night, Derek found a small group for gay strugglers wanting to follow Christ. He started going to meetings led by a man who had been out of the gay lifestyle twelve years. He and his wife led the group. There he met many men and women who were deciding to give God, rather than sexuality, control over their lives. "It was very difficult for me at first,"

Derek admits, "because I still believed gay was all I was and all I could ever be. And there was part of me that habitually wanted it. Let's face it; sex can be habitual, even addictive, for the heterosexual or homosexual. I had to learn to change how I was thinking about my need for sex. Sex is a pseudo-connection for a hetero- or homosexual's need for intimacy. Processing my thoughts and struggles with other Christians who struggled helped me find the thought pattern driving the habit. I started learning how to disconnect the motor of my thoughts before taking me down a road I no longer wanted to travel."

With the weekly support and encouragement of this group of men and women, Derek has abstained from homosexual sex for almost eight years now. I asked him why he hasn't gone back and if it's been a struggle. He admitted there have been struggles along the way with pornography, but not with acting out sexually.

"My greatest struggle was during a time when I was feeling disconnected relationally at church. My gay friends came around about that time, asking me where my Christian friends were, kind of taunting me by saying they cared more than my church did. That was difficult. But now, I can see those relationships for how unhealthy they were. There was such emotional dependency, almost like a spiritual cannibalism, because you want him and he wants you in a very possessive kind of way. It's a true, genuine feeling, but it grows out of other needs in your life not being met. That's why so few of these relationships really last. The peace I have with God far outweighs the darkness I once felt."

"The gay community would probably think your choice insane," I told Derek. "Feeling like it's unfair that you can never be fulfilled sexually. What do you think?" I asked.

"I think one day I will be married," Derek said. His comment surprised me. After knowing him for years, I had never heard him say this, nor did I expect it.

"Really?" I asked. "Is that new?"

"Actually since being here at Gateway," he said.

"Why's that?" I asked.

"I think I feel empowered and encouraged, like I matter," he told me. "As I've become more assured of myself as a male, I can tell that I'm happier with myself and I'm not afraid of the opposite sex. I found myself really bonding to one woman—she was a lesbian who also came to Christ and has been straight for six years. As I connected with her, I found myself attracted to her like never before. I think I will one day be married."

Messy but Moving Forward

That, of course, won't be true of every gay who chooses God's alternative lifestyle. It's messier than that. Most do not report a change of orientation. As a church, we must struggle in the tension of loving and accepting gay people seeking to follow Christ, recognizing their orientation may never change. Some people have left Gateway feeling unsupported as struggling gay Christ-followers. Others have felt very supported and have started a group for other strugglers at Gateway wanting to follow Christ. One male couple came to Christ and on their own decided to live together as friends but stop having sex. It's messy and far from perfect, but there's clear evidence God is at work, redeeming gay people, moving them forward in his direction.

Derek has some wisdom to share on how the church can be a light shining into the gay community. Here are his suggestions:

1. Welcome gay people to church. Genuinely care about them as people who matter.
2. Be patient with people and encourage them to get support in a group of fellow strugglers wanting to follow Christ. Be a friend to gay people even if you don't have a support group available. It doesn't have to be about being gay but about being a human as God intended. Let them see that gay is not all they are, they have other needs only God can meet through his community—meet what needs you can.
3. Straight men don't need to be afraid of gay men. Friendship does more than anything else. One of the biggest confidence-builders for me was being invited by guys at church to play volleyball. I said I didn't know how, and they offered to teach me, saying they'd love to have me on their team. That built my confidence as a man among men.

In a world high on tolerance, the Christian church cannot afford to neglect our greatest asset: Grace. We must live out the tolerance, mercy, and transforming power of the God who offered more than tolerance—his own Son for the sins of the *whole* world. As we demonstrate not only the righteousness of God, but also the compassion he has for creatures in a broken, lost world, people will see the hope and power of God in fresh ways. This breaks down the barrier of tolerance keeping many from considering Christ.

But even the most tolerant must also confront truth. How do we remove the barriers to truth without discarding the truth? That's what we'll attack in the next section.

STUDY GUIDE

Culture Check

1. In Matthew 21:31 Jesus tells certain religious leaders that the prostitutes are entering the kingdom of God ahead of them. Why? What does this say about the heart of Jesus? How does your heart reflect the heart of Christ toward all people, including gay people?

2. Read 1 Corinthians 6:9–11. Go down the list and check off the sin categories listed that people in your church probably still struggle with as Christ followers. How many categories did you check? Why do you think churched people sometimes treat some of these struggles with sin differently than others? If God alone can make any of us clean, what does this imply?

3. How will you answer the question, "What does your church think about gays?"

Small Group Questions:

1. Why do you think homosexuality has become such a divisive issue in our culture?

2. Read Matthew 21:31. Jesus never condoned sexual sin of any kind, yet here he tells certain religious leaders that the prostitutes are entering the kingdom of God ahead of them. Why? What does this say about the heart of Jesus? How does your heart reflect the heart of Christ toward all people, including gay people?

3. Read 1 Corinthians 6:9–11. Go down the list and without naming names, check off the sin categories listed that people in your church still struggle with as authentic Christ-followers. How many categories did you check? Why do you think churched people sometimes treat some of these struggles with sin differently than others? If God alone can make any of us clean, what does this imply?

4. Read Leviticus 18:22 and Romans 1:26–27. In what ways are these verses really pro-gay (there as a warning to protect gay strugglers)? We can never change or fix another person, that's not our job, but we can invite gay people into a place where they might come to trust a God who loves them, then allow Christ to fully do his will in their lives in his timing (not our wills or our timing). Talk about your personal struggle in doing this for your gay neighbor.

PART FOUR

The Struggle with Truth

Artist: David Reed

The Humble Truth about Truth: Creating a Culture of Truth-Telling Humility

We must know where to doubt, where to feel certain, where to submit.

Pascal

I was high on LSD at a Grateful Dead concert when my intellect turned from atheist to a believer in God. It was an awesome and sobering experience (especially not knowing if I could be forgiven for all I had done), but I could no longer deny God's reality. That began my eleven-year journey on a search for Truth."

Leigh grew up in Massachusetts in a family disillusioned with Christianity and church. She often heard her mother rant against right-wing conservative Christians who thought they knew what was true and right for everyone. In a small, predominately church-going town, Leigh felt ostracized by kids in school.

"They would badger me about not going to church," Leigh recalls, "yet these judgmental church kids were the most promiscuous, wild students in my high school. I wasn't really into drinking or drugs. I was actually a good, moral kid, so the arrogance mixed with hypocrisy really turned me far from Christianity. At graduation, a Christian pastor came and spoke, and I remember being so angry that he was pushing his beliefs on me."

In college, Leigh embraced atheism, even subscribing to atheistic journals to buttress her beliefs. Several years out of college, she met a guy and fell in love. He happened to be a Deadhead, an ardent follower of the band the Grateful Dead. "My boyfriend introduced me to LSD, and from the first hit, I felt like I had the answers to life. Honestly, I never really liked the Grateful Dead, but traveling around with these groupies turned out to be like living with one huge, loving family. They formed a real community of people—everybody shared, loved one another, and created a very safe environment—it was great. I loved everything about it . . . except . . . the Dead often played songs with lyrics about God or Jesus.

"I kept feeling like Jesus was being shoved down my throat," Leigh admits, "even in these Grateful Dead concerts. I really took offense to that. Then one night, as the Dead opened with a song that referred to God, something clicked. It was a very sobering experience. I had always hated people telling me I was sinful, yet in that moment, I realized it was true. I realized there was a God who loved me anyway, and I knew I needed to find out more about this God."

Leigh moved back to Massachusetts, away from the drug scene, and started pursuing God. Because Christians seemed so arrogant and unloving, she didn't even think to look for this God of love in a Christian church. Instead, her pursuit led her to take a job at a Yoga center.

"I started reading all kinds of books on spirituality. I became very works oriented. I turned vegetarian, donated to Greenpeace, meditated, chanted, used crystals and Tarot cards, prayed the Rosary . . . I tried everything in order to be closer to God. For eleven years, I did these things seeking the truth about God. One day I saw a bumper sticker that said, 'All paths lead to the same Truth.' It perfectly summed up what I had come to believe."

The Postmodern Challenge

For Leigh, the journey to faith in Jesus as the Truth was a long and winding road. Though Leigh had some knowledge about Christianity, she knew little about the Bible. Most of her understanding was from a negative, distorted view of Christian faith. In her search for God and truth, her frame of reference began from a post-Christian, postmodern outlook on truth and religion. Many people today begin their journey toward the truth of God from the same starting point.

Now that we live in an increasingly secular society, we must understand the struggles people have with truth in order to build bridges into the culture. Many people today view Christianity from a worldview that taught them through the media and public education that:

■ History, especially religious history, like in the Bible, was written or selected by the powerful few with a motive of oppressing and controlling the weaker masses (especially women, slaves, minority populations, etc.). Therefore, history must be deconstructed and viewed from its biased context, realizing there is no "true" unbiased history. The assumption is that the biblical writers wrote with this bias. Those who compiled the Scriptures selected as authoritative and "from God" only those books that benefited their controlling interest. So the Scriptures cannot be trusted as accurate history but simply as another viewpoint from antiquity.

- Truth and moral norms evolve out of social context for the purpose of mutual benefit and survival, but they are relative to that context or culture. No truth is absolute because no one person or society can know or understand all things. Truth is really our interpretation of the world from our own subjective point of view.

- Therefore, arrogance about truth comes from a desire to control and subjugate people. People who think they have "The Truth" are the source of most all religious wars, intolerant acts of hatred, and bigotry in the world. Arrogant truth is the greatest evil.

■ ■ ■

Postmodernity is definitely redefining truth, but so what? Culture has redefined truth for thousands of years, yet the truth of God can still penetrate any culture. Intellectual debate about truth has its place, and many books stake out various positions within the church and without. If you are unfamiliar with postmodern philosophy and its effects, I would refer you to some of these books.[1] What I want to focus on is the practical "so what" we must understand to create a culture where the Leighs of our world have a fighting chance of finding the truth about Jesus.

Much has been written about the way our current generation processes truth experientially rather than rationally or linearly. But the eclectic diversity of our generation makes it impossible to pigeonhole them in this way. Different people need different approaches. What we have found that helps people overcome this postmodern struggle with truth boils down to a mysterious interplay of four different ways of approaching it: humble truth, pragmatic truth, rational truth, and incarnational truth (incarnational truth will be explored in the next chapter).

Leading people into truth in our world today requires culture creation that pays attention to all these approaches while recognizing God's Spirit mysteriously at work, drawing unique people homeward in unique ways (even starting with Grateful Dead concerts). Let's look at how God uses each approach, and often all of them together.

Humble Truth

The greatest resistance to Christian truth happens when Christians come across as arrogant rather than humble—so we must first create a culture that reflects the humble nature of Jesus.[2] People today are repulsed by a tone of superiority or arrogance about what's true. From their worldview, *nobody* has a lock on truth. Therefore, being humble and forthright about the real limitations we have of ever knowing *all* truth becomes paramount. Humble truth does not shy away from presenting what we know to be true and why we believe it's true, but it never uses truth as a club to beat people into agreement.

I remember watching a debate at Willow Creek between a well-known atheist and a Christian apologist. We had just launched Axis, our church-within-a-church for twenty-somethings, and many of our young leaders had invited skeptical friends to the debate. Intellectually, the Christian tore apart the arguments of the atheist and clearly won the debate. But debriefing with Axis leaders afterwards, we found out their skeptical friends agreed that the Christian won the argument, but most were so turned off by his demeaning attitude toward his opponent, it convinced them even more that they didn't want to become Christians.

Paul, who had great skill in debate and reasoning, reminded us of the priority of love over being "right," when he reminded the Corinthians that "knowledge puffs up, but love builds up."[3] Knowledge must take a backseat to love as we present truth in a postmodern context. Remembering most people are not primarily asking, "What's true?" but rather, "Do I want to be like you?" Don't get me wrong, knowledge is *very* important, but not to those who can't hear it.

■ ■ ■

Leigh moved from Massachusetts to Austin after several years, met Steve, and got married. When they first came to Gateway, her resistance was high. Leigh recalls:

> I had tried Hindu meditation retreats, Unity churches, and very new-agey churches still searching for truth. It felt too nebulous. Gateway wasn't like that, it was clearly a Christian church, but I felt that if God led me to Gateway, maybe there was something I needed to understand about Jesus.
>
> Still, on the inside, I was kicking and screaming intellectually. I felt very put off that you had a group of missionaries. To me that seemed like going where you weren't wanted, changing people's cultures, pushing your beliefs on others. I didn't want to be exclusionary. I didn't want to start

quoting Scripture at people. I didn't want to feel like anybody else was wrong. I didn't want be like "those Christians." I have very liberal friends. If I had anything to say about Jesus, except that he was a teacher among many, I would be labeled a freak.

But I was looking for a community of people who cared about each other, and I could sense that with Gateway. So after a month, I got involved in a mom's group. I had a real attitude, but whenever I'd come back at them with my issues, I didn't get an attitude back. I sensed genuine humility from the leader, who constantly encouraged me to be myself and question openly. She welcomed me like a friend and tried to understand my point of view while explaining the Bible's point of view with integrity.

■ ■ ■

Postmodern people grow up with the assumption that "what's true for you is true for you, what's true for me is true for me, and what truly matters is that we can respect each other with our differences." When a church leader attacks others' views, though that leader may be technically correct, most people will just turn him off like another TV preacher. I learned this by making many mistakes, turning away some otherwise genuine seekers, and sensing God's gentle rebuke. Defending the battle for truth this way loses the war for life. But what this means is that there may just be better ways of helping people find truth.

Admitting Our Limitations

James came to talk to me about his struggle with Christianity being the truth. That felt arrogant and uneducated to him. He had taken many sociology and religious studies courses in college, read books by John Spong and Karen Armstrong explaining Christian faith as merely a sociological or evolutionary development, so he distrusted the motives of believers. He had been hanging around Gateway for a while. Throughout our discussion, it felt like we were digging a trench going back and forth on tangential issues, and he kept asking why he should believe me over these scholars who saw Christianity more as useful myth. I emailed him the next week seeking to humbly admit my limitations, yet clearly focus the issue.

> James, I was thinking about our conversation, and I wanted to try to clarify some things. First, Christians are not always right! But some Christians (myself included) may come across as if we think we know everything and have nothing left to learn—especially from those who don't have the "truth" like we do. That is arrogance and actually against the teachings of

Jesus. Jesus had to rebuke Peter (one of the twelve disciples), telling him he was deceived, yet Peter was as sincere a believer as you can get. The point is this, no human has a lock on all truth, and every human can be deceived. We can all be deceived by our own "motives," and tend to guard our own position simply because it gives us security. This often causes us to not be willing to consider things that go against our current beliefs (or even lack of belief).

I don't know if you remember from reading the book of John, but as Pilate was trying to decide whether to crucify Jesus, he asks Jesus if he is the king of the Jews. "Jesus said, 'My kingdom is not of this world . . . [but] you are right in saying I am a king. In fact, for this reason I was born, and for this I came into the world, to testify to the truth. Everyone on the side of truth listens to me.'

'What is truth?' Pilate asked" (John 18:36–38).

What is truth? I think Pilate's probably right that if it's simply up to limited, finite humans to figure out what is true, who could possibly know? Think about it, how could you or I or any author read the millions of books written, study all areas of knowledge, and then synthesize it all into an absolutely "true" understanding of everything? Not possible! If you think I'm subjective in proclaiming my understandings of what I've learned about God, you're right. There is a lot about God (and even myself) of which I know nothing. But why would you think John Spong or Karen Armstrong or other writers are any more "objective"? No one is purely objective, or unaffected by the influences of others, and every writer has a point he thinks is "true" — or more true than others — that he hopes you see too!

But what does this mean? Many postmodern philosophers say it means the word "truth" has no real meaning other than "strong opinion." But what if God, the Universal Creative Mind, who alone understands all things and can know what is true (reality as it actually is), decided to communicate his mind to flailing humans? If we could determine with some assurance God really has communicated, that would be our very best shot at knowing what is true — a lot less risky than trusting spiritual advisors (like me) or scholarly opinions. That is why in our conversation, I was trying to get us to focus on what I think is the primary question, "Has God revealed truth about himself and about us?" If the answer is "no" then it's simply my subjective opinion. But if there is good reason to believe God has penetrated our world to reveal some truth (as I think there is), then we can know at least some things are true. This is what the prophets and those who wrote about Jesus claim.

I believe that ultimately, Truth is a person. And if you can approach finding truth about God more like you'd approach getting to know a person, it might help. Because the fulfilling part of knowing Truth personally comes with experiencing his love—that really is the whole point! It seems like you've been doing religious learning, but have never fully given yourself to God—in an act of surrender.

A person could stand by a swimming pool for a while watching people swim, walking around and around the pool observing. He could analyze why they take the risk, question whether it's safe to take the risk, and whether water can really hold a person up. He could scrutinize and dissect why and how others swim, study the properties of water in detail, and read stories of people swimming and others who drowned while swimming. But if after all that learning, he walks away from the pool and says, "Swimming just didn't work for me," it's because he never dove into the water. You can't actually swim if you never dive in.

I hope in this intellectual process you don't miss the point of faith in Christ—to know and experience God's love personally. And that will always require not just your head, but also ultimately your heart fully yielding to God. I know you can't force it, but I hope the intellectual wrestling will convince you to take the plunge.

It is important for leaders to be able to humbly admit our human limitations of knowledge. But the fact that I cannot know all truth does not mean I cannot know any truth! Humble truth allows us to admit we're not always right as fallible humans, yet it points out that we can know some things as true about God, even though we can't know all truth. Often, this opens the door for people to continue seeking truth.

Practical Truth

Unlike James, for many people, truth just isn't an issue at all. Most people are not on a search to figure out what is true for everyone, but they do want to know what will be true for them. Often this becomes a matter of pragmatics, of what "works." But leaders must not miss this opportunity because nothing "works" better than doing life with God.

Practical truth is what got Leigh in the door of our church. She had heard about Gateway and even told her husband, Steve, who was adamantly antireligious at the time. She intended to come check us out, but her resistance to attending a Christian church kept her from actually stepping foot in the door. When a marital crisis escalated to the point of Leigh moving out, it was Steve who first came to Gateway. That weekend the service was about letting God teach us to love with his sacrificial kind of love. Steve, feeling convicted and hopeful at the same time, called Leigh in tears after the service and asked if she would move back in and start going to church with him. Learning about faith and how it intersects their practical, daily struggles kept Steve and Leigh coming.

n n n

Leaders must communicate not only the reasons why Jesus is the way, the truth, and the life, but also the "so what" of knowing and following this truth. This is what we focus on teaching in our weekend services, how life with God—living in God's kingdom rule—actually works. We find some postmodern people almost have to try on the clothes of the gospel before making the purchase. Some practically test the waters of acting like God is real, even before taking the plunge of full faith in Christ.

Let's Get Practical

The first time I met for breakfast tacos with Bob, he told me his story of growing up going to church in the Northeast yet never understanding the ritual or feeling like he belonged. Bob was not a believer but wanted purpose for his life and work. Although he was making hundreds of thousands of dollars a year as a young single guy in sales, he had lost motivation to work and feared getting fired if he didn't hit his year-end sales targets. In our first breakfast meeting, he admitted to me that living for the pleasures of sex and materialism had left him feeling empty. After a long conversation about his struggle to believe the truth about Jesus, I made a suggestion.

"Bob, for the next few months, try an experiment. Act as if God were really there," I recommended. "Pray to God as a friend who knows you better than you know yourself. Do your job wholeheartedly to honor God, and follow God's wisdom regarding money and relationships, and just see what happens." Three months later he called me for a follow-up meeting. Bob's excitement was evident.

"Man," Bob exclaimed between bites of his Rudy's breakfast tacos, "I'm really changing, and I can see how much better this way is. I've gotten into a men's small group that's been awesome, and I'm growing! I like it. I don't know how it happened, but since doing as you suggested with my work, I closed every single deal by year-end. Some of them were just unbelievable how they happened—almost miraculous. I ended up with my best quarter ever!"

"That's awesome, Bob!" I said. "I don't doubt it, but I'm always amazed at how God meets people in personal ways when they truly seek him." I was quick to warn him that miraculous deal-closings don't always happen. "But I do think God is trying to help you see that he cares about every area of your life," I said, "and he wants you to know him intimately—that's why he did all he did through Christ."

"Yeah," Bob confirmed, "I'm coming to really believe he's there, but I still have questions about Jesus. And I'll be honest, changing my habits with women has been challenging, but I'm trying, and I can see now how unfulfilling and messed up my views were. The really neat thing is that I met someone I'm interested in for all the right reasons. We're both trying to honor God with our relationship, and it's gonna be really hard not getting sexual, but we're trying! I don't want to screw this one up."

What I see happening in Bob's life, I've seen with so many in our postmodern society. As they begin to tiptoe into the waters of practically understanding and even experiencing the wisdom of God's ways, this often leads them to open up to the truth of Jesus. It doesn't always fit our categories of how faith works, but I'm convinced God doesn't always work within the bounds of our professions anyway!

It Is Good News

The gospel of Jesus, the good news that life with God is now freely available for all, *is* good news because it really *does* work. The truth about God is immensely practical, not only for eternity but even for today. In fact, I'm not sure there is such a dichotomy between normal life and eternal life since Jesus said, "This is eternal life: that they may know you, the only true God, and Jesus Christ, whom you have sent."

> Every week I come and you challenge me to think. Many times I feel like you are talking directly to me about my weaknesses. I feel challenged and sometimes uncomfortable. Sometimes it takes me a couple of days to process. I love that!   —Lori

Maybe part of the reason the church is losing the battle for truth is that the quality of life the Living-Truth produces is not that evident in our churches. Knowing God in truth produces an eternal quality of life, and the impact is wonderfully freeing and life-giving to our relationships, our work-world, and our moment-by-moment experience of life. Jesus said, "If you hold to my teaching, you are really my disciples. Then you will know the truth, and the truth will set you free."[4]

Leaders need to test whether they are living the truth and then communicating how practically life-giving this truth truly can be. Our goal is not to get people to "convert" by repeating one prayer. The goal is to love God and people, living out of the fullness of life in God's kingdom, inviting all to come and enjoy the fruits of his life in us, because the door has been flung wide open through Christ. A prayer for salvation is the beginning of

I first opened my heart to even trying church and seeking God after relocating to Austin. Once I made the first step to go to Gateway, God went to work. I began to ask questions, attended Christianity 101, got involved with Comfort and Hope, and found a small group that was very supportive of my quest to understand who and what God is all about. God began the process of healing my broken spirit and revealed many things about my life (current and past) that needed healing. I experienced his grace well into this process, when I was led to confess a sin that had been weighing heavily on my heart for years—a past abortion. The healing process was very, very hard, but God is so good. Through this healing process, I became a Christian and committed myself to Jesus. I see God's work every day in my life now. I look for him in every situation, and I can see how clearly he knows just what I need personally. Nothing compares!   —Brooke

relational confidence with God, but the goal must be to help people trust God in very mundane, practical ways more and more every day.

We make truth practical by telling stories of practical faith and by teaching how to actually do life with God (life in the kingdom of God). We ask the "so what" practical questions of all we teach on weekends, so that people can be doers of the Word, not just hearers of it. What we find is that people who are not on a search for "what's true" are still on a search for "what's life-giving." We challenge people to live "as if" God and his words were true and to see if it doesn't produce in their lives something better than they have right now. As they come to realize that God's truth actually produces the quality of existence they've longed for—of increasing love, joy, peace, better relationships, less worry, and so on—they often open up to the Truth who leads them into all truth.

But this is not to say we believe truth is only pragmatic. It just means that God's truth *is* pragmatic, and we can't fail to explain how faith works practically, because this is partially how emerging generations approach finding truth. But even the most postmodern, post-Christian people often need more than just pragmatics; they still need reasons to believe Jesus is *the* Truth.

Rational Truth

One stereotype that must be dispelled is that emerging generations no longer think logically or rationally or linearly, no longer want reasons as a foundation for faith, and are only interested in experiential ways of knowing truth (as in an experiential style of worship). You almost get the impression that the only people left in postmodern America are artists and poets, and specifically the ones who are nonlinear in their thinking. This stereotype makes for good antimodern church rhetoric, but our generation is much more complex than that. I have encountered engineers who were nonlinear, postmodern thinkers in religious matters; but I have also seen postmodern poets, musicians, and very artistic nonlinear people helped immensely by "proving from the Scriptures that Jesus was the Christ,"[5] just as Apollos and Paul did publicly.

Koby[††] grew up in Austin in a family that didn't actively seek to know God. Her way of spiritually sorting out the world came mostly through writing poetry. Vocationally, she holds creative workshops on teambuilding and leadership. The way she processed the truth about Jesus reveals the mysterious interplay we have often seen between "God moments" as she calls them, reasoning about truth, and community.

Before coming to Gateway, Koby's only real source of "spiritual" input came from reading *The Celestine Prophecies* and *Synchronicity*. Three years later, she made the decision to be baptized but even then struggled with the decision until she

> *I saw your series "I Doubt It" on your website, which my fiancé stumbled across. We listened to the message "Is the Bible True?" We were impressed with the clip and decided to attend. I haven't attended a church in about nine years and haven't really thought much about starting back up, but I must say that I think I'll keep coming every Sunday.* —Tom

could get a "crash course" from us on other world religions. Listen as Koby reflects on her journey toward truth as she prepared for her baptism:

> Growing up, I did not have the opportunity to go to church because my dad was and still is opposed to God and the church. The few times I was invited by friends, I felt awkward and honed in on as a guest.
>
> It wasn't until the year of the Millennium that a series of what I call "God moments" brought me to Gateway to begin exploring my spirituality. In a creative workshop at work, we did an activity called "Lost Treasures," an experiential activity designed to reveal core values. We were asked to write down on four pieces of paper the four things most important to us. I wrote down friends, family, health, and spirit. One by one we had to give up one of those things, tearing up the paper and throwing it away. Had you asked me going in what I thought would be the last value standing, I would not have said "spirit." But that exercise made me realize that if you have spirit (spirituality), then you really still have everything else. This simple exercise got me thinking.
>
> I had always believed in God but have questioned the idea as well. Not having grown up in church, I never felt comfortable in one because I had never read the Bible or knew what the pastor was talking about. When they asked me if I had been "saved" I thought it meant going to church.

But I wrote letters to God and poetry that was spiritual in nature, and I prayed. Before this workshop, I had prayed to God to help me broaden my circle of friends. The week after this exercise, I decided to try meeting new friends online. The first person I met online invited me to Gateway. The fact that it was in a movie theater (which I thought was cool), and my recent questioning, led me to give it a try.

I met almost every person that walked through the doors that day, and the band played a song I actually recognized during the offering, certainly not what I expected from a church. I truly enjoyed my first visit.

But what made me come back the next Sunday was the series topic: "God, Jesus, and the World's Religions." The topics were the exact questions I had been pondering, "Can we prove God exists?" "What's with all these world religions?" and "Who is Jesus?" They were my questions. Coincidence? I think not! So I came back again, and again, and, well . . . almost three years later, I'm still here.

Since that first day, I have been growing and changing through the messages, connecting with others in small groups, with accountability partners, and involvement in ministries. I believe in God. I believe that Jesus died for my sins. I don't need to be part of any one religion to know that in my heart. But now, a new beginning to my story begins with my baptism.

> For what the caterpillar sees as the end of its journey
> God sees a butterfly as unique as me
> Fly, fly butterfly. . . . fly free.
>
> Koby

Leading people into truth requires a culture that approaches truth with humility, teaches God's truth practically, but does not neglect the rational. As Koby's story indicates, we find that often it's a mix of several approaches that God uses to mysteriously guide people into truth. The mystery of it we can only embrace, but the culture we can help shape. In culture creation we cannot neglect the rational, but we must be careful with it.

Prioritizing Rational Truth

In a world that begins with the assumption that "nothing's absolutely true," leaders must be careful not to get lost focusing on less important "truths" and cause spiritual skeptics to miss seeing the Truth of Christ. I have watched Christians get caught up debating the "truth" of evolution versus creation, or the literal truth of controversial Bible passages, or arguing about abortion or homosexuality, or whether there is absolute moral truth. These are important issues, but all of secondary importance. When a person begins an authentic relationship with God, often these issues resolve in time. We have found arguing these less-central "truths" just confuses the main issue with skeptical people. What is the main issue? The primary issue comes back to where Paul would start—with the person of Jesus . . . The One who is Truth.

Paul focused on the truth about the Messiah first, even in pagan, relativistic Greece: "As his custom was, Paul . . . reasoned with them from the Scriptures, explaining and proving that the Christ had to suffer and rise from the dead."[6] Paul would seek to prove (presumably from the Old Testament prophecies) to both Jews and Gentiles that Jesus came from God just as foretold. He would explain to those ignorant of the Scriptures by using the bridge of their pagan poets and philosophers that "God overlooked people's former ignorance about these things, but now he commands everyone everywhere to turn away from [worshiping things other than God] and turn to him . . . and [God] *proved* to everyone who this is by raising him from the dead."[7]

I cannot "prove" the Bible is inspired by God, but most convictions of truth Christians argue about are based on this belief. So to argue that "the Bible says it, so it's true" with people coming from no prior knowledge or conviction about the Bible is futile. You can't convince someone the Bible is truth because it comes from God, when the only way to know it's from God is because the Bible says so—that's circular.

> I had convinced myself that Christianity was a blissful diversion to everyday life. About a year ago, prompted by my friends, I started going to Gateway and reading books like **The Case for Christ** and **Letters to a Skeptic**. When you talked about "Is the Bible True" and "The Case for the Resurrection" then had the Q&A, I started believing the historical facts behind the Bible and exploring what it meant for my life. That led me on a process of studying Scripture and discovering that following Christ is an integral part of human life we were meant to live. —Jake

We can break out of this circular reasoning, however, by showing that God has done something miraculous in foretelling of the Messiah. If I can help people just focus on answering the "Who is Jesus" question, this is central to discovering all knowable truth!

Every year we do a series on the weekend to help people see the reasons to believe, often focusing on the prophecies of the Messiah. I've been amazed at the numbers of skeptical seekers who suddenly see the truth about Jesus because they realize that the prophecies of the Messiah reveal something only God could do—foretell the future over a 1500-year period and have it correlate with actual, verifiable historical events outside of the Bible.*

Leigh expresses how much this helped in her journey toward truth:

> A close friend who considers herself open-minded to all religions said to me, "You know those people at Gateway believe Jesus is God."
>
> "They do not," I insisted. Yet as I started to listen, I heard more and more about Jesus being God's self-revelation. I didn't know anything about the Bible except I had been told it had been changed over the years, a book of myths. I was walking my son in the stroller one day, and I remember praying to God saying, "If there's really something to this Jesus thing, I'm gonna give you thirty days, and I'll just focus on Jesus. If this is what you want for me, come lead me and guide me." I started reading the Bible for the first time, and I know it was the Holy Spirit guiding me, because I not only understood it, I couldn't get enough of it. I couldn't wait to read more about Jesus every night.
>
> I kept giving God thirty-day extensions to convince me. During that time, the church did a series called "Prophecies of the Messiah." Those messages changed everything for me. That was the key to my intellectual resistance. Seeing God's fingerprints in prophecy, confirmed by history, made me realize this is real—even for people who think the way I think. Suddenly I wanted everyone in the world to hear this. I bought tapes to give away to friends. I was telling everybody. It just made so much sense. Not long afterwards, I worked through the pre-baptism study, and that's really when I understood the grace of God offered in Christ. I asked him into my heart and my life. After eleven years of searching, there has been a change in me this year that's hard to describe. There is a happiness and relief I hadn't expected. I have a focus I didn't have before. Now that I see God through Christ, God's identity has become clearer to me, and I now know how I can relate to God.

Leigh's faith and growth are solid, and I see Jesus leading her into more and more truth by his Spirit, just as he promised.[8] But first she had to accept the One who is Truth. John writes about this personal nature of truth when he writes to the one "who knows God's truth—the truth that lives in us and will be in our hearts forever."[9]

---

* Gateway's messages are available online at *www.gatewaychurch.com*. Just follow the links to Weekend Messages archives: *Prophecies of the Messiah—Divine Humility* series.

This relationship with the Truth becomes the epicenter of discovering other truths in a relativistic world. Once people can begin to personally trust Jesus, they pragmatically see the truth of God's wisdom. They also can see how Jesus treated the Scriptures. I find this path from the Truth to "the truths" often clears the way to understanding God's mysterious superintending of the writing of all Scripture. So all these approaches work together leading people into truth, but not always in predictable, orderly ways—there's a mystery to it.

The Mystery of the Truth

God works in mysterious ways. This reality has been neglected by modernity, which was obsessed with dissecting and describing and objectifying and controlling everything.

But in a postmodern world, leaders have a new opportunity to help seekers see God's mysterious work because people are more open to it. In most everyone's journey of faith, there are times when God seemed to be gently tapping them on the shoulder. If we can make people aware of the mystery of the Truth, who personally pursues wayward people, they become more open to responding to him.

But teaching and storytelling about God's mysterious behind-the-scenes work may require us to take God out of the box of predictability. As the Scriptures make clear, sometimes God does downright mysterious, unpredictable things.[10]

■ ■ ■

Shae, the Stanford student I mentioned in a previous chapter, had many intellectual problems with Christianity. "A girl in my dorm one night explained the 'sinners prayer' to me," Shae recalls. "But it just didn't sink in. I saw no relevance for God at all in my life. I had put up such a strong wall against God. Everything religion represented was judgmental, anti-intellectual, closing off your mind to new ideas, intolerant of others, and oppressive toward women. I had this idea that Christians cared so much about the afterlife that they didn't care about social issues all around them. I couldn't escape the responsibility we have for making life better on this planet. I couldn't see how you could know and trust God, yet take responsibility—faith felt like a cop-out to life."

But what caused Shae to open up and truly seek would cause most modern Christians to shudder. Shae recalls:

> I had joined a dance troupe after moving from Stanford back to New
> York. It turned out to be a spiritual dance group. They would stand in a

circle, hold hands, and pray before class. At first it freaked me out, but it was a loose kind of prayer, so I loosened up. Some prayed to Christ, some to God, some to the Divine Spirit, some to the Great Goddess. Over time, I began to pray in a very generic way.

One night, I was dancing on the beach in a drum circle when I had an epiphany (I don't know what else to call it). I had a direct sense I just knew there was a Greater Being who cared about me and I wasn't alone any more. It was a vision of a figure dancing with me—not male—and a ribbon extending into the sky from me to some force in the universe.

Looking back, I think it was God revealing himself to me in a way I could relate to. For instance, I always had a hard time with God being a "he." To have a sense that God was there in the presence of women, somehow tied to me by a ribbon, helped me. I always saw the use of male pronouns for God as a way to keep women under the dominance of men. God knew exactly what I needed to break through my resistance.

Now I felt I couldn't go back to my atheism because I knew there was some Greater Being. I tried the Unitarian church but felt I was at a college lecture. The next April, I came to Austin and went with my aunt to a Good Friday drama telling the story of the crucifixion. I realized in a moment why people cared about Jesus. During the performance I had a similar vision of a ribbon connecting me to this Higher Being as during the dance before. I also had this sense that I needed to be in Austin to understand more about this Higher Being. I moved to Austin and, not long afterward, came to believe in Jesus as my Lord.

Shae bought a Bible and began consuming it. She came to Gateway, plugged into a small group and service opportunities, and took every opportunity to learn about the truth of Jesus. Three years later, Shae and her husband lead a small group of their own and now are exploring full-time ministry. Her faith in Christ is solid, yet the mysterious path she traveled getting there transcends modern categories. Her questions of truth were overcome by the mysterious work of God.

■ ■ ■

Truth, we must remember, belongs to God alone. As people are restored into right relationship with the Truth, then by his Spirit he guides people into all truth just as he promised. Church leaders must understand this multidimensional process of culture creation by which our postmodern, post-Christian world arrives at truth—through humility, practical understanding, rational reasoning, and ultimately the mystery of God's guidance.

And as Leigh and others demonstrated, there's still an experiential aspect of culture creation that may be the most influential of all: Incarnational Truth. I rarely find people in this day and age who find faith without experiencing the Truth come alive through the Body of Christ first.

STUDY GUIDE

Culture Check

1. Are you communicating truth with humility or arrogance? Are you winning the argument but losing the person? How would you know?
2. What ways could you lead your church culture to better re-present the truth of Jesus with a humble approach? A pragmatic approach? A rational approach? A relational approach (relational will be covered more in the next chapter)?

Small Group Questions

1. What struggles have you experienced (personally or with others) regarding truth and Christian faith? Read John 14:6–9. Are Jesus' statements meant to be exclusive or inclusive? Why?
2. Which approach(es) had the greatest impact on you finding faith— a humble, pragmatic, rational, or relational approach? Share why that approach helped you.
3. Read Philippians 2:5–11. Why is a humble approach to truth important? Jesus conveyed uncompromising truth in an attitude of humility. How can we (personally or as a group) be more like Jesus to those around us?
4. Read John 8:31–32. Why is it important to convey practical truth to the world around us? What practical issues relate to Christians and non-Christians alike, and how does faith in Christ practically help?
5. Read 1 Peter 3:15. Why is it important to be prepared to convey rational truth? How prepared do you feel? What steps can you take to become better prepared? (In the next chapter we will consider conveying relational truth as a group in more detail.)

Tribal Truth: Creating the Culture of Incarnational Truth

This is the church of the living God, which is the pillar and support of the truth.

1 Timothy 3:15 NLT

Hey, John and Melissa," I said, as I walked out of my office to greet this good-looking couple who appeared to be in their late twenties to early thirties. "I know you're both extremely busy, so I really appreciate your taking the time to meet with me. Come on into my office and grab a seat."

John's sharp but casual dress was less corporate than I expected for a partner in one of the most prestigious law firms in the state, but then again, he was the youngest partner too. Melissa's fair complexion and blonde hair contrasted perfectly with John's dark complexion and neatly trimmed goatee. John was Samoan by nationality—together they looked ready to take on the world. I felt a little sloppy in my jeans and untucked shirt—standard Gateway casual and acceptable attire in most of young, high-tech Austin.

"I appreciate your willingness to share your stories with me," I began, after spending a few minutes hearing how John and Melissa met and how their first year of marriage had been for them. Melissa had just gotten baptized, but I knew John was still wrestling with some questions. "I understand your small group played a big role in sorting through questions of truth and faith for both of you," I said. "I wanted to hear your stories to understand what has helped or hindered you in seeking truth about Christian faith."

"I grew up agnostic in Colorado Springs," John began. "I wasn't staunch atheist—just didn't know or care honestly. In college, I studied aerospace engineering but took lots of philosophy classes. It seemed modern philosophers had pretty much given up on knowing much of anything. But I had two phi-losophy professors who intrigued me. Both turned out to be Christians, so I decided to read the Bible out of curiosity. After reading it, I just couldn't under-stand how intelligent people could believe miraculous accounts like I read. So after that, I set it aside for years."

"What piqued your spiritual curiosity and got you coming to Gateway?" I inquired.

"I went to Harvard for my law degree, then eventually got recruited to a law firm here in Austin," John explained. "Ironically, what got me thinking about spirituality again was Stephen Hawking's *A Brief History of Time*. He's an atheist, but reading it made me realize that if there is the possibility of other dimensionalities, then there is the possibility of God and 'super' nat-ural events. That's when a friend invited me to Gateway. The main thing I've liked about the atmosphere here and in the small groups is that this church is more like a teaching church. It's okay to ask questions and people will explain if they know, but they're also comfortable saying 'I don't know on that one.' There's just an atmosphere of openness and honesty. That allows me to explore faith with other people rather than just by myself. While I haven't made a decision regarding Jesus, I feel I continue to make progress. Three years ago I was still agnostic. Now, I feel certain there is a loving, inter-active God running things. And I'm becoming increasingly convinced that this God is the God of Christ."

"What about you, Melissa?" I asked, thinking she had been kind of quiet. "Tell me a little about your spiritual background."

"I grew up back East in an Italian Catholic family," Melissa started. "I don't think it meant anything to my mom or dad. They took me to church until I was confirmed, just to appease my grandmother. After that, we all pretty much stopped going to church. I couldn't tell you anything about the Bible, and church gave me zero comfort but plenty of guilty feelings about never being good enough. It's something I've struggled with ever since, and especially in coming to faith in Christ. In high school, we read *Siddhartha* and *The Tao of Pooh*, and it just didn't make sense to me that everyone who wasn't a practicing Catholic was going to hell. Still, I felt really guilty com-ing to Gateway at first, like I was being bad because it wasn't Catholic."

As we continued to talk, I put together the pieces of the puzzle that led Melissa to faith and that helped John overcome many of his struggles. I saw a pattern we've seen over and over of the power of community in this jour-ney toward faith.

"We decided to get into a Taste of Community small group," Melissa told me. Taste of Community is a six-week, no-obligation try at a small group.

"Our first meeting," Melissa recalled, "I thought, Oh my gosh, what am I getting myself into? They're all a bunch of crazy Christians!"

"Why?" I laughed, watching Melissa come alive—clearly feeling free now to express her experience.

"The way they were all talking 'God talk'—God this, God that, God everywhere, and they were talking about how they had given themselves up to God completely. That freaked me out at first. But they all went around the room that night and shared their experiences, and I realized it was their choice. They weren't just playing a Christian game. As they each shared their stories, they had very similar pasts to us, and I realized they are actually just normal people who have decided to make God an integral part of their lives. When I opened up and told them where I was coming from, still questioning, many said they'd been there too. I found out our group host who is now our leader grew up Muslim, others grew up in a variety of religious contexts—most had strayed far from God and church, but had since found an authentic faith in Christ. Some were brand new to faith, but one guy's dad was a pastor, and he could quote the Bible backwards and forwards. The first three months of that small group helped me come to faith in Christ more than anything else."

"That's what I've seen over and over again!" I exclaimed. "Why is that? What was it about the small group community?" I asked.

"In our first small group," John interjected, "we really respected the leaders and people but just didn't really connect."

"You were in another small group before this Taste group?" I hadn't realized this. They had actually been in another small group for almost a year, but there was something different about the Taste group that helped them on their faith journey. I wanted to understand it. "How were the groups different?"

"In the Taste group," John explained, "lots of people were not in church previously, so I realized they were coming from the same place I was. Whereas it seemed like in the first group they were at a different life-stage than we were, most with kids. They were all raised in a Christian environment and hadn't strayed away or questioned. I felt they wouldn't understand where I was coming from, so I didn't really open up."

"Who was in that group?" I queried. As John told me the names, something struck me! It wasn't the backgrounds—I knew that two of the couples in that first group came into Gateway from either agnostic or Jewish backgrounds and came to faith in Christ. Actually, they had a lot in common with this couple, but the irony was that John and Melissa never really heard their stories or got to know them past the surface level. Their leader led great Bible study but had been unable to get the group to be vulnerable.

What I began to see, talking with John and Melissa, is that it was vulnerability and transparency in the Taste group that helped them connect and journey toward faith. Having people who shared their struggles and victories and got into each other's lives helped them see real faith in action. This environment, modeled by the small group leader, helped them process their own beliefs and struggles and move toward faith faster than years of our sermons and seminars and Bible studies. I had seen this relational aspect of finding faith many times.

"What was it in those first three months that helped most?" I asked Melissa.

"I guess that it was okay to experience ups and downs. One day to desire pursuing God, then the next to feel like I was questioning everything that was happening. I found out that battling with ups and downs was normal and even the path to spiritual growth. Plus, I had a lot of guilt to overcome. Talking about this with the small group, getting into the Bible, and seeing how people applied it to their lives really helped. Opening up about personal struggles with anger helped me to see how they dealt with similar things but also let me see how giving God control rather than trying to control everything made life a lot easier."

"Yeah," John tagged on, "I'm just a very skeptical person. But on an emotional level, there's a resistance to believing. Subconsciously I know it's gonna mean a big change in my life that I might not want to make. I think I do still have some valid intellectual questions, but I know it really comes down to an emotional resistance."

"That's incredibly perceptive," I replied. Most people do not realize that intellectual arguments are almost never the final bulwark of resistance to God's leadership. Fear that God's way will be a net loss of life tends to be the final barrier.

"But getting to know these guys in the group has helped?" I asked.

"It has!" John responded. "The most powerful thing for me with the small group is that if I ever have a problem I need to talk over, I've got four guys I can call to have breakfast with, hang out with, and talk. I respect them, we're friends, and they're all Christ-followers. I have friends outside of church, but they're all atheists. I can't really talk to my atheist friends about these personal issues in the same way."

"So just having others you can relate to who allow you to process your struggles has actually helped with the barriers to faith?" I asked.

"Yeah, it has!" John said. "A great lawyer once told me, when you're trying to convince people of the truth of a case, don't try to tell a jury what they're supposed to think. When you start telling people the way things are, the first thing they do is start looking defensively at all the data to see if anything is wrong with what you've said. Better to lead people through questions, beginning where you have common agreement, so that they come to their own conclusions. Even though you directed them through the questions, they will be more willing to accept your conclusion because you helped them engage in discovering it for themselves."*

The Power of Community

John's and Melissa's spiritual journeys represent a trend we have observed over and over: many people process truth in community.

Over the past two decades, I have noticed a significant shift from the rugged individualism of the previous generations to a craving for community. This longing to connect with a group of close friends has a stronger intensity and greater importance in processing truth than in previous generations. Although young adults today are far less likely to join civic associations than previous generations, they highly value loosely structured friendships. This has had a profound influence on how people tend to process their views and beliefs.

Many adults grew up looking to their peer group for validation and authority. As more and more families blew apart, parents generally became less involved and less directive. Permissive parenting became more the norm, so kids looked more to their peers to process issues of right or wrong. More and more families opted for two incomes, leaving kids with more time interacting with friends than family. The natural result had an effect on the processing of beliefs and views. If teens had a question about life or ethical issues, Mom and Dad were less available and less authoritative, so teens learned to process issues with their friends who formed an alternative values-clarification system.

Group processing of what's true or what's right feels natural for emerging generations. Not everyone processes this way, but we have discovered that finding faith often happens more like it would in a tribe than as a collection of autonomous, isolated individuals. Often in countries where tight-knit tribes or people groups exist, it is rare that an individual will break away from his people to follow Christ. To do so means cutting himself off from his very sense of identity his tribal community has given him since birth. To do so, that individual must feel very connected to his "new tribe" of Christ followers. And the best way for this to happen is if this new tribe includes those

---

* Six months after this interview, John came to faith in Christ. It was a three-year process, involving a practical, rational, and relational approach.

of the old tribe, so that groups of people find faith together. Sometimes a whole people-group will decide together to follow the God of Jesus, and the whole tribe will change beliefs.[1]

Urban Tribes

Our society feels much more tribal than individualistic as we move forward into a postmodern future. Ethan Watters chronicles this tribelike trend in a book called *Urban Tribes: A Generation Redefines Friendship, Family, and Commitment.* In it Watters discusses the way many singles in cities are clustering together in close-knit groups of friends who may delay marriage into their thirties, but who have formed a kind of social family away from family.

After gaining notoriety for coining the phrase *urban tribe*, people bombarded Watters with emails from all over North America and even Europe, telling stories of their own "tribe." Most were communities of young people, mostly college-educated singles in their twenties and thirties, who delay marriage due to a combination of career demands and fear factors. Often they form diverse groups knitted together by threads of social ties—friends of friends of friends. But over time, they prove to provide an important support network. Watters elaborates, "Many tribes told me that they had pooled money to send an individual member on vacation ... groups would pitch in to build decks, paint rooms, or remodel each other's houses. Tribes were also adept at quickly mobilizing to come to the aid of individual members in acute distress."[2]

This tribe often provides relationally many of the "one anothers" described in Scripture for Christian communities, so they can become important in the life of a single. This community also has a lot to do with how people process their worldview. Watters recalls a similar theme in emails from other urban tribes: "We stitched together our life philosophies from song lyrics, sacred texts, our college social psychology classes, our parents, our bosses and coworkers, *The Simpsons* ... for us, the answer to the question 'How do you live a good life?' was not something handed down from on high. We were making up answers—riffing them—as we went along."[3]

People today are not likely to throw these important, tribal connections out the window to seek "truth" all alone. But if given the opportunity to see Christ's community functioning in authentic, loving ways, and if they feel included in a small group community or serving team, this allows a subconscious willingness to "change tribes" that I think often precedes coming to faith today. Many times spiritual seekers change tribes before they change beliefs.

Often, when a person finds faith, she is told to dissociate with old friends. While new Christ-followers need new spiritually supportive friends around them, if encouraged to live out their faith boldly without discon-necting from the old tribe, many see whole groups of friends eventually find faith. A former bar manager who came to faith through involvement with Gateway's Arthouse and Comfort and Hope ministry wrote saying, "God really gave me such a wonderful gift when he had an employee invite me to come to church. And now many of my friends have followed me to Gate-way, friends I expected to lose when I got involved with church. In fact, my relationship with my best friend has been restored and is growing because we are now both growing spiritually." This is how the majority of people have come to Gateway—one friend inviting another.

Truth by Association

Marketers have understood this relational aspect of deciding what's true or right. People decide what they value and trust by association, not just by proposition or argument. In the fifties and early sixties, ads would seek to convince consumers of the superiority of their product. Fast-forward to the late nineties and you see marketers for Apple Computers taking out expen-sive billboard space filled with a picture of Gandhi and only two words in barely visible print in the bottom right corner: "Think Different." The name *Apple* or the word *computer* doesn't even appear, just Apple's logo associated with the image of a kind of person customers would admire. But marketers have understood something about the postmodern mind—decisions often are made more by relational association than facts!

Unlike a previous generation, most adults we interact with are not ask-ing the question, "What is true?" As mentioned already, the assumption of the day is that everybody's "truth" is equally valid as long as it doesn't hurt others. They don't ask "What is true?" so much as "Do I want to be like you and your friends?" "Do these people reflect who I want to become?" Nobody asks these questions out loud, but it has become clear to me that these have become the pipelines through which truth often must flow. "You say this is the truth . . . but what does this truth of yours produce in a life?"

Once people experience the Body of Christ re-presented in commu-nity—they *see* it. They experience the truth. Then they begin to ask, "Now what do you believe and how can that work in my life?" Some Christians might see this as a challenge to truth. I think it's the primary way God intended truth to transfer!

The Body of Truth

The more I read about God's view of his church, the more I realize how the biblical model has always been to present Truth incarnate. Ephesians chapter four paints a picture of the church we've been trying to emulate at Gateway.

> He is the one who gave these gifts to the church: the apostles, the prophets, the evangelists, and the pastors and teachers. Their responsibility is to equip God's people to do his work and build up the church, the body of Christ, until we come to such unity in our faith and knowledge of God's Son that we will be mature and full grown in the Lord, measuring up to the full stature of Christ. Then we will no longer be like children, forever changing our minds about what we believe because someone has told us something different or because someone has cleverly lied to us and made the lie sound like the truth. Instead, we will hold to the truth in love, becoming more and more in every way like Christ, who is the head of his body, the church. Under his direction, the whole body is fitted together perfectly. As each part does its own special work, it helps the other parts grow, so that the whole body is healthy and growing and full of love.[4]

This passage starts off saying those leading the church are to create a culture where all God's people figure out their unique gifts and ministry in serving each other in community. It's a community effort! But as we all get involved serving and growing in community, something else is happening; the Body of Christ is formed.

The Scriptures claim that God revealed himself on earth in the form of a Jewish male body two thousand years ago. Jesus showed the world the exact representation of God's being in human flesh.[5] According to Scripture, Jesus ascended into heaven, but God still has a human "Body" on earth.[6] God's Body is now formed out of a multitude of diverse parts made up of unique people connected together by Christ who is the head. Ephesians chapter four goes on to say that as we grow united in faith, our goal is to re-present the mature, full-grown "stature of Christ." The best measure of Christian community is whether people experience what Jesus is like through our skin.

As leaders teach "the truth in love" about how to stay connected to Christ and serve others in community, "we will hold to the truth in love, becoming more and more in every way like Christ, who is the head of his body, the church." And the way we know we are successful is when people who come in contact with our community experience God's Spirit animating his Body in all its parts, "healthy and growing and full of love." This is how people experience the Truth incarnate!

Ephesians 4:21 goes on to say we "learned the truth *that is in Jesus*."[7] Jesus said "I am the way and *the truth* and the life."[8] Jesus is the Truth in the flesh, and even though people who encountered him two thousand years ago might not have understood every propositional statement about truth, when they experienced the Truth with skin on, many believed and followed. So when we are functioning as the community of Christ, his Body, people experience the Truth as he makes himself known through his community, and many believe and follow! This incarnate Truth overcomes postmodern relativism, agnostic cynicism, and pragmatic skepticism.

For this reason, our primary goal from day one has been to connect people into small group communities. We teach people how to be a unified community, building one another up in love, using their gifts to serve others in response to the leading of Christ.[9] And what we have seen over and over resonates with what Jesus said would happen in his last recorded prayer, "My prayer is not for them alone. I pray also for those who will believe in me through their message, that all of them may be one, Father, just as you are in me and I am in you. May they also be in us *so that the world may believe that you have sent me.*"[10]

Incarnate truth does not neglect propositional truth but presents it in love with skin. And as people hang out and experience it, they find something so otherworldly and unique, they often find themselves compelled to believe in Jesus. It happens with Harvard grads and it happens with hippies, as Laura's story demonstrates.

Experiencing the Body

There's nothing "usual" about Laura. She stands out as an iconoclast in every way. Her dirty blonde dreadlocks contrast her youthful, innocent looking face. Her pot-smoking, hippie-style life clashes against the backdrop of growing up a missionary kid whose mom translated the entire New Testament from Greek to another language. She knew all about the "truth" of Jesus, growing up in church and Sunday school every week, but she never *knew* the Truth.

At age eighteen, she rejected all her parents stood for. Christianity felt cold to her, nothing but an intellectual pursuit of strict discipline. In search of freedom and love, she began drinking and drugging, met an artist and married him. Soon after, he got a job offer in computer animation that brought them from Pittsburgh to Austin.

"They say when you come to Austin, you either find yourself or you lose yourself," Laura recalls. "I did both. I longed for a community of people who truly cared about others and the plight of our world. When we came to Austin, my husband and I volunteered at several nonprofit organizations and found ourselves attracted to a community of people feeding the hungry, building bikes for ghetto kids, and starting community gardens. This hippified subculture felt very real, very open and accepting, and extremely unstructured—the exact opposite of the way I grew up.

"I soon found we had a lot in common with this community: We hated all the same things. We hated pollution, so we would live in a self-sustainable way. We hated hunger, so we would feed the homeless. We hated capitalism supporting slave and child labor, so we boycotted franchises. We hated war, so we protested it. We hated government, our parents, and anyone who would interfere with our revolution to change the world, one joint at a time."

One day Laura was hanging out at Barton Springs with her friends. Barton Springs is a beautiful oasis of environmental sensitivity in the center of the city—home of the protected Barton Springs salamander. It's a natural spring-fed, giant clear-water pool surrounded by lush vegetation and gently sloping grassy knolls where people come to sunbathe and swim. A group of Laura's friends had come together to swim and hang out. That day began a series of life-altering interactions leading her into truth. Laura recalls the events in an email:

> As I sat staring off across the pool, a good friend turned to me and said, "Laura, you're the most peaceful person I've ever known." I turned to thank him, but as I looked him in the eyes, another thought oozed into my brain. "I'm not at peace, I'm so stoned right now I can't even remember your name, and you're a good friend!" In that moment I realized, this is not the peace I'm longing for.
>
> My search led me lots of places, but every time I would get there, I would still feel miserable. At that point however, Christians were nothing but SUV-driving, consumerist, metro-sexual, urban-class, Republican yuppies. They were the enemy!
>
> A nightclub owner I knew and really respected told me about Gateway. Because I liked him, and because it met in a movie theater, I decided to check it out. I wasn't prepared for the emotional impact. I knew intellectually all about Christ, but I had never experienced real community, real love, so I rejected Christianity. But every time I would come to church, I would be bawling my eyes out. I started attending pretty regularly when I wasn't too hung over. Deep inside, I wanted someone to come up to me, but it never happened in the dark theater. Something kept bringing me back though, something that was missing in the other community, something I sensed I wanted in this church scene.
>
> It amazed me that I never felt judged for dreadlocks, looked down upon for being well below the poverty level, or shoved aside for coming to church reeking of cigarette smoke. I felt drawn to this community, yet torn by associating

with a group my friends hated. I kept making excuses for not getting in a small group. I usually sneaked in the back after the offering and slipped out right after the service. I greatly valued my anonymity. Yet Something was drawing me closer. I remember after one service, weeping silently until the room had emptied. I remember wishing someone had noticed me in that dark theater, I wanted someone to put an arm around me and pray for me. But after a while, I was glad I had not been exposed. I wanted to be held, but I didn't want to be held accountable for my lifestyle. For years, I went to church like this.

Then my life hit a telephone pole and I crashed. I left for three months of training in New York, pursuing my dream career. I returned to find a broken house and a broken heart. My husband had left me. After taking my things to Goodwill, he moved his stuff out, leaving me jobless, broke, and broken. For months I was a basket case. My old friends kept saying, "Get over it." "Get a new dude." "Get a new job." "Move on." They didn't understand my grief. That's when I opened myself to the generous, caring arms the church community had opened to me all along.

I now believe God lives in people, and through a community of people I saw God's love. It was beautiful, and something I wanted to see in me. I joined the Divorce Recovery support group at the church the week my divorce papers arrived in the mail. In that group I found support and comfort from strangers. For the first time, I had people listen, and I felt understood. I had worn out most of my old friends, and when I needed them most, they began to disappear. But in this support group, I could process my pain, and hear others tell me, "You're feeling just how I felt, and there is hope." I began to feel a lot of love from the church in a very tangible way.

Thinking that things couldn't get worse, the porch on my house collapsed. I couldn't find a job, I couldn't break-even selling my house, and I couldn't renew my homeowner's insurance with a collapsed porch. Facing foreclosure, I was distraught. I remembered that Joey, whom I had played softball with at Gateway, led the church's Habitat for Humanity ministry. At church, I asked Joey where I could get cheap materials to rebuild my porch. Several Saturdays later, I was blown away when Joey and his small group showed up with pickup trucks full of materials. Joey had taken up a collection to help, and he and his small group spent three Saturdays building a huge, beautiful porch on my house. In my time of trouble, all my friends I had invested years of my life into were nowhere to be found. Yet here these men, who didn't really know me, were generously giving time and money to serve me.

I found a job working nights in a factory, not a dream job, but it paid the bills. When my car broke down, I was biking ten miles of highway at 3:00 a.m. When Joey's small group found out, they contacted the Benevolence Ministry at Gateway that helps people in crisis. They took it on themselves to make sure my clutch got fixed. The love I experienced when I had nothing to give overwhelmed me. I started to see what God must truly be like through all these people.

For the first time since my husband left, I wasn't consumed with loneliness and hopelessness. I felt inspired to study the life of Jesus. As I read through Matthew, I felt as if I had never heard any of it before. Jesus was so cool! I began to open myself to the truth about Jesus, but still resisted "giving in."

It was Christmas season and the sullen realization overtook me that people who barely knew me cared more about me than the people I had poured my life into for years. My family was far away, I no longer had in-laws, my friends had forgotten about me, and self-pity was my main comfort. Then I met Jeremy and Susan at a mid-week Gathering service. We made each other laugh, and they invited me to share Christmas dinner with them. They prepared a feast and gave so much of themselves. As I got to know them, I felt the peace that they had found rubbing off on me.

A week later, I found myself at a New Year's Eve party full of church people, the last place I ever expected to be on New Year's Eve. I was blown away by the kindness of these churchy folks — these Starbucks-drinking, Wal-Mart-shopping, Republican enemies!* But instead of sharing things in common that we hated, this diverse group shared things in common that we loved. I met the Massengale family that night. Their kids are my age, yet the respect and honor they have for each other feels like the example of what family could be like, what God must have intended. Sometimes now I go to their house just to watch them all interact. They are human, they are Christ-followers, and they are a beautiful family, even if they don't recycle!

Through seeing people loving me I began to see the truth of what God is like. I wanted to be like that and give other people that same experience. I started to really believe what one person said to me, that I had a God-shaped void in my life and that only Jesus could really make me whole again. I never wanted to call myself a Christian. I had such a negative stereotype of a plastic, Bible-thumping facade. But I started to realize that all Christians are just people, like me. They struggle just like I'm struggling. Some just express it differently.

So now I'm a Christ-follower. I want to do God's will, and I call myself a Christian. Now that I have found peace, I realize peace doesn't come in a

---

* Our church is actually about half Democrat, half Republican.

pipe. Now that I've found community, I see that real community comes through Christ. Community is like salve on the wound of humanity because we were built to be interdependent on each other. Now I'm a part of real community, the kind I was searching for all along, and we're changing the world . . . one life at a time.   —Laura

An Organized Organism

Creating a culture where the Body of Christ can function to re-present Jesus requires organization. At first, that may sound contrary to the organic, relational style of ministry I have described. But if you think about it, if we are to function as an organism, a body, the very word implies organization. In fact, the human body has an amazing level of organization. Every cell has a unique roll to play as it inter-relates with others to make up the tissues, which form the organs. A complex interdependency exists between these organ systems to coordinate body functions. Without this integration, communication, and transportation between organ systems—the body is dysfunctional.

Early in the life of a new church, the organization tends to resemble a more amorphous embryonic form where cells have not fully differentiated. Every person functions in multiple tasks, and only a few Body functions have developed. There may be a worship service, a few small groups, and the necessary serving teams. As a church grows, so must the organization, as the early church describes in Acts 6. We try to connect every person in community (small group or serving group communities), which might be analogous to the various tissues that make up the organs of a human body.

As the church organizes and leads to allow cell differentiation, more individuals find a unique part to play in the Body. They combine with others whose complementary gifting, life experience, and passion form the various ministries, or organ systems, of the church Body. But all these systems must coordinate rather than compete, and they must communicate rather than isolate.

I have been amazed at the way the Lord redeems unique individuals, with unique life experiences and gifts, and begins to form new ministries around them like new organ systems of a body. For instance, our Divorce Recovery ministry helped Laura. Divorce Recovery began because Julie had her own divorce crisis. A friend invited Julie to church, where she experienced the grace of Christ through his Body. After finding faith and growing, Julie realized she had a desire to help others find faith and healing through the pains of divorce. So she assembled a team, and started our Divorce Recovery ministry.

The larger a church gets, the more important it becomes that these systems of small groups, ministries, compassionate outreach, teaching, budgeting, and assimilation stay coordinated, cooperating, and connected to the Head (who is Christ)—doing it all out of service to God, not for personal power or prideful gain. This is a constant challenge for leaders: to realize the Body is always changing and growing, requiring increasing levels of organization and coordination. Only then can it grow up as a unified, coordinated, healthy Body that is full of love.

From a Tiny Seed to a Giant Tree

Have you ever wondered why Jesus didn't come during the age of global media? If God wanted to get the message out about his grace, wouldn't it have been more strategic to wait for satellite TV and the Internet? Jesus could have done all his miracles on the air—impressing viewers worldwide. Surely word would have spread like wildfire, and though there would still be doubters and skeptics, millions would have tuned in to watch. His teaching would not only be broadcast around the globe, it would be recorded and preserved perfectly. Surely Jesus could have done a better job representing himself to his TV audience than others have done in his place. So if God wanted all people everywhere to hear and learn of his love and grace, why didn't Jesus come during our century of mass communication?

I am convinced it wasn't because God made a strategic marketing mistake. I'm certain God knew exactly what he was doing, and as the Scriptures declare, "When the right time came, God sent his Son."[11] But maybe the message God intended was never meant to come wrapped only in words but always through a living, growing Body. Maybe God's real message of life found in the gospel is best communicated life on life. Maybe only person-to-person is the truth accurately re-presented: that there is a God who loves you, and he will teach you to love others as you follow him. Maybe that's why God entrusted his message not to mass communication, but to simple fishermen, thieving tax collectors, prostitutes, and misguided zealots who had experienced the Truth incarnate, and it changed them.

As I read Paul's letter to the Thessalonian church, I see the same pattern. Paul says, "Our gospel came to you not simply with words, but also with power. . . . You know how we lived among you for your sake. . . . You became imitators of us and of the Lord. . . . And so you became a model. . . . Your faith in God has become known everywhere."[12] Paul says he lived among them, caring for them like a mother cares for her children, encouraging and urging them on in faith like a father would his kids. He imparted not just a message, he says, but his very life.[13] And God's Spirit infused his Body with life so that the message rang out, and people from all over were drawn to Christ.

We have witnessed the same pattern of God's Spirit at work life-by-life. Jesus says the kingdom of God grows in this manner ... from a tiny seed planted, it organically grows up into a large tree that benefits many. Let me trace the life-by-life chain of events that led Laura to follow Christ, and you can see this pattern at work.

Life by Life

I met Nate†† when he was a brand-new Christ-follower. He joined with a small group of ten people, before Gateway even had a name, and we moved our meetings to his house (we call those core-building days the "Nateway" days). Within a year, Nate started leading his own small group along with Steve††, who had also rejuvenated a stagnant faith as a part of our core group. Nate invited others who found faith in Christ, like Jeff and his friend Craig. In time, Craig met Trent* at a recovery meeting and invited him to Gateway. Trent started following Christ, recovered from a cocaine addiction, and invited Alison who also began following Christ. After getting married, Trent and Alison launched our Recovery ministry and brought many others to Gateway. Soon Nate discovered a passion for serving those in need through mission trips to Mexico and Peru and needy areas of Austin, and he and his wife now lead our missions efforts.

Meanwhile, Steve invited two friends from MBA school he used to party with, Tammy—who brought her future husband, Ron, and both eventually found faith—and Kenny††, a wild man who seemed least likely to succeed as a Christian. But against all odds, Kenny decided to follow Christ, and Steve invited him into his small group. Kenny had a desire to connect others from the beginning. He met Koby† online, and invited her. Koby found a small group, came to faith in Christ, and started our Big Brothers Big Sisters (BBBS) mentoring ministry. I'll never forget Koby as a one-year-old Christian, down in the river, helping me baptize her BBBS little sister, Maria, whom she had mentored and led to faith.

Soon Nate, Steve, Kenny, and Koby were watching God do an amazing work in and through them as they all led small groups and ministries of their own. Steve joined our board of directors and eventually came on staff overseeing new church initiatives. Kenny, a systems analyst, used his abilities and

---

* Trent's and Craig's stories are found in chapter 4.
† Koby's story is found in chapter 9.

passion to connect others to start our Frontline teams and connections process, and eventually he joined our staff full time.

Steve invited his old roommate, Joey,* to join his small group. Joey felt far from God because he was far from perfect, but as he hung out with Steve and his new friends from church, Joey experienced something he wanted. He realized he didn't have to be perfect to let God into his life as he witnessed God's life-changing work in Steve. Joey opened his heart to Christ. Soon Joey got involved helping build houses through Gateway's Compassion ministry (started by Kenny's future wife, who also found faith at Gateway and had a passion for those in need). In time, Joey discovered his gifts of leadership and administration and began to lead our Habitat for Humanity ministry.

As Joey continued to grow, he became an apprentice small group leader and eventually birthed his own small group, through which his friend, Carl, came to faith. One day, a young woman with dreadlocks stopped him in the hallway to ask about materials for a porch. Because Joey had experienced the culture of incarnational truth, it felt natural to him to lead an arm of Christ's Body to reach out in response. That's how Laura found faith. In just six years, the branches of the tree have spread out far beyond what I can trace here.

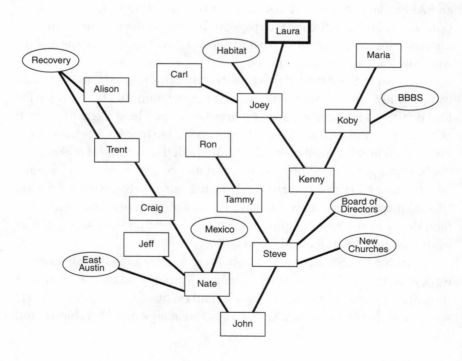

---

* Joey's and Laura's stories are found in chapter 10.

We are the Body of Christ, and since the truth is found in Jesus, people experience the truth in us when we lead and organize and grow in unity and love as the re-presentation of God in the flesh. The spoken message of the God-inspired words of Scripture must never be minimized. But in an increasingly broken world, relationships matter more than ever. Relational connection in community becomes the key to finding faith for many.

As a leader, have you created a culture where the truth of Christ can not only be heard in word, but experienced by the world around you through his Body? Do people see themselves in an interdependent way as they serve one another and the surrounding society? Have you organized so that new believers can grow to form new groups and ministries to function as various organ systems of a whole Body? The incarnational truth found in the Body of the community of Christ will change our postmodern world.

But the Body grows in a broken world only if there is hope! The greatest challenge facing the church in the wake of the Postmodern Experiment is brokenness. That's what we'll struggle through in the next section.

STUDY GUIDE

Culture Check

1. Read Ephesians 4:11–21 and 1 Corinthians 12 carefully. When you think about the people you lead, is a Body the best metaphor of what you're leading them to become? If not, why not? In what ways is your local Body functional? Dysfunctional? Agile and expressive? Paralyzed?

2. Read John 17:20–21. How can you better lead people to function together as a unified Body to love, serve, and heal a broken world around you?

3. If spiritual seekers required months or even years of experiencing the Truth of Jesus by interacting with his Body, how would this happen with your church or group? Do people experience the truth of Jesus re-presented?

Small Group Questions

1. Read 1 Corinthians 12:7–27. This says if you are a Christian, you have a ministry (work of service) to perform as a unique and necessary part of the Body that re-presents Christ to the world. Discuss what unique part you can each play.

2. Read Ephesians 4:11–16 carefully. This says that as we use our gifts to serve one another and the world around us, and as we grow up together speaking truth in love, together we will re-present Jesus (a full-grown, mature view of him) to those around us. How can we do that together as a group? Why does it take a whole community of faith to accurately convey the truth of Christ relationally?

3. Read John 17:20–21. How do you think our unity affects this relational aspect of people discovering the truth?

4. If your unbelieving friends, neighbors, or coworkers needed to experience relational truth by hanging out around your Body for months or even years before believing, how might that happen? What do you think they would experience?

5. What can we do to better function as a Body together? What ways can we tangibly re-present the truth of Christ to the world around us?

The Struggle with Brokenness

Artist: Jessica Gilzow

All God Intended You to Be: Creating a Culture of Hope

[Most people] lead lives of quiet desperation.

Thoreau

With our world in the throes of the Postmodern Experiment, broken lives abound. Henry David Thoreau had it right: "[Most people] lead lives of quiet desperation . . . an unconscious despair is concealed even under what are called the games and amusements of mankind."

My guess is that the pain of our generation may not be unique across the history of time, but its depth and breadth makes concealing it more difficult. Between the pains of growing up in nuclear family blowup, abusive situations, or as the unwanted generation, I find most people are secretly running from the evil twins of despair and shame chasing close behind. Pile on the prevalence of divorces, addictions, abortions, sexual compulsions, and workaholism—and emerging generations are left gasping for hope.

As I read back over so many emails from seekers and believers alike, I found the word "hope" whispered again and again through pages of low-grade desperation. But you would never know it passing these people in the office or on the street. These everyday people often feel like they are the only ones struggling up the steep hills of life.

As leaders, we must create a culture of hope in our churches, ministries, and small groups. We must teach, model, and create environments that breathe hope into our hopeless world. "For everything that was written in

*"Eternally Damned; On Earth and After!"
That's what I imagine is written in the Book
of Life next to my name. Why else would I
be so miserable and so alone? Why does it
seem that I'm destined to forever live without any kind of happiness? What is it that
God wants me to learn from all this suffering? I've already failed at one marriage.
What kind of lesson is this? "Here, make all
these mistakes, and then live with them,
with no bright light at the end of the tunnel.
Here, hand your heart over to someone, let
them crush it, then they can throw it on the
ground, stomp on it, spit on it, jump on it a
few more times (just for kicks), then you can
have it back. Then wait a while, and let
someone else do it. Don't worry about the
pain; after all, it only lasts a lifetime." If this
is all I'm good for, then why am I here? I
didn't ask for this; I certainly don't want it.
But can I give it back? No. How could I possibly have angered God so much that he
would dole this kind of punishment out to
me? Is there anything I can do to get myself
back into his good graces? Why doesn't he
just take my life? Why doesn't he just cast
me into hell and be done with me? Guess
that wouldn't be painful enough, either.
Guess I've got to suffer here first, before I
get cast into hell. Guess I've earned it. But
if this is fate, if this is all I deserve, why can't
I just accept it? Why do I keep hoping . . . ?
I just want to know why; that's all. And
maybe if God does have some kind—any
kind—of happiness in store for me, at least
that would make life a little more bearable.*
                                        —Anonymous

the past was written to teach us, so that through endurance and the encouragement of the Scriptures we might have *hope*."[1]

If we do not create a context for hope and healing, people will keep acting out of their pain in sinful ways. We all know we were intended for more! But we all need hope, that despite all our screw-ups and mis-guided stabs at life, we can still become all God intended us to be.

A Harbor of Hope

People are out sailing through the seas of life with no Navigator on board. They think they're sailing toward life as they follow the siren song of "doing it my way," but they keep running aground, dam-aging their lives on the hidden shoals of sin.

The Christian community must become a safe harbor from the storms of life that beat them up. The problem compounds, though, when seekers come into our churches or groups and rather than hear the predominate message of hope in Christ—that the Creator of the seas wants to come on board and navigate them toward life—they hear only that God is mad about the reefs they keep hitting. They're not about to let an angry navigator on board, life's miserable enough already. But until they let God navigate, they will keep run-ning aground, and they will never become all God intended. But often, leaders spend more time talking about shipwrecks and reef-avoidance than how to let the Navigator navigate!

Tom appears tough and all together on the outside—shaved head, stocky, intellectual, and doing well in business—but listen to the undercurrent of an email he sent me:

> I found Jesus a few months ago. I'll admit, my walk hasn't been straight, and it's still somewhat of a struggle, but I don't feel that sense of doom that I used to. I feel redeemed. I've been reading a lot of literature on Christianity's history lately (being the anal-retentive, logical, pain-in-the-butt I am), and figured out why I always felt bad the times I tried several other churches. They were either steeped in traditions I couldn't understand or seemed to only preach gloom and doom, not the "good news" of Christ, as it seems he intended.

What Good News?

Tom's comment elicits an important question: Is life with Christ *good*? Is it really good news that we hold out to a world in search of hope, or is it more bad news? Do we believe Jesus' words apply to today, "The Spirit of the Lord is on me, because he has anointed me to preach good news to the poor. He has sent me to proclaim freedom for the prisoners and recovery of sight for the blind, to release the oppressed, to proclaim the year of the Lord's favor."[2] Is it still the year of the Lord's favor, good news for poor, blind, oppressed people? Do we believe we have a message that ordinary, sinful, struggling people would see as good news for them if they only understood it?

I believe the problem comes from our wrong perception of the goodness of God. The church often fails to accurately portray his compassion for hurting, broken, sinful people. Creating a culture of hope in which God can heal our broken generation starts with the leader's view of God. What I realized ten years into ministry was that my perception of God was not that great, and the life I was leading was defined more by what I didn't do than by the life-giving experience of the liberating freedom Jesus promised.

Jesus came, died on the cross, and overcame the grave.... Why? To give us life! Jesus said, "The thief's purpose is to steal and kill and destroy. My purpose is to *give life* in all its fullness."[3] "This is how God showed his love among us: He sent his one and only Son into the world that we might *live* through him."[4] God longs to wake us up to give us the fullness of life. So why is it so hard for people to believe?

I think Dallas Willard nailed it when he said,

> How many people are radically and permanently repelled from the Way by Christians who are unfeeling, stiff, unapproachable, boringly lifeless, obsessive, and dissatisfied? Yet such Christians are everywhere, and what they are missing is the wholesome liveliness . . . of God's loving rule. . . . "Spirituality" wrongly understood or pursued is a major source of human misery and rebellion against God.[5]

Jesus rebuked the religious leaders of his day because they had an inaccurate perception of God and no compassion for broken people. They focused on teaching people how to conform by outwardly making sacrifices. They taught extensively about not breaking God's laws (reef avoidance), and yet Jesus rebuked them saying, "You load people down with burdens they can hardly carry, and you yourselves will not lift one finger to help them."[6] He also said, "It is not the healthy who need a doctor, but the sick. But go and learn what this means: 'I desire mercy, not sacrifice.' For I have not come to call the righteous, but sinners."[7]

> *This is the place where I learned to see God not as a rule-giver, but as a life-giver. A Father who wants to give me good things and include me in on the good things he's doing.*
> *—Jerry*

God's love and mercy for a hurting, broken world is indescribable. But if we don't work hard at describing and demonstrating it, people won't believe it.

Stop and assess your view of God. As a leader, has your experience of Christ in your life been good news or merely sacrifice? When you see people who don't know God, do you find yourself compelled by love to try to explain and show them how much he loves them and wants to bring life to them? Do you believe the good news that God still brings hope for healing and vision for life? Do you believe he will use you to show mercy to a hopeless world?

Lindi's story showed me early in the life of our church that if I will hold out hope to broken people, the God of all compassion will not fail them.

It Counted

In the first year of starting Gateway, I got an alarming email. I sat staring at the words on the screen, praying for wisdom as the gravity of the situation became clear. Lindi wrote:

> I have been attending Gateway for a little while now, trying to find some kind of purpose or hope. People say God is here, but I don't feel that, nor does

it make the pain any less. My job as a hospice social worker is to comfort the hurting. But where do I go when I'm in the same boat? The church has never been there in the past, at least not for me, and yet I still hope. I wish I could tell you how terrifying it is to write. The fear of being known haunts me. During the past few months, I have been thinking about my own death and how to hasten it along. I am trained to recognize signs of suicide risk, and I am getting in pretty deep.

As the words ripped through my mind, I sat back in my chair, stunned. *Lord, what do I do? She's at the crossroads of life or death. Show her there's still hope. I don't have a clue what to say, you've got to show me.*

I read on. Five years ago, Lindi married her husband, trusting him with all her heart. Three years later, she discovered an affair that ripped her heart in two. After nine months of separation and his many vows to be faithful, she trusted again and reconciled. Within a year, her husband committed adultery with still another woman.

Lindi continued:

> I am able to recognize signs of abuse with my clients, but I was blind to the fact that it was happening to me. I am haunted by memories of things my husband said and did, and I can't make any of it go away. If the only person who claimed to love me could betray me in such a horrible way, how could I think anybody else would accept or care about me? I filed for divorce last month, and now I feel a whole lot of guilt. What does God really think about divorce? I have never felt so alone. Enough. I already regret sending this, but I will. . . .
> —Lindi

I felt a panic come over me as I finished reading. Again I prayed for Lindi, and as I did, I found myself moved to empathy for this woman I barely knew. I knew she came to Gateway claiming to be agnostic, poking at others' beliefs, but now I could see through these emails the pain stabbing through her protective wall. She was attractive and witty but stone cold, I recalled, with a biting edge that kept people at a distance.

Lord, what do you want to say to her? As I started to email a reply, a passage of Scripture popped into my head—Hebrews 11—all about God's heroes of faith. It's one of my favorite chapters but has nothing to do with suicidal hopelessness! I pushed the thought away and kept writing. But the more I wrote, the more I felt compelled to read Hebrews 11. I stopped emailing and read. As I got to the last part of the chapter, about so many followers enduring horrible suffering in faith, the thought kept coming to me: It counted.

But Lord, this isn't what she needs to hear! I prayed. She doesn't even have faith—she doesn't even believe in you. Why did I think about Hebrews 11?

I decided to step out in faith and include it in my reply. I wrote telling her why there's still hope, how God has led her to our church for a reason, and that he loves her more than she can imagine. I shared about God's grace offered in Christ. Then at the end, in faith, I paraphrased the story of all the people of faith who suffered and how God saw it all, witnessed all the horrors they endured, and it counted in his eyes. I encouraged her to seek God and let this count for something good.

She emailed back five days later:

> Of all the things you wrote, the one sentence that I found so very comforting was God saying, "But I saw what they endured, and it counted." Why that means so much to me, I don't know, but it does. I remember asking my ex-husband what was my reward for forgiving his first affair. It seems as though there is no honor in "doing the right thing," yet maybe, if there is that God you speak of, maybe it means something to him. It is comforting to contemplate the possibility that he sees the turmoil that no one else can and that he cares and it does matter. That God would be worth checking out. Thank you for putting that in your letter.

I still get choked up realizing the amazing compassion of God, and the mystery of how he can use ordinary, messed-up people like me, and through our words and thoughts, convey his message of hope. I often feel so unsure and inadequate, and yet he has demonstrated again and again, he really does mysteriously meet people in personal ways if we can just get them to reach out in hope. Through Lindi, God demonstrated to me early on that I must encourage people to seek him, because he will be found—sometimes in surprising ways.

Lindi continued to attend church and even began to attend our first small group connection. I prayed that people would show her love by seeing past the sharp-edged cynicism that guarded her wounded heart.

She had shared with me in other emails an even deeper source of her despair. Having grown up feeling she didn't really deserve love, she would blame herself and heap condemnation on herself for everything. Her past haunted her with a vengeance. She would ponder her brother's suicide, and wonder what she did wrong to keep him from reaching out to her for help. Though she had been the victim of rape, she put the blame on herself saying, "I should have fought harder, I should have screamed louder." She had lost a baby and felt she was the cause because she couldn't maintain proper weight during pregnancy. She felt angry with herself, scared, untouchable.

This voice of shame echoed through her every memory, deceiving her into believing that God could never love her either.

Angels at Barnes and Noble

One Sunday, our message was on hope—hope grounded not in some questionable outcome or situation or even relationship, but hope grounded in the power and promise of God in Christ. At the end of the message, I addressed those like doubting Thomas, who just couldn't believe there is hope. I told them, "Jesus invites you to reach out with the hand of faith and say, 'If I can really find lasting hope in you, remove my doubt.'"

Lindi decided to take me at my word and seek to learn more about Jesus. She left the movie theater where we met for church and drove to Barnes and Noble. Lindi made her way to the Christian section, not knowing what she was looking for. As she stared in bewilderment at all the books, wondering how to find the right book to help answer her questions, a man walked up and stood right beside her. She thought it strange the man would stand so close but assumed he had a specific book he needed.

To Lindi's shock, the man reached out and pulled a book off the shelf right in front of her, then turned to her and said, "You should read this book," and handed it to her. She looked at him, wondering why a total stranger would do that for no reason, then looked down at the book in her hands. Curious, she opened it and glanced at the contents. When she looked up again a few seconds later, the man was gone!

She wrote me an email the next week, "Your God is continuing to show me things. I guess they are things necessary for my own healing. The signs are unavoidable." She told me of the "angel" at Barnes and Noble and said, "The book he gave me, *He Still Moves Stones*, has helped me in ways I wouldn't have thought possible. Then your God sent another message," Lindi confided, "through a grieving widow tortured by guilt and anger. As I counseled her, she told me her husband had an affair eighteen years earlier. Now, after his death, she is struggling with all the regrets and guilt related to all the anger she carried for so long. After she left, I felt paralyzed by the impact of her words. It began to seem necessary and even comfortable to consider forgiveness...."

A week later, Lindi wrote,

> I am amazed at how far I have come in the past two months—from the depth of "the dark night of the soul" to a view of the light that is just now breaking through. God found it in his heart to save my life. It was what you wrote in one of your first letters that has stuck in my mind—that

sometimes the greatest act of faith is simply hanging on until it gets better, and God knows what we're enduring and it matters to him. You have no idea what the simple act of writing those things to me did to help me take a closer look at your God. You have helped me see a God that I had never seen before — one who is compassionate instead of condemning. Today I bought a Bible that I could understand, and finally, I prayed to your God and he became my God.

Picture God

I'm convinced I have good news for every single person. Every single person wants to become all he or she was intended to be. It's the funny thing about humans compared to other creatures. We alone know we are not yet as the Creator intended. I seriously doubt cats ever feel anxious about whether they'll reach their full potential. But all humans know they have potential to be more. We all instinctively know there's a life out there we were created for, but we can never fully seem to live it.

People long to become all they know they were intended to be, but they can't without God. One of the greatest challenges leaders face is correcting misperceptions of the nature and intentions of God, so people will trust him. I am convinced that I will never be able to adequately describe the depth of love God has for every single person he created. I am also convinced that if people are not better persuaded of God's goodness, they will never take steps toward trusting him. But if we can convince them to take steps toward trusting him, he will meet them and reveal more of himself. Their spiritual eyes will begin to see. So a large part of creating a culture of hope has to do with painting accurate, compelling pictures of the loving, compassionate nature of God toward hurting, wayward people.

The Evil One has done a great job of making God look like the mean, bad guy who wants to rob people of all life—destroy their fun, deny their dreams, make them marry someone they aren't attracted to, and then send them into a profession they hate against their will. I often say to our church, "If God really wanted to destroy your life, do you really think he'd need your permission to do it? Of course not! So why does he respect your will? Because he wants your love—willingly given."

Jesus said Satan is a liar and the father of lies, and these lies about God come through the evils of this broken world—passed down generation to generation. Because of people's broken pasts, they often put the faces of other people, abusive authority figures, distant fathers, or mean-spirited Christians on their mental image of God.

Jesus Hates Me This I Know

Kevin approached me after a Sunday service and said, "I'm kind of embarrassed to say this in church, but every time I hear the word 'Jesus' or see the word in the song lyrics, I think of a hateful person."

"Really," I said astounded. "Maybe you're picturing humans who have not accurately represented him. Have you ever read the eyewitness accounts of Jesus' life?" I asked.

"No, I haven't," Kevin honestly replied.

I explained God's free gift of forgiveness, and I walked him through Romans 8 showing the love and life God offers. I suggested he read the book of John to see what Jesus was truly like.

Three months later, I gave a message on the parable of the prodigal son, a graphic visual Jesus used to help people "get it" about the love of God the Father. Ted Beasley, Gateway's other Teaching Pastor, created a powerful multimedia piece, retelling the prodigal son story in a personal way. Afterwards, I told a story about an epiphany I had with my children. At a moment when I experienced my heart so filled with love for my kids, so desiring their best, it hit me—*I'm an imperfect father*. And in that moment, I sensed God telling me, "I'm a perfect Father, and I love you even more than you love your own children."

Here's what I realized in that moment: if God is love, then all human love is simply borrowed from him. So I asked the congregation to imagine the way they feel about the person they love the most. And then I whispered, "The Father loves you even more."

After that service, Kevin came up with tears in his eyes and could barely get the words out, "I get it! I finally get it."

■ ■ ■

See, words are not enough to change people's view of God. The graphic effect of an evil world has etched a distorted image into people's minds and labeled it "God." Leaders must find creative, graphic ways, just like Jesus did, to paint accurate pictures from Scripture of the God who is defined by the word "love" and whose intentions lead us into life. Using imagination, multimedia, video, music, graphic illustrations, and all the arts help connect to the world people live in and bring the Scriptures and God's true identity to the mind and the heart.

Hope through Life-Giving Services

Christian Schwartz studied one thousand churches in thirty-two countries to determine the universal principles that globally seemed to be at work in growing, healthy churches. He came up with eight characteristics common in these churches worldwide:

- empowering leadership
- gift-oriented ministry
- spiritual passion
- organizational structure
- holistic small groups
- loving relationships
- need-oriented evangelism
- inspiring worship services[8]

The last two define how we have gone about creating a culture of hope—through life-giving services that offer the hope found in Christ to spiritual seekers, and not just through propositional words, but good news connected to real-life needs.

People do not change without motivation. But the root of motivation comes from emotion—a connection to the heart as well as the head. And there's no greater motivation than the hope of being all we were intended to be. It's a need we all share in common.

Emot-ivation

While channel surfing one night, I landed on a PBS program talking about how motivation for change usually does not come from logical persuasion but from emotional connection. It gave an example of when the Mexican government, concerned about literacy rates among male adults, launched a mass-communications effort to persuade male adults to learn to read.

> I have been to your church three times now. I have tried to describe the experience as "alive" and "authentic" but even these words do not quite define it.   —Nola

After spending millions of pesos on educational materials, the effect was virtually zero. But when the largest television network ran a soap opera, infusing adult male actors with positive messages about reading, enrollment of adult males in literacy classes increased 800 percent in one year.[9] Miguel Sabido, creator of the program, explained that the social, economic, and cultural conditions in these dramas must reflect, to the last detail, the social realities of people's lives so that viewers will think "there's someone just like me doing that."[10]

But identifying with lead characters marked only the first step in the process. The real goal was to persuade viewers to change their behavior. The key, Sabido reported to the *Boston Globe*, lies in creating the "doubter" character who questions the proposed new behavior and gives the viewer an outlet for his own doubts and skepticism.[11]

In a world where people secretly fret, worry, and despair about meaning and purpose, they need a church service to engage them where they really live. As we provide outlets for their real questions, doubts, and struggles, they can better see how doing life with God navigates them into the life they desire.

The worship service can create a culture of hope that inspires seekers and believers alike to clearly see who God is, to envision the life he intends for them in a specific realm, and to motivate them to trust him in that area. In a broken generation longing to live in freedom, this life-affirming message of God's kingdom now available, "on earth as it is in heaven," motivates. Leaders must create inspiring services that bring hope into every area of real life, while confronting and explaining why sinful patterns destroy this life.

Rebecca's comments touch on the mysterious way God can use the entire "feel" of a worship service to move the heart toward hope:

> I never thought I would be excited about going to church. I am not even sure how I ended up going here. I hate to say it, but the fact that I wasn't pressured for money made me not afraid to come back after that first day. I left that day with an indescribable feeling. I wanted to break into tears the entire service. Not for any particular reason, just an overwhelming feeling of love, purpose, and joy. Gateway reunited me not only with Jesus Christ, but also with my sense of self and humanity. My faith is greater than ever.   —Rebecca

Creative Motivation

For us, creating life-giving services has revolved around the right team of creative people who truly understand the culture we aim to reach. Our music matches that of Austin, dubbed "The Live Music Capital of the World." JJ Plasencio, our music director, toured the world with the band Sixpence None the Richer. He's a world-class musician who left it all for our mission: "To help unchurched people become a unified community of growing Christ- followers." He came to Gateway when we had 250 people meeting in a movie theater (in fact the day he auditioned, we had church in the theater showing the *Exorcist II* and the power kept shorting out!).

JJ has a heart for seeing people far from God become worshipers of God. When we're selecting music, he chooses worship songs to engage the head and heart on the topic of the day. The style of music is relatable to seekers as well as believers, the sound and quality matches that of any club

> *"I look forward and get excited to go to the Sunday services, the Gathering, and the Bible studies. This is definitely a new experience for me. Every day I am blown away by the contrasts in my life. This commitment and new walk with God has just been amazing. The joy and peace I feel now is so awesome. It is like I was just released from a concentration camp and I suddenly have life. The contrast from feeling oppressed to suddenly having peace and joy is impossible to describe. It is like you've said, "supernatural."* —Joanie

or concert, and the lyrics are understandable, even if a seeker doesn't believe them. We expose seekers to the worship of Christ's community, but we don't drown them in it.

JJ and others wrote many of the worship songs we sing to express in words our common experience of God's goodness and provision. If appropriate, on Sundays he may use a song known in the secular culture that brings up a spiritual question or issue or points toward the topic. Sometimes our band will play a song while a video or a photo essay shows on the screens, giving visual texture to the lyrics. The transferable principle is to use music that communicates in whatever culture you're trying to reach, and to use the song within the context of the motivational path of all the elements of the service.

Learning from MTV

From the beginning, Ted Beasley has been our creative arts genius behind much of the vibe of Gateway services. He has a gift for molding words and images into a powerful medium of communication. Often Ted and the team will create a multimedia, video, or drama that God's Spirit uses in surprising ways when combined with the message of Scripture.

A number of years back, a popular secular song conveyed the image of running through life. Ted and the team combined emotionally moving photos telling the story of life, from birth to the grave. Underneath the images, thought-provoking questions echoed the hopes and dreams we all have along the path of life. As the powerful swell of music and lyrics ebbed and flowed, we were taken on a visual journey across the longings of one life in a matter of minutes. Right afterward, I spoke about "Making Life Count for Eternity." Seekers and believers alike felt a palatable motivation to respond to the words of God about making life count, now and forevermore.

We've heard people say that whenever they hear that song now, they are reminded to make life count. In this way, we let secular radio serve as a spiritual reminder throughout the week. Just as MTV has had a powerful effect on our generation, we use media in this same way to powerfully reinforce a spiritual message.

Individual elements such as rockin' music, movie clips, video, art, or multimedia do not ensure a motivating or life-giving service. We find we must constantly evaluate whether we are connecting the dots, using creative elements to really connect the message of Scripture to real-life issues, or if we are falling into the trap of doing creative elements to "wow," entertain, or be cool. The latter never motivates spiritually.

My British neighbor, who never went to church in England, once told me, "When I come to your church, it's not for great music or video or comedy, but for the spiritual message." This is important to remember. It's not using the arts or humor that matters; it's using them well, in spiritually inspiring or motivational ways.

So as leaders, we must never forget that the creative elements serve the message of Scripture or else they merely distract. But when they voice real questions and raise real issues in creative, identifiable ways, and when these elements tap into the life-giving experiences of humanity—the joy of laughter, the pain of our sorrows, the longing for hope—they can motivate movement toward trusting the God who gives life.

A Place for Preaching and Teaching?

That brings us to the thorny subject of preaching and teaching. Honestly, I have a visceral reaction to the word "preaching" because of all the negative connotations associated with an attitude of arrogance. Nevertheless, I still believe there is an important place for the biblical idea of *kerygma*, the Greek word often translated "preaching." In Scripture it most often means "proclaiming" this good news from God. Jesus went about proclaiming that God's kingdom-life was available to all people. He told his followers to go and proclaim this message as well.[12] It was a message of great hope for ordinary, hopeless people in need of spiritual, emotional, and physical healing.

Some emerging leaders who understand the postmodern context warn that the death of preaching and teaching is imminent, saying, "[Preaching] is a violence toward the will of the people who have to sit there and take it."[13] They ask why one person has the right to speak for God, and they assert that this sets up a power imbalance in the church.

I think the real problem today is not with the biblical idea of preaching and teaching. Surely God's Spirit has not revoked these gifts he gave the church.[14] The problem lies with the attitudes of some preachers—one of arrogance and "near-perfection" rather than humility and real-life transparency—and the content of many messages—predominantly bad news, boring news, irrelevant news, or nothing new. When seekers come to church, they usually know something's broken . . . but they are not sure there's hope for something better. Humble preaching and teaching are still necessary for proclaiming the hope of God's available kingdom-life. And multiple gifted teachers bring health and balance to a church.

Jazz Teaching

Some emerging leaders claim authentic teaching is needed today. And if you've read the previous chapters, you know we're all about authenticity. But some define "authentic" teaching solely as "improvisational"—meditating on the text, scribbling a few notes, and being okay with whatever comes out—kind of like playing jazz.

It takes tons of effort to improvise jazz music. Great jazz players practice and memorize scales and riffs and progressions and rhythmic patterns to be able to improvise. Personally, I believe very few people can improvise teaching the Scriptures in ways that truly connect and motivate. Some can and I envy them, but it usually comes from lots of practice. I'm not that gifted. For me, it takes a tremendous amount of work and effort to be clear, compelling, and biblical, yet authentic in delivery. It's a labor of love I work at with lots of prayer.

I think I would do more violence to people by winging my messages, rather than working hard to recognize the average eight-minute attention span, to anticipate natural resistance and questions people might have, to be aware of biblical terms or characters needing explanation, and to think hard about the "so what" questions that derail listeners if not taken into account. I cannot do justice to the Scriptures or the listeners without prayerful, laborious preparation. On our last all-church survey, we asked what people liked most about the church. A guy who was not a Christian, but who had been attending a few months wrote, "I understand what the hell they're talking about." Our staff loved that one.

It's worth the hard work to help people "get it." People vote with their feet. If they feel violated by an inauthentic messenger, you'll know it, because they'll show it with their attendance. Personally, I think the problem with preaching and teaching may be that it's just plain hard work. I know young pastors in Virginia Beach, Los Angeles, Cincinnati, and Dallas who all have thousands of young unchurched people showing up each Sunday. All of them work hard to craft out a biblically sound message that takes the listener into account. And most all of them write it out verbatim, then go the extra mile to serve people by going over and over it until the delivery is heartfelt and natural. With preparation comes the freedom to make Spirit-led deviations during the delivery. When people can relate, when you work hard to grapple with their real questions and issues, when your message helps people process God's Word in light of the "so what" questions of everyday life—God uses it to bring hope.

Putting All the Pieces Together

Some emerging pastors also doubt whether preaching and teaching really has any long-term behavioral impact. To a degree, I agree. If you do not connect messages with next-step opportunities, there will be minimal lasting impact. The truth is, people only retain about 10% of what you verbally say. If they see something visual along with the words, the retention rate may jump closer to 50% of the message. But involve them in doing something with it, and retention rockets upward toward 70%—it makes a lasting impact.[15]

For that reason, our teaching team works hard to connect the teaching to the relational or organizational life of the church. The messages teach the truths of Scripture and help create culture by reiterating the most important values and behaviors dear to God. But messages can also motivate people to take next steps: connecting in community, serving with their spiritual gifts, putting intentional practices in place. That's when people begin to become all God intended. And when all the pieces come together, God powerfully uses catalytic teaching to bring hope and life through the whole Body, and that becomes contagious.

Jack is a martial arts black belt. A high-tech engineer, he came to Gateway as a single dad raising two young boys. Listen to the power of hearing the "good news," which motivated Jack to get involved using his gifts.

> Before Gateway, my life was just a maze. I felt lost, never knowing if the person I knew myself to be—or at least hoped to be—would ever come out. I wasn't a very good person growing up, never had a good family experience, and didn't have God for most of life. Gateway marks a point in my life when I finally saw myself the way God intended me to be. This seems to be a bold statement of clarity, but it doesn't scratch the surface. The main thing that Gateway has helped me to understand is that I matter, not just in the scheme of things, but like a piece of a puzzle . . . as an essential part, a unique piece of God's great plan.

Jack started to see God at work in every part of his life as he learned how to do life with God. Motivated by a message on community, he found people to surround himself with who helped him break out of his shell. As a result, he started taking risks he otherwise shied away from taking. "One day after hearing a message about spiritual gifts and passions," Jack recalls, "I took a leap of faith and emailed our children's pastor about teaching children. Now

I can't picture myself serving in any other capacity. For the first time, my life has more meaning than I could have ever imagined."

As he grew spiritually, Jack saw his life changing, and that even changed his heart toward his ex-wife, Anne. When he invited her to Gateway, she came. She found support and healing through the Comfort and Hope ministry, and began to open her heart to following Christ as well. Today Jack and Anne serve Gateway's kids together.

This has been the pattern we have seen over and over. Life gives life. When God's message of hope begins invading the hearts of people, motivating them to action, meeting their real needs spiritually, they change. And life-change is contagious. Seekers invite seekers even more than believers do. The change and newness of life is fresh and liberating and full of hope.

But amidst all the good news, I can just hear the dissonant voices questioning, "But what about sin? How do you address the fact that our sin is serious business to God? Do you ever tell people the truth—that often their behavior destroys the life God intended?" Absolutely! In the next chapter, we'll look at a few areas where sin patterns enslave our broken generation and explore how to communicate God's laws of liberation.

STUDY GUIDE

Culture Check

1. If you look honestly at your personal fears, worries, actions, and motivations—what does your behavior indicate about your deep-held views about God? Is it more the real God or an imposter you're serving?

2. In what ways do your services and the culture of the church breathe hope of the good news of Jesus into a hopeless world? Where is hope needed in your context?

3. The Evil One has blinded the eyes of the unbelieving, making God seem like the enemy who takes away real life. What are some creative ways you can show people a clear picture of the living God?

4. People tend to act in line with their motivations. What do you think most motivates the actions of the people you seek to reach and minister to? How can you creatively help them align their motivations with doing God's will?

Small Group Questions

1. Where do you need hope right now?
2. Read Romans 15:4. How have the stories and words of Scripture brought hope to you in the past. What might bring hope to your situation in the present?
3. Do an exercise to determine what your conception of God is truly like. On one side of a sheet of paper, write down descriptive words or phrases of your impression of God and/or your parents growing up. On the other side, write down what you've always hoped God was like deep in your heart. Discuss which side aligns more with what Jesus was like. When you evaluate your fears, worries, actions, and motivations—what does your behavior indicate about your deep-held views about God? Is it really God you're following, or more of an imposter god?
4. How does our view of God affect our willingness to trust him?
5. Read John 10:10 then Luke 11:46. Does your view of the Christian life feel more like Jesus' description in John 10:10 of an overflowing life or more like the burdened religion of the Pharisees described in Luke 11:46? Why?

chapter

12

Mental Monogamy: Creating a Culture of Sexual Wholeness

Ours is a culture crying out for intimacy, but only able to conceive of accessing it through sex.

Mike Starkey, *God, Sex and Generation X*

Janice—they're definitely living together. They aren't married yet," Nancy proclaimed to her small group leaders. Nancy and Jason had stayed behind after small group to confer a growing suspicion about the new couple, Amanda and Ken. Janice and Bob had been leading a small group for years. They knew the Bible inside and out, had studied it cover to cover, but they had never dealt with a situation like this before.

"They're really a sweet couple," Janice replied. "Do you think they know it's wrong? The past few months they've been coming, they act like we would never think twice about it—like there's nothing wrong with it."

"Well, regardless," Bob jumped in, "it's our responsibility to tell them. Doesn't the Bible say in Leviticus, 'Rebuke your neighbor frankly so you will not share his guilt'?"

"You know, maybe they're just roommates," Jason suggested. "A lot of men and women live together as roommates these days. Maybe they're not even sexually involved."

"No, they're definitely sexually involved," interjected Nancy. "Amanda told me the reason they started coming to church had to do with relationship troubles she and Ken were having. She told me about a bad fight they had in bed one night that made her realize they were missing something. They're not platonically sleeping in the same bed!"

"Well, it's our responsibility to do the right thing," Bob reminded them. "First Corinthians 4:3 says clearly that sexual immorality is a sin. Jesus said, | 223

'If your brother sins, rebuke him, and if he repents, forgive him.' I think we need to tell them it's wrong and they need to move out."

"And we need to be ready to help them do the right thing," Janice added.

"Let's make a plan right now," suggested Jason. "We can stick around. This is important."

Assessing Trajectory

Let's hit pause in our story for a second and evaluate. Although a dramatic re-creation of dialogue, this actually happened at another church in our town. Amanda and Ken later came to Gateway and conveyed this story.

As a leader, what would you do if a couple came into your group living together? If your church or small group reaches its arms into the real world, this situation will soon come your way. What's the right thing to do? Stop and reflect on how you would handle this situation. What Scriptures might guide you? How might Jesus respond?

When Amanda and Ken came into my office a year later to talk, they reminded me of a stray puppy, wanting to be loved but so afraid of getting kicked again. A young couple in their midtwenties, as they entered, I could see the tension in every muscle made ready to run. They openly told me why they felt scared.

"Last year, Ken and I decided we needed God in our lives," Amanda shared after taking a seat and bantering a few minutes about trivial things. "So we went to a church nearby and got into a small group. We were both feeling so isolated. Our relationship was headed south, and we felt we had no real friends around us. We both sensed we needed God."

"But it turned out to be a nightmare for us," Ken interrupted. "We love Gateway, and we want to get into a small group, but Amanda can't take that kind of pain again."

"What happened?" I asked.

"We had been going to this group about two months," Amanda explained. "I was so excited because I felt like my life was turning around. Ken and I were growing spiritually, we weren't fighting all the time, and for the first time in years, I felt like I had the chance to make some really close friendships with the couples in our small group."

"They were really nice people. We thought they were our friends," Ken said. "Then one night, the leaders invited us over to dinner. It wasn't a small group night."

"At the time," Amanda interjected with a look of sadness, "I was so excited thinking I might finally have some good friends to grow with spiritually—people who would be good for me."

"Obviously, something went wrong," I said, anticipating the bomb coming. I was trying to assess where this couple was spiritually, but it was hard to tell. I realized they lived together. Usually in a situation like this, my goal is to listen and ask questions long enough to determine not just where people have been but which way they are headed. Someone with an immoral past can be headed in the right direction, yet get derailed by spiritual leaders who hammer on what's currently wrong, rather than encouraging the forward movement. Likewise, a Christian might look good on the outside but be headed the wrong way and truly need that good old Levitical rebuke.

"After dinner," Amanda continued, "they sat us down and told us we were in sin for living together. They made an ultimatum that we needed to move out right away to stay in the group."

"Not only that, they already had it all planned for us," Ken explained. "I was supposed to go live with Nancy and Jason, and Amanda was supposed to go live with Janice and Bob until we got on our feet financially—starting that night! We felt totally cornered and ambushed. They didn't seem to care what we thought. It really hurt Amanda. She thought she was going to make close friends but felt more of the condemnation that made her hate church people growing up. We left that night and never went back."

"We felt so burned," Amanda admitted, that we stayed as far away from church as we could get. But we went through so many trials and tribulations during our year away from church, and we still felt like there was something missing. My grandmother lives in the retirement home next door, so we finally got up the nerve to come here. We want to get connected in a group, but I'm just afraid of getting hurt again. That's why we wanted to talk to you. Will that happen again? I want to know Gateway's view. I just don't understand why it would be wrong to love each other. And why is it wrong to live together? We're just trying to make sure our relationship is strong instead of plunging into the cycle of marriage and divorce like our parents did."

Knowing how burned they had been, I backed up and heard both their stories, asking many questions about their spiritual and family backgrounds. It turned out Amanda came from a very harsh, strict family that used occasional religion like a billy club. She had suffered sexual abuse by a member of her family. The rigid rules couldn't keep her family together, and the pain of their divorce haunted her.

Neither Amanda nor Ken understood the grace of God offered in Christ, but Amanda felt she desired to turn her life over to God since coming to Gateway. As I explained the good news of God's free gift, she confirmed she wanted what Jesus did to count for her and wanted to follow him. Ken believed in God but still was not sure about surrendering to Christ. After really seeking to understand the trajectory of Amanda and Ken, and reassuring them about God's love and forgiveness, I explained some of what we will talk more about in the rest of the chapter—how to help people move forward from here.

Which Way Forward from Here?

Leaders today face the challenge of helping people understand that God's ways bring life. In a post-Christian world in the wake of the Postmodern Experiment, which gave birth to the sexual revolution, simply telling people, "The Bible says it's wrong," holds little authority. But leaders cannot afford to retreat into holy huddles, cursing the darkness. We must walk forward into it and turn on a light. Jesus said his words are truth that liberate—that bring life and freedom to every aspect of existence.

In a post-Christian world, rather than presuming the authority of Scripture on everyone, we must work harder to understand and explain to people *why* God's ways are truth that lead to life. We must spell out for them why doing things our way instead of God's way destroys life. The more you understand human nature, relationships, and the social effects of sinful actions, the easier it becomes to see why God's ways protect and provide life for people. This is especially true with sexuality.

So going back to our couple living together, let's ask the overmarketed question, "WWJD—What would Jesus do?" Fortunately, in this case, we can see what Jesus actually *did*. He put first things first. John chapter four records an account at Jacob's well in Samaria. Jesus met a woman with a relational past about as checkered as you can get. She had been married and divorced five times, and she was currently hooked up sexually, living with a guy. Jesus knows all this, so what does he do? He begins where she has need.

> When a Samaritan woman came to draw water, Jesus said to her, "Will you give me a drink?" (His disciples had gone into the town to buy food.) The Samaritan woman said to him, "You are a Jew and I am a Samaritan woman. How can you ask me for a drink?" (For Jews do not associate with Samaritans.) Jesus answered her, "If you knew the gift of God and who it is that asks you for a drink, you would have asked him and he would have given you living water." "Sir," the woman said, "you have nothing to draw with and the well is deep. Where can you get this living water?" (John 4:7–11)

Jesus first values her by asking her for a drink. She is astonished that he pays any attention to her since Jewish men were forbidden to associate with Samaritan women—he bridges relational barriers. Then he tells about a better source of water to meet her thirst. Jesus starts from her perceived need (for physically convenient water), and he proceeds from there to her spiritual need. Jesus knows how thirsty for love this woman must be, but to tell her to "stop trying to quench her thirst for love with men," before giving her something to satisfy her soul, simply won't work.

> Jesus answered, "Everyone who drinks this water will be thirsty again, but whoever drinks the water I give him will never thirst. . . ." The woman said to him, "Sir, give me this water so that I won't get thirsty and have to keep coming here to draw water." He told her, "Go, call your husband and come back." (John 4:13–16)

"Go get your husband and I'll give you this eternal kind of water," Jesus says, knowing full well she's living with a man. She's half-honest. "I don't have a husband," she replies. Now, instead of condemning her, Jesus matter-of-factly explains that he already knows she's had five divorces and is now shacking up with another man. That's all he says. He makes no moral commentary, does not insist she "do the right thing and stop sinning." He simply acknowledges her real condition.

She changes the subject. He allows her to shift away from the pain of her real need to an esoteric theological question. But Jesus steers back to the real issue—which by the way is not the sexual/relational mismanagement of her life, but putting God first, heart and soul, in spirit and truth (authentic worship). "God is spirit, and his worshipers must worship in spirit and in truth,"[1] Jesus tells her. Jesus knew that until she had living water springing up in her soul, flowing out of a right relationship with God, she would forever drink from muddy water.

The text makes no mention of Jesus rebuking her sin or telling her to move out immediately, even though it says Jesus stayed there two more days. All it says he did was offer himself as her Savior! Obviously, even with the covers of her past pulled back and her sins exposed, she felt more love and grace than condemnation. The text says she ran to her friends in the village basically saying, "You've got to come meet this guy—maybe he's the Messiah we've waited for."[2] And many, it says, found faith in Christ through the testimony of this woman.

First Things First

As leaders in a post-Christian world drowning in moral relativity, we must focus first on making sure people are rightly related to God and truly willing to follow Christ. Then we can guide and direct them to the freedom of following his ways. If we try to force people to morally approximate the gospel before they have the source of life-giving water, we spiritually dehydrate them.

But once they've experienced this life-affirming gift Jesus offers, and if we patiently guide them to tune in to God's Spirit, in time, they often make right choices on their own accord. Especially as they understand why God's wisdom works.

Alison and Trent were living together when they came to Gateway. Both were addicted to crack. From a static standpoint, they would never fit in most churches. But from a dynamic standpoint, their movement toward full surrender to Jesus astounded me. Trent surrendered his life to following Jesus from his first day in church, got into recovery, and has been sober ever since. He invited Alison, who had already entered recovery. After finding a solid spiritual foundation and a track record of growth, they could hear truth spoken in love as a prompting from God.

Alison recalls, "I had been living with Trent when a leader at Gateway made it abundantly clear that my lifestyle was disobedient to God. His words resounded that of the Lord's voice and prompted what I had been denying . . . and through prayer and God's grace, Trent and I both sought to move in line with God's desire."

This leader put first things first, making sure Alison and Trent knew the grace of God and were intent on following Christ, then out of a trusting relationship with this leader, Alison could hear hard words as from the Lord. Trent and Alison decided to honor God relationally, they're now married and, years later, lead our recovery ministry.

Do not focus on the static situation, but on the dynamic movement. Listen attentively to a person's story, then ask, "Which way forward from here?" Help people move toward Christ regardless of their past.

Our Sexual State of the Union

Of my first seventeen premarital counseling appointments, thirteen of the couples were living together. The cultural times have changed, and we must be prepared. In the 1950s, it was pretty easy to publicly decide to save yourself sexually for that one special person and a lifelong commitment. Society reinforced the belief that this was good and chastised alternative behavior, sometimes in hurtful, destructive ways.

For instance, in the fifties, actress Ingrid Bergman was chased out of Hollywood for conceiving a child out of wedlock. It was a major scandal. But just consider the contrast. In the 1990s, when actress Connie Seleca and entertainer John Tesh mentioned that they were *not* going to engage in sex before their marriage, Hollywood treated the couple in almost as shame-inducing and derogatory a fashion as they treated Ingrid Bergman decades before.

If you're a single adult, the prevailing message you get is that if you are normal and healthy, you will have sex. Otherwise there's something wrong with you. To save your sexuality for the context of a committed, loving, life-long relationship sounds archaic and downright detrimental.

Listen to how Watters, author of *Urban Tribes*, talks about the norm for the postmodern urban single.

> Only conservative politicians continued to give lifestyle advice as if it were still in style. It was pretty easy to read this for what it was: political posturing. George W. Bush's advice that we abstain from sex before marriage was an excellent example. Given that many of us were delaying marriage until we were thirty or thirty-five, his just-say-no-to-sex rhetoric read like a blatant pandering to the Christian Right or willful ignorance of social trends or both.[3]

Americans have been brainwashed with messages about their sexuality. The average young American will watch over 14,000 sex acts (or references to sex) with corresponding messages about sexuality every year on TV. This means that during the sexually formative decade between ages thirteen and twenty-three, emerging generations probably receive close to 100,000 messages about sex through the media, the vast majority outside the context of marriage.[4] If repetitive commercials stick in our minds and influence our buying decisions, how has Hollywood trained us with this brainwashing about sex? Has it really improved our lives or given us the freedom to love with an intimacy that can last?

Not surprisingly, the Alan Guttmacher Institute indicates that by age nineteen over three-quarters of American teens have had sexual intercourse.[5] The National Marriage Project says that about half of unmarried women between ages twenty-five and thirty-nine will have lived with an unmarried partner.[6] If you engage the culture as a leader, you can expect over half the single population to think living together is a good idea, and most will have had sex by age nineteen. So the question is not how to go back to the fifties, but how to help emerging generations move forward toward sexual wholeness from here.

The Moral Majority tried to change society's moral behavior with external pressure but had zero effect. That's because just as Jesus said, "Out of the *heart* come evil thoughts, murder, adultery, sexual immorality. . . ."[7] Condemnation may achieve temporary conformity, but it doesn't instill lasting change of heart.

As leaders, we must be prepared to take people from their broken sexual past and help them move heart and soul toward God's plan for sexual wholeness. And we must educate and inspire others, especially teens, to wait. This can actually be a life-affirming discussion, even for sexually active people, when clearly explained. But we must assume that God's ways will *not* make sense to them until explained.

We do not claim to have the perfect way to talk to people about God's will for their sexuality, but we *have* had a lot of experience due to the number of singles in our church. We try to teach on God's restoration plan for our sexual relationships yearly in our services, quarterly in our premarriage weekend, and in every premarital counseling appointment. Surprisingly, I have found amazing willingness from the vast majority of couples to move forward in God-honoring ways, when we create a culture for sexual wholeness.

To help this be practical, the remainder of this chapter will take you into a real-life counseling conversation. The situation and conversation came predominately from one couple; however, I have taken the liberty to include several common issues or questions taken from other actual counseling appointments and put them in Joseph's voice. I have done this hoping it will be beneficial to see the most common points of resistance and the way we typically try to respond to help move people forward.

Counseling for Mental Monogamy

Joseph and Tanya came into my office for premarital counseling. As they sat down, Joseph scooted his chair close enough to grab Tanya's hand. They came to Gateway and within three months both decided they wanted to follow Christ and were baptized. From previous conversations, I had already inferred they were living together.

Joseph grew up on the West Coast and lived there all his life until moving to Austin. Joseph had been sexually active since puberty, but sex had never brought Joseph closer to what his heart longed for ... assurance that he mattered and was loved regardless of whether he succeeded in life. He came from a broken home and lived with tremendous pressure to prove himself.

Tanya grew up in Austin, stretched between the chaos of a physically abusive father whom she felt never loved her and a mother who tried unsuccessfully to kill herself several times. Tanya knew her father had cheated on her mother on numerous occasions. Her mother spent Tanya's teenage years confined to a mental hospital, while Tanya and her older sister were left with their angry, compulsive dad.

All of Tanya's friends agreed that you could never get love to last without sex, and it just made sense to live together before marriage. Determined to create the family life she never had, Tanya moved in with her first boyfriend at age eighteen, thinking he was the one. After four years of discouragement, the relationship blew up and wounded her greatly. She tried again, living with a guy for six months, but it ended badly as well. She met Joseph several years later.

They planned to attend our Gateway Encounter Marriage (GEM) weekend, where we have couples do a marriage readiness assessment to pinpoint strengths and potential stumbling blocks.[8] They came to talk about some of the struggles they were having with communication since getting engaged. Realizing some of their struggles related to moving in together and trying to act married without the commitment of marriage, I shifted the subject.

"Tell me about your views on living together and sex before marriage," I asked, "because I find this has an important bearing on your future together."

"Well, we are living together," Tanya stated.

"I think it's been good," Joseph added. "It's how I knew I wanted to marry Tanya."

"So I'm assuming you're sexually involved. Am I right?" I asked. Both nodded affirmatively. "Here's what I find with most couples I counsel living together. With so much divorce, you want to insure that your relationship will last before getting married. This is a good thing. And word on the street says the best way to insure that a marriage relationship will stay together is to try it out first. Is that what motivated you two to move in together?"

"For me, I really love Tanya," Joseph began, "and with the bad family past we've both endured, we want to make sure it will work. Kind of like test-driving a car before you buy—you don't make a twenty-thousand-dollar decision without really checking it out. So I've always felt like living together is a great way to check things out and make sure you can make it last before getting married."

"Plus saving money," Tanya added with a hint of sarcasm. "Actually, I was opposed to living together, but I gave in," Tanya reticently admitted with a side-glance toward Joseph. "I used to think it would help, but I made that mistake twice. I think that's part of the struggle we're having, we moved too fast."

"Well, now that you're both Christ-followers, let me explain why God's wisdom works best. Because God wants to help you truly make it last. The real problem is that the current thinking actually hinders us from getting what we really want—in fact it trains us for just the opposite. Most people still want a loving, intimate, lasting relationship where emotional intimacy and sexual fulfillment grow over a lifetime together. I assume that's what you both want. Am I right?"

"Of course," Joseph stated.

"Sure!" Tanya concurred. "And we already see some things that aren't working. That's why I knew it wasn't best to move in together. But for some reason, I keep ending up in the same place."

"Well, look, here's the deal," I said. "Regardless of what you've done in the past, it's not too late to honor God and honor yourselves with your sexuality and relationship. Scripture tells us to keep the marriage bed pure—meaning save sex for marriage.[9] God says this to protect you. He wants you to have the best marriage and sex life imaginable, but in a way that doesn't hurt you or others. You can allow him to make you sexually whole and prepare you for lasting intimacy where it counts most—in your mind—by practicing mental monogamy."

Research Reality Check

"Word on the street may say living together will insure success," I continued, "but you need to know that recent research says the word on the street is wrong! I know you both want to honor God, but even if you didn't, I'd still advise you against living together. Here's why: Rutgers University did extensive research on living together before marriage. Have you seen that article we have on the resource table called 'Should We Live Together?'"[10]

"No, I haven't seen it," Tanya said, "but I have a feeling I'm gonna wish I had."

"If not, you can go online and read the research for yourself, but let me read you some highlights." I got up and grabbed a copy I had seen in the "need to file" pile of papers next to my desk. Sitting back down, I continued, "From their nationwide study, Rutgers researchers say, 'Virtually all research on the topic has determined that the chances of divorce ending a marriage preceded by cohabitation are significantly greater than for a marriage not preceded by cohabitation.'[11] They quote another national survey that found couples who live together before marriage 'have a hazard of dissolution that is about 46% higher than non-cohabitors.' A lot of words, but let me translate that for you: Living together doesn't help, it hurts! The only good reason to live together is if you want to increase the already 50% odds of divorce by almost another 50%."

"But I know people who have great marriages that lived together first," Joseph retorted.

Sensing he might be getting a little defensive, I said, "I often find couples never think they will be a statistic because they feel their love is special. I'm sure it is, but realize that this isn't my opinion, it's secular research saying, 'No positive contribution of cohabitation to marriage has ever been found.'[12]

And it's not just Rutgers—*Psychology Today* says, 'Living with your partner before tying the knot may help you pay the rent, but it could cost you the relationship, new research suggests.'"[13]

Everybody's Doing It!

"Look," I said, "I know what everybody's doing. But everybody's getting divorced too. Yes, you can point to marriages that make it after living together, but as a friend of mine likes to say, 'Is it possible to go from the top to the bottom of Niagara Falls in a barrel and survive? Yes—some have. But there's a much safer, wiser way.' With only 50% odds as it stands, why would you choose to increase your odds of divorce? You wouldn't gamble your savings with those odds; don't gamble your most important relationship."[14]

"Well, we already have," Joseph stated matter-of-factly. "But why would living together be any different than marriage? What difference does a piece of paper and a ceremony make?"

"None!" I replied. "It's not the paper or wedding, it's the commitment that makes the difference. And even though you've already lived together, I'm not saying you're doomed. But you may need to change your thinking about marital commitment. Jesus said, 'At the beginning the Creator made them male and female, and said, "For this reason a man will leave his father and mother and be united to his wife, and the two will become one flesh." So they are no longer two, but one. Therefore what God has joined together, let no one separate.'[15] God's intent from the beginning was for two people to come together in a lifelong commitment toward oneness, becoming one spiritually, emotionally, and physically. It's the picture of loving, trusting, unconditional unity that mirrors the unity and love of God. That's why it's sacred. When you give yourself physically without giving yourself heart and soul in committed love, sex becomes something we use for *our* purposes rather than for God's intended purposes, and it ends up hurting others and us."

Sexual Duct Tape

Sensing I had their attention, I continued, "That's why over thirty times in Scripture God tells us to avoid casual sex (sexual immorality)[16] and to reserve sex for marriage—when you have a lasting, lifelong commitment. You've both opened your hearts to Christ, so I assume you want to follow him and his will for your lives. Is that a fair assumption?"

"Yeah," Tanya said first and Joseph nodded, "I've been trying to grow, but I feel like I keep screwing it up."

"The only question I have," Joseph asked, "is why would it be wrong if we really love each other? I mean, I'm not for casual sex or using people—I know that's wrong. But if we love each other, isn't it just a way to express your love and make you closer?"

"That's a good question," I said. "It is a way to express your love and commitment—that's why God created it. But sex isn't super glue. It can't keep a marriage together without committed love. I find many couples use it to try to hold their relationship together, but it works against them. Sex doesn't establish commitment or intimacy—it requires them. We learn from the street that if you want to make a relationship stick—have sex. And God created sex for spiritual bonding. In fact, researchers have found an actual chemical bonding effect that sex can stimulate in the brain.[17] So it has a sticky, bonding effect. But when we use sex in our dating relationships, it acts like duct tape.[18] Duct tape does a great job of sticking two things together. But when it's used to try to stick two people together who are not committed for life, and the relationship ends—what happens? We rip the duct tape off. Ouch—it hurts. Then we date again, use sexual duct tape again, break up—rip it off. Ouch—it hurts. Why does it hurt at first?"

"Because it really mattered," Tanya suggested. "It meant something."

"And because deep down," I explained, "we feel something tear from the soul that God never intended to be torn. But when we keep taping and ripping, taping and ripping, what happens? After a while, it doesn't hurt so much, does it?"

"You become callused," Tanya said, intercepting my thought.

"Exactly," I agreed. "Sex has lost its spiritual stickiness because it was never meant to be used and reused in multiple relationships—it was meant for one monogamous bond. And when we use it like duct tape and then get married, we enter marriage thinking about sex and our sexuality the wrong way. We haven't learned mental monogamy—to think about sex as exclusive for a permanent and lasting bond. And so it doesn't stick at all in marriage—we've trained our minds to be discontent sexually by taping ourselves to many different people, or imagining sex with many partners."

"But we do intend to get married, so maybe it's just like we're already married in God's eyes," Joseph suggested.

"How long until your wedding date?" I asked.

"In May, about five months," Tanya said.

"Well, if I were in your shoes," I said, "even though it will be hard, I'd decide to stop having sex, move out, and do all I could to honor God and honor each other in preparation for marriage. Your marriage is worth whatever it will cost. Use the next five months to learn to practice mental monogamy. I counsel a lot of people living together, and most say, 'We're already committed.' But when you live together, the only commitment (if you're honest) is to stay until you find something you can't stand. But that doesn't build trust. So allow God to retrain your minds to think about marriage and sex as a unique, sacred bond. Work on what will stick you together for life, your spiritual and emotional intimacy. If you get that right, the sex and living together will work, and it will last!"

Joseph had that deer-caught-in-the-headlights shock in his eyes.

Tanya glanced over at him and casually said, "I've been saying this same thing because I learned all this the hard way."

God, Sex, and Sanity

Feeling they needed some hope, I said, "Look, people think God's ways are outdated or that he just wants to ruin our fun, but neither is true. God wants to show you how to have what I'm sure you both really want: growing intimacy, respect, contentment, and sexual love that gets better every year because your love grows deeper every year. This only grows out of a commitment of our whole person to another whole person for our whole lives. God is not opposed to sex. He created it. It's beautiful. Dr. Drew didn't make sex pleasurable; God designed it that way."

Joseph squeezed out a strained laugh and said, "It's hard to think about it that way for some reason. God and sex just don't go together."

"Growing up," Tanya chimed in, "the only association I had between God and sex was guilt."

"That's part of the problem," I said. "We run and hide from God rather than realizing he already knows what's up and has our best interest in mind. God thinks sex is good. A whole book of the Bible, the *Song of Solomon*, is devoted to the beauty of romantic, sexual love in marriage. But like every good thing God has created, we can misuse it. And when we do, it hurts others or us. God's not opposed to sex; he's opposed to premarital sex, just like I'm not opposed to my son playing with a dog, but I don't want him playing with a wild dog. I'm opposed to anything that might hurt him because I love him. So there is a good, natural, God-given desire that we can affirm as sexual beings. But just like any desire, God expects us to tame it and rule over it, and not let it rule over us. The desire for food is good, but if I compulsively think about food or can't control or limit my eating as he intended—that's broken. And God gave us the ability to control our sexual appetites as well.

It's Not Hurting Anyone

"But I still don't see how it's harmful," Joseph said. "If two people consent and love each other, it's not hurting anyone—really. Why would God oppose it? He created animals, and they're not monogamous."

"But animals aren't created in God's image either," I reminded him. "God makes relational covenants with us to give us spiritual security—it's what we need most—and he created us to enter into trusting lifelong covenants with each other. Animals can't make loving covenants or rebel against God's ways like we do. You don't see animal Hitlers or animal Mother Teresas. Let me explain it this way. We can be free to express our sexuality outside of marriage, because God gives us the ability to go against his will. But it potentially costs us a greater freedom. Jesus said if we follow his ways, we will be free—that his desire is to give us maximum freedom, including sexual freedom. What we fail to realize is that the freedom to express our sexuality outside of a marriage covenant costs us a greater spiritual freedom to be fully monogamous and content with one person. It also costs our entire society."

"How so?" Joseph questioned, obviously not convinced.

"I think the statistics tell the story pretty clearly. You weren't at Gateway back when we did the 'God, Sex, and Sanity' series. Let me grab my talk file." As I walked over to the file cabinet, I added, "See, from an individual perspective, we don't see any harm in sexual freedom outside of God's intended design, but just imagine what God sees. Imagine all the pain and hurt God has to watch people endure because we abuse his purpose for our sexuality."

"What statistics are you talking about?" Tanya questioned.

"Basically what's happened in our society since the Sexual Revolution of the sixties," I said as I pulled the file and sat back down at the table. "We used to think our problem was sexual inhibition. We were just undersexed. So we knocked down the traditional walls of sexual morality for the purpose of freedom—the goal being maximum fulfillment in our sexual pleasures. And with that aim, we 'freed' sex from the context of marriage. But what's been the result of this revolution? First, not more fulfilling sex. It says here that 57% of couples say their sexual relationship is not satisfying or fulfilling—so more sex has not equaled more satisfaction according to recent research."[19]

"Man, if that's true, why do you think it's so high?" Joseph questioned.

"I think we've trained our minds to think about sex in wrong ways, and it's backfiring on us. In much more painful ways than just dissatisfaction," I said. "Following the Sexual Revolution, the divorce rate tripled from 1962 to 1981.[20] The teen pregnancy rate soared. Today, 40% of teens will be pregnant before age twenty, 80% of those out of wedlock.[21] Nearly one of every three babies in the U.S. is born out of wedlock, the highest anywhere in the world.[22]

"I wouldn't have thought it was that high," Tanya said, "but I know several friends who have had abortions already."

"The sad part," I continued, "is that children lose both ways. Statistically, kids conceived out of wedlock are at much higher risk of all kinds of pains and problems,[23] if they even survive the womb, like you mentioned. The number of abortions doubled until 30% of pregnancies were terminated in the early eighties.[24] This 'free love' movement of the sixties turned into herpes in the seventies and AIDs in the eighties. It's hard to conceive of all the pain God sees.

"He sees the one out of four adults estimated to suffer with some form of sexually transmitted disease, and the number has been rising—it's an epidemic.[25] Not only does it hurt adults, but more and more babies are born with birth defects caused by STDs every year as more people get infected. God sees all of this pain," I said, looking up from reading my notes. There was no comment, so I continued.

"On top of all this, pornography grew into a multibillion-dollar industry, including billions made from child pornography[26]—abusing children for twisted sexual gratification. Today, one out of six adult women surveyed has been raped or sexually assaulted, and more than half of those were under age eighteen when it happened![27] One government report estimated one out of four little girls and one out of ten boys are sexually abused as children![28] We've lost control."

"Whoa," Joseph said, obviously shocked by what I had just read. "That's horrible."

"It's painfully horrible," I said. "Those leading the Sexual Revolution thought they were tearing down obstructive walls around freedom, but it turns out they were tearing down protective walls—primarily around kids and families and marital security. We are a generation that has experienced a lot of pain directly and indirectly from tearing down these moral walls. We have freedom to have sex before marriage, but choosing this lesser freedom has cost us a greater freedom and a lot of pain. I have counseled so many women and men in their twenties or thirties who are still feeling the painful effects of sexual abuse. They don't just forget what happened, because sex is not just physical, it's emotional and spiritual as God designed."

I paused, feeling like maybe I had started hammering a little too hard. I noticed tears pooling in Tanya's large brown eyes. "Are you okay?" I asked her.

"Yeah, just give me a second," she said, grabbing a tissue off my desk to blot back the flow of pain. She sniffled as Joseph and I both sat waiting, feeling the tension in the air.

"As you were talking," Tanya began, "I just started picturing all the pain and hurt I've experienced since childhood . . . all because . . . ," she paused, but couldn't go on. Tanya covered her eyes with the tissue, and Joseph moved closer and put his hand on her back to reassure her. "I've just experienced so much pain. My father's affairs, all the confusion I've felt living with different guys but never seeming to get closer to what I really want. And I don't know how I keep getting myself back in this situation. Joseph and I are engaged, but we've got some real problems to work through."

Joseph tried to keep stroking Tanya's back, but slowly pulled his hand away, resting it on the arm of his chair, obviously feeling uncomfortable.

"Tanya, I'm sorry if I triggered some painful memories or if I got too worked up," I apologized.

"No, it's okay," Tanya answered, as she regained her composure. "It's something deep down I've known but don't like to think about. Maybe it's all connected somehow to these patterns I'm seeing. I just want to figure it all out and do it right for once."

"Listen, you're not alone," I said, hoping to comfort her. "And it's not too late. It's never too late with God. God is with you now, and he wants to help you both grow spiritually into the people he intended you to be. As he guides you in that, he will be preparing you for a lasting kind of love." I looked over at Joseph who was sitting in silence. "Joseph, you all right?"

"Yeah, I'm fine. I kind of feel like the bad guy for some reason," he admitted.

"Why do you feel like the bad guy?" I asked.

"I don't know. I guess I don't feel like I've tried to hurt anyone, but somehow I'm associated with all of that. Does that make sense?"

"I think I understand," I offered. "Look, the truth is we all screw up. We all go our way more than God's way and hurt others and ourselves. That's why Jesus died on the cross in our place. So we can know that God doesn't stand ready to condemn, but to forgive and to do life with us—to grow us up into the people he intended. That's why he wants us to listen and follow him with our sexuality. When we honor God, it protects others and us from pains we never think statistically will happen to us. And we may avoid being a statistic, but we all contribute to society's greater pain when we ignore God's will. That's the lesson of the Old Testament—sin affects the whole community, even if we don't realize it."

"I guess I see that and I feel bad." Joseph replied.

"Well just remember, you stand forgiven," I reminded him. "God's grace allows us to learn from our mistakes and grow with his guidance. His design for our sexuality is not just for our protection but to provide what we really want."

"So what can we do positively?" Joseph asked.

"Let's shift gears," I said, "and talk about how to move forward from here. I find the most important place to start is with your thinking. You have to train your mind for mental monogamy. The problem is that we've been training our minds to think about sex in detrimental ways."

Training for Mental Monogamy

"God wants to train us to have patience, control, and a committed view of sexual love, so we can build emotional intimacy—which is 80 percent of great sex. When guys use sex to prove their manhood or just for a 'feel good' fix, they're training themselves to view sex only as a means of self-gratification. That's the opposite of what our mindset needs to be for growing marital contentment and satisfaction.

"Sometimes women use sex to keep a guy around or to have some control and power in the relationship. But this too is manipulative—it's about using sex to get her needs met rather than a giving of herself in trusting, lifelong commitment. When we train our minds to use sex for self-centered needs, it backfires on us in marriage, which is probably why the majority of all married couples today are not satisfied with their sexual relationship.[29]

"When we have sex with multiple partners or when we use pornography to sexually stimulate ourselves, we train our minds to be discontent with just one person. So what happens when you find that special person, get married, and it's the same person in the same bed every night? You become discontent and critical, killing the intimacy God planned for you. When you consider how society has trained us to think about sex, it's not surprising that nearly half of all marriages have suffered an affair and the isolating, devastating consequences."[30]

"That many people really cheat on their spouse?" Joseph asked astonished.

"I can believe it," Tanya added, "just looking at my own family and the people I work around. Office flings happen all the time."

"I guess I never thought about it happening when I got married," Joseph admitted.

"Nobody thinks any bad consequences will come their way, which is why so many keep doing what feels right in the moment. But learning mental monogamy right now is the best prevention against these future pains," I said.

"Well, we've screwed up pretty badly. Where do we go from here?" Joseph asked.

"It's never too late to start honoring God," I said, "and you'd be surprised at the healing and wholeness he can restore if you're willing. God has great compassion regardless of your past, and willingness is all he needs. Jesus was once confronted by an angry mob of religious leaders who caught a woman in the act of adultery. So they brought her to Jesus to test him, asking if they should stone her to death since she was guilty. Jesus said, 'Whoever has no sin throw the first stone.' After they dropped their rocks and left, he looked at her and said, 'I don't condemn you, go and sin no more.'

"I'm feeling like I still took a few hits," Joseph said honestly.

"Well, you guys are not alone," I assured them, "and I know many who have taken steps toward honoring God's will and seen great benefit. Decide today to start honoring God and yourselves with your sexuality. Make a plan to move out and agree to put protective boundaries up so you can reserve sex for your marriage, from this day forward. Work on emotional and spiritual intimacy, and ask God to begin developing mental monogamy in your attitude toward sex. When you start thinking sexual thoughts, catch them, and immediately open the windows of your mind and let God's light in. Just say, 'Lord, look at what I'm thinking. Where's this going? Will this give me what I really want? Show me where it will lead me.' And then you flip over to the positive. Start thinking about what you really want. 'God, I want great sex—I want sex connected to deep, intimate love. I want to be able to be married and be content. I want to be mentally faithful to my spouse. I want sexual wholeness.' Affirm what God wants for you and what you really want, and watch what happens. God will retrain your thought processes toward mental monogamy."

Joseph and Tanya struggled with the decision for another six weeks and then finally agreed to save sex for marriage and moved into separate houses until the wedding. I find that when most couples realize it's in their best interest and that God is trying to protect and provide something better, they are willing to honor God. Sometimes I find I have to move into increasing confrontation as people grow spiritually but remain unresponsive in this area. But I can't tell you the number of couples at Gateway who have come in living together or sexually active, have come to faith, and have moved into God-honoring relating patterns.

As you listen to a couple's story to understand their spiritual trajectory, make sure they are rightly related to Christ before trying to force moral conformity. Seek to help them move forward by encouraging them and teaching the personal and social value of mental monogamy. Organize premarital events, men's and women's groups or seminars, and provide materials and resources to help educate people, so they understand *why* God's ways work to give them lasting sexual and marital intimacy. Create a culture for sexual wholeness, and you'll see God's Spirit change hearts and heal lives.

In our sex-crazed culture, sometimes sex becomes an addiction—one among many addictions that a leader must be prepared to face when reaching a broken generation. How do you create a culture for healing an addicted generation? That's what we will discuss next.

STUDY GUIDE

Culture Check

1. Do you think your church culture would welcome a cohabitating couple who were seeking, or does your culture expect even those who are not Christians to morally approximate the gospel? How could you change that?
2. Do you teach about sex and help people understand why God's wisdom works for long-term marital intimacy? If not, why not? Can the church be silent on the most talked about, watched, and exploited subject of our culture?
3. What's your plan for helping people involved in premarital sex, or married people still mentally trained by a broken view of sex, to move toward mental monogamy and the restoration of the mystery and wonder of sexual intimacy?

Small Group Questions

You may want to have men and women sub-group for discussion.

1. How did you learn to think about sex growing up? How did that view differ from God's design? How was it in line with God's design?
2. What struggles does our society face because of the training about sex we receive through the media and elsewhere?
3. What struggles do you face with sexuality and/or mental monogamy (i.e. thinking of sex only in positive, marriage-centered ways as opposed to fantasy with others)? What is the greatest source of your struggle?
4. What are some ways we can re-train our minds to view sex in positive, God honoring ways?
5. What are some ways we can help each other grow spiritually in this area?

chapter 13

Recovering an Addicted Generation: Creating a Culture of Healing

You broke the bonds
and you loosed the chains
Carried the cross of my shame

U2, "I Still Haven't Found What I'm Looking For"

You know, Martha, I've been very successful in life by all outward standards. Most all of the goals I set for myself I reached. We've had a great life materially. But I'd give it all back . . ." His voice started to crack as I witnessed one of the few tears I'd ever seen in my father's eyes. ". . . I'd give it all back if I could just have my health and my family."

We were visiting my father at M. D. Anderson Hospital, the premier cancer treatment center in Houston. Over an agonizing year and a half I had watched my father slowly atrophy to the point of needing help just to roll over in bed. The man who represented the pinnacle of strength and ability in my teenage mind had been stripped of everything by a smoking addiction that would soon claim his life at the age of forty-seven.

When I think back on the many Sundays I sat in church next to my father as a child, listening to theological musings that somehow flew right over the gritty reality of the addictions my father fought alone, I just get angry. How could our family have played church for so long with so little real impact on everyday struggles? Maybe that's why I left the church as soon as I was old enough to rebel.

I'm convinced addiction is the hidden secret in the church today. It's everywhere, but we hide it well. I long for Christ's community to be a place of healing for people like my father—whose deep wounds, inflicted by his own father's brokenness, fueled the addictive behaviors that robbed him of peace and drove him to an early grave.

In a generation spawned in brokenness—broken families, broken childhoods, broken lives—addictions rule! The current generation struggles with addictive behaviors more than any previous generation this century, yet I fear the church is caught flatfooted, not really knowing how to respond.

Jesus went to a party that Matthew threw for his tax-collector friends—the reprobates of society. So the religious leaders asked Jesus' followers: 'Why does he eat with tax collectors and "sinners"?' On hearing this, Jesus said to them, 'It is not the healthy who need a doctor, but the sick. I have not come to call the righteous, but sinners.'[1] I think Jesus' sarcasm gets missed. The religious leaders were far from righteous—they would soon crucify him. His point? He came for all who *realized* they needed help.

Addictions drive people into a state of absolute helplessness, a state Jesus referred to as spiritual poverty.[2] And he called it a "blessed" state to be in—why? Because it cracks our shells of denial (in which we all tend to hide) and forces us to recognize our deep dependence on God. But isn't it ironic that those so close to this "blessed" condition, in need of grace and truth, would not be welcome in church groups?

John Townsend tells of consulting for a large Christian organization about small groups when one of the executives asked him, "What difference do you see between groups for people with problems and groups for normal people?"[3] Reflecting on this encounter, Townsend points out how blind church leaders can be to our own neediness and brokenness (there *are* no perfect people). The Bible indicates we are all in this abnormal broken state of trying to "play God," and as the parable of the Pharisee and tax collector indicates—the only *real* difference between us is whether we recognize it or deny it.[4]

There are two extremes the emerging church must avoid to create a culture for healing our addicted generation. First, we must not force those with addictions into hiding from God and running from the church community as happened in the past century with alcoholics—they need God and they need community *before* they get better.

But we also cannot just invite them in and hope for healing. We must be prepared with groups and programs or know of outside resources available to help set free those enslaved to addictions.

The Roots of Recovery

When you understand the history and principles of the Twelve Steps, you realize how God will use recovery as a tutor so that through an understanding church, people can truly know the God revealed in Jesus. Though many Christian churches have looked down on the Twelve Steps because they do not directly acknowledge Jesus, the Steps have more in common with Christianity than most realize. One of the most common criticisms made of the Twelve Steps by non-Christians is that the Steps are entirely *too* Christian.[5]

In retrospect, it appears the recovery movement was an act of God's divine mercy when the church didn't know how to "fix" messy alcoholics and decided they weren't welcome until they could clean up their act. (Alcoholics in 1935 felt less than welcome in most churches.)

The Twelve Steps were devised in the recovery movement of the past century, but they're really as old as the Bible. In fact, Bill W., who wrote down the Steps, acknowledged that they came straight from the pastor of Calvary Church, Dr. Sam Shoemaker, who led Bill W. to faith in Christ through a small group called the Oxford Group.[6] Keith Miller has written an excellent book, *A Hunger*

The Twelve Steps of Alcoholics Anonymous

Step 1: We admitted we were powerless over alcohol—that our lives had become unmanageable.

Step 2: Came to believe that a Power greater than ourselves could restore us to sanity.

Step 3: Made a decision to turn our will and our lives over to the care of God as we understood him.

Step 4: Made a searching and fearless moral inventory of ourselves.

Step 5: Admitted to God, to ourselves, and to another human being the exact nature of our wrongs.

Step 6: Were entirely ready to have God remove all these defects of character.

Step 7: Humbly asked him to remove our shortcomings.

Step 8: Made a list of all persons we had harmed, and became willing to make amends to them all.

Step 9: Made direct amends to such people wherever possible, except when to do so would injure them or others.

Step 10: Continued to take personal inventory and, when we were wrong, promptly admitted it.

Step 11: Sought through prayer and meditation to improve our conscious contact with God as we understood him, praying only for knowledge of his will and the power to carry it out.

Step 12: Having had a spiritual awakening as the result of these steps, we tried to carry this message to alcoholics and to practice these principles in all our affairs.

Reprinted with permission of Alcoholics Anonymous World Services, Inc.

for Healing: The Twelve Steps as a Classic Model for Christian Spiritual Growth. In it he shows how the Steps are simply biblical spiritual disciplines that allow the God of mercy and grace to live his life in and through us.

Just as God heard the prayers of a Roman soldier, Cornelius, and led him to Peter to learn that the God he worshiped sent Jesus for his sake, we have seen many people in recovery find faith in Christ. We acknowledge God's work in their lives and simply point out to them that the God who healed them wants them to know him personally and know why he's so forgiving and merciful. Maybe God wants to teach his emerging church what Peter realized that day with Cornelius: "I see very clearly that God doesn't show partiality. In every nation he accepts those who fear him and do what is right."[7]

Not Far From the Kingdom of God

I grabbed a cup of coffee and reviewed what I had learned about the Steps while I waited for Karla and Greg. Steps 1 through 3 are all about restoring relationship with God, Steps 4 through 7 focus on restoring a rigorously honest relationship with self, and Steps 9 through 12 work on restoring relationship with others. We were meeting for premarital counseling, but I also knew neither of them were Christ-followers, both had been divorced, and they had lived together for four years.

It was our third meeting when Karla's past Step work showed through in her rigorous honesty with me. I had taken out a Bible and read from 1 John 4:7–9 about all love coming from God.

"I have to be honest," Karla said apologetically, "It's freakin' me out to have you read from the Bible and talk about Jesus. I'm having a hard time concentrating."

"I'm sorry," I said, "Why does that freak you out?"

"I don't know. Probably what was pounded into my head by my father. He was a professor of physics and a devout atheist, so even reading from the Bible gives me the heebie-geebies."

"You told me you believe in God, right?" I clarified. "When you think of God, who do you picture?"

"I don't know. I guess somebody who really cares and is loving and kind. Someone powerful because I sure needed power I didn't have to get sober ... and someone honest. That's a big part of recovery, getting past blaming and covering and learning to speak truthfully."

"You know, Karla, you just described the God of Jesus," I ventured. "I believe God has done something amazing in your life and Greg's life, and I really don't think it's any coincidence that you came to Gateway or that we're here talking. The God who rescued you from addiction did it because he loves you, and he wants you to know him better. He wants you to know, like that verse I just read points out, that he loves you so much there's nothing he wouldn't do for you. The reason he is so merciful and patient and willing to forgive all our shortcomings is *because* of what Jesus did for us. Jesus came to both show us what God is like relationally and to give us the reason we can have confidence he won't condemn us. And as it says, he wants to show you how to really live. You've already started to see that, right? The freedom of turning your will and life into his care?"

"Yeah, it's amazing," Karla said looking out the window. "You know, I think I just need to get over it and learn more. I don't think it's a coincidence either."

"Just keep an open mind," I suggested, "and I think you'll discover that a lot of your fears about Jesus are unfounded."

■ ■ ■

Greg and Karla got in a small group and started reading the Bible and other books explaining Christian principles of recovery. Six months later both were baptized, professing their belief in Jesus as the one who saved them— from addiction and from life without God. I'm convinced that the God of all mercy had been at work for years through their recovery, even though, like Cornelius and the Ethiopian eunuch,[8] they did not understand their Creator's identity at the time. And acknowledging the validity of God's work of healing opened the door for complete confidence in relationship with Christ. Our ability to speak the language of recovery, understand its biblical roots, and point people onward toward God's full revelation in Christ will pay huge dividends in the emerging church culture.

A Path for Healing

Not only must the emerging church and emerging small groups be a next step for Twelve-Steppers to know God better, we must be a place of healing as well. Many people come to church to find freedom. They hear they must be saved by praying the "sinner's prayer," accepting God's forgiveness offered in Christ. They do it and get baptized. Often they are led (or misled) to believe their problems will immediately disappear. True healing, however, often requires a lengthy process of righting the wrongs and uncovering the lies of the past. God can heal us immediately, but more often he takes us along a difficult path that forces us to continually depend on him, because only in him do we find true life. If he immediately healed us, we would immediately turn back to our independent, self-centered ways.

Unless churches and small groups address these very real struggles and give encouragement and spiritual direction to people suffering from addiction, compulsive behaviors, or abuse, they will soon feel they don't fit, or worse, that their faith didn't work since they still struggle. If self-defeating behavior is denied, ignored, or minimized, then our religion has become a shield to hide from life's realities, and we've missed our calling as a healing force in the world.

Cycle of Addiction

The apostle Paul reminds us, "Even though 'I am allowed to do anything,' I must not become a slave to anything."[9] For the church to have a healing influence, it must understand the slavery of addiction. Just telling people it's immoral or wrong won't set them free—we need to create the right cultural context for healing. Our generation struggles with addictions to alcohol, drugs, pornography, tobacco, spending, sex, eating, working, dieting, and gambling to escape the pain of brokenness. Extrapolating the statistics, it appears that potentially half of early twenty-somethings today struggle with some addiction.[10] Gerald May, in his book *Addiction and Grace*, defines addiction as "any compulsive, habitual behavior that limits the freedom of human desire."[11] May goes on to explain five essential characteristics that mark true addiction. They are:

- Increasing toleration—always wanting or needing more to feel satisfied.
- Withdrawal symptoms—negative reactions to the removal of the addictive behavior.
- Self-deception—mental defense mechanisms such as denial and rationalization invented to counter attempts to control the addiction.
- Loss of willpower—an inability to conquer the addiction despite the illusion of control.
- Distortion of attention—a preoccupation with the addiction that usurps our concern for the true priorities of life, especially God.[12]

Dr. Patrick Carnes notes that at the core most addictions are fed by a cycle of shame. "Addiction is much bigger than any specific compulsive behavior, because it can manifest itself in any number of ways and still be the same problem. If we compartmentalize addictions, we miss the core issue of shame."[13] Shame can be defined as feeling that "there's something unacceptable about me at the core" and yet still possessing a drive to "do it right" and prove "I am acceptable."

When children grow up in families that are both rigid and detached emotionally, addiction often follows.[14] They learn to ignore their needs for love, acceptance, and approval since they can never get these needs met no matter how hard they try. Yet the deep longing to have these God-given needs met doesn't ever go away. These needs keep reasserting themselves, and even as adults, they often feel they fail to live up to the standard of performance necessary to "earn" acceptance.

Eventually, they find relief from the pain by "acting out" in a way that is often extreme. Yet this acting out brings comfort because they temporarily feel "good" or "alive." Almost immediately, though, feelings of being horrible and unworthy follow. Once out of control, the addict tries to regain control by "acting in." So a smoker will ironically become a neat-freak, constantly cleaning house to feel clean and in control. Or an alcoholic might compulsively diet or save or work harder to feel better about himself. But this attempt to do better never relieves the isolation and disconnectedness shame creates, so the pain builds and builds. Like clockwork, he acts out again seeking relief, and around and around the karmic wheel of shame he goes.

This underlying cycle of shame gets broken only when grace meets truth in a person's life. When a person learns to take responsibility for her actions, only then can she put her life and will into the care of God who will love her and give her the power she needs to overcome.

But this act of surrender usually only comes when the pain becomes intense. Until the pain is severe, people who struggle find it very hard to look honestly at their harmful behavioral patterns because to them, admitting wrong means admitting "I'm unacceptable."

The Voice of Shame

"Robert, are you having sex with your girlfriend?" I asked. I had been meeting with Robert with the intent of developing him into a leader.

"We're intimate, but it's not getting out of control," Robert replied.

"What does that mean?" I probed for clarity, knowing what Robert had revealed to me about his past. Robert told me one day why he thought his first marriage had failed, confessing that he always gets sexual and then things move too fast. He grew up in a very perfectionistic, detached family, which caused him to stay emotionally detached from others. As a Christ-follower he told me he now wanted to enter relationships in a healthy way in the future and asked me to help him with this goal. Yet I sensed old addictive patterns overtaking him in this new relationship.

"A little petting, but that's all," he said with nervous laughter.

"Robert, you're going down the same old path you told me destroyed past relationships. This is not God's will for you. You need to stop and put up new boundaries immediately." I felt I needed to be frank.

"I'll pray about it," Robert said.

I had numerous conversations in the following weeks, finding out the petting included much more. The more I tried to remind Robert what he had confessed before about desiring to change, the more I sensed he didn't want to hear it. Finally I asked to meet with him.

"Robert, this isn't about you and me," I said after feeling resistance to my plea to back off the sexual intimacy. I read 1 Thessalonians 4:3 out loud about not defrauding others with sexual intimacy outside of marriage. Then I said, "Robert, this is God's command. It's not my opinion against yours. I love you and care about you, and that's why I hate to see you heading in a path I fear will destroy another relationship. But if you choose to continue, I can't let you lead others as long as you're unwilling to follow Christ in this area."

Suddenly Robert became extremely angry, cussing at me and telling me he wouldn't take any of my #%*&@. He threatened to leave the church. As I tried to talk to him, I realized what had happened. I sincerely believe to this day that when I explained to Robert why he couldn't be a leader, all he heard was his father's voice of shame. Robert heard, "You have let me down, you are bad, and you are no longer worth anything to me." No matter how hard I tried to tell Robert I loved him, that I thought he had tremendous potential, and that I wasn't giving up on him, all he felt was total rejection.

The voice of shame can be so strong, people need lots of love and support to be able to differentiate their compulsive acting-out from their worth as people. Communicating love for the person while speaking truth about the behavior can be very challenging, and you won't always succeed. Leaders must remember that changing people is not our job, creating culture for change is. When you walk through the stages of recovery with someone who *is* willing, the payoff for everybody is enormous.

For that reason, leaders must understand what enslaves people and the path to help set them free. Let's walk through the challenges of the three most prevalent addictions in our generation: drug and alcohol addiction, tobacco addiction, and sexual addiction.

Substance Abuse

The number of persons age twelve or older with substance dependence or abuse (alcohol or drugs) has increased from 6.5% of the population in 2000, to 7.3% in 2001, to 9.4% in 2002. But when it comes to twenty-somethings, that rate jumps closer to 20%.[15] If you want to reach emerging generations, one out of every five to ten people you interact with will struggle with alcohol or drug dependency. It's not just college drinking we're dealing with—cocaine use by young adults has gone from 1% during the sixties to 15% in 2002, and if you minister to young adults, nearly one out of four will have used a hallucinogen like Ecstasy.[16]

Of course, the challenge in all recovery is overcoming denial. The nature of addiction deceives us into thinking, "I can stop any time" or "It's not a serious problem because I'm still functioning fine." This is where speaking the truth in love comes in.

Too often, when we confront others, it is not done in care or concern for their well-being, but in anger because we have held back from speaking until we become fed up with the person. Confrontation about the problem then comes across as rejection of the person, often triggering his shame-induced fight-or-flight mechanism. Instead, we must learn to move in closer in love as we boldly speak words of truth at the Spirit's prompting. We must not forget to ask God to guide us to be his instruments, since he alone can break through with grace and truth.

Confronting in Love

"You know, honestly, I still drink but it's not a problem like it used to be," Mike confessed to the men in our small group.

When he said it, a warning light started flashing in my head, so I began to pray, "Lord, what do you want me to do?" Mike had opened his heart to Christ a year before, but I sensed he still struggled with his old demons. Mike was a manager with a lot of responsibility, so as long as he could perform at work, life was okay in his book. But I knew Mike had come out of a past of drug dependency and any regular drinking could easily ensnare him again.

"Mike, how much do you drink, honestly?" I probed, continuing to pray for God to shine his light on anything dark or deceptive.

Instead of reacting defensively, Mike got honest. "I probably have two or three beers every day, maybe more sometimes."

"How do you feel about that?" Larry asked.

"I don't know. It doesn't bother me." Mike sloughed it off.

To me, it felt like denial. But I didn't know how to lovingly confront it, so I kept praying as others talked. Then, like a flash, a scene from my past appeared in my mind, and I thought of Mike's fourth grade son. Suddenly I felt compelled to tell him my story.

"You know, when I was in middle school, my father would come home and have a few beers each night. It helped him relax, he said. The truth | 251 was, my father had a drinking dependency. I loved my dad more than I could imagine, but when he drank, he was a different person. He felt it made him loosen up and be more loving, but it made me want to puke. I'll never forget one night when my dad came home, and I had been looking forward to hanging out with him, but he decided to 'run to the store.' My mom begged him not to get beer, but he came home with a six-pack and polished it off. After my dad went to bed early, I told my mom, 'You know, Mom, if Dad were to die, and I had to write a book about him—I'd have to write two books. One I would call, *My Dad, My Greatest Hero*. It would be about a father who is the most loving, wonderful man in the world. The other book would be called, *My Dad, the Drunk*, and it would be about this man I don't like very much. And right now, I'm not sure which book would be longer.' My mom woke my dad up to tell him what I said, and that night he decided he had to quit drinking completely. I'm so glad he did, because I only had four more years with him—and they were the best years of my life with my dad."

Mike sat there staring straight ahead, almost in a daze. He didn't say much after that, and neither did I (assuming my point was missed). The group continued on. The next day Mike called me.

"I don't know what happened last night, but as you were telling me that story, I felt a kind of tingling all over my body—it was like the words were piercing into my soul—I was almost shaking. I knew God was telling me I have to quit. I don't want to do that to my son. I want to be a father he'll remember and be proud of."

God broke through his denial. Mike admitted his powerlessness and decided to seek help. Since then, he has stopped drinking and has grown tremendously in his knowledge of God's Word, studying it voraciously. He now helps in our recovery ministry.

Denial

Denial doesn't often crack as easily as it did for Mike that night. Oftentimes, the addict must come to the end of himself, and that usually happens only through a tremendous amount of pain. Christians often look at pain as bad—something we must always pray each other out of or help fix. But sometimes pain can be a friend if it drives us to the end of ourselves and into the arms of God. This means leaders must become comfortable letting people go through painful consequences at times. We can express sadness for the pain they are going through, and lovingly support them, yet firmly point out truth about their behavior. Only then can we walk supportively with them when they're willing to get help.

One of the greatest challenges with getting people into recovery has to do with the deceptive nature of addiction. On the one hand, the person has no power over the addiction, but on the other hand, her unwillingness to admit she's powerless keeps her stuck. Most addicts will try to avoid recovery meetings because pride tells them, "I'm not one of *them*." In other words, there's this judgmental stigma placed on "those people" who go to recovery meetings, even by those who are just as powerless.

So the church can be a starting point for recovery if we create a safe environment where people can admit brokenness. Sometimes it requires intervention by friends or leaders to help a person see she is powerless and needs to get over her false pride of not being one of "them." Yet the church usually cannot provide the level of support 24/7 that recovery from substance abuse requires in the first ninety days (daily meetings and accountability during this ninety-day phase produces the best results).

There is also the need for a sponsor who has been through recovery. If a church does not have the resources for a full-blown recovery program, it's best not to try to take the place of recovery groups. Instead, provide referrals and Christ-centered support for spiritual growth that gets people into recovery and then beyond recovery. But to get people started, leaders must assume addictions exist and creatively find ways to bring people out of hiding.

A Confessing Culture

"I need to confess something, though I really don't want to." Dave sat staring at his feet, ashamed.

Dave, Peter, and I were in a corner of the room, huddled up during our Leadership Community meeting—our monthly meeting with all the serving team and small group leaders of our church. Our staff had prayed about what our leaders needed, and the consensus had been to talk about the need for open confession. We realized that over time, leaders often feel forced to be incongruent—to pretend.

So I read from the passage in James where he tells us to confess our sins to one another so we may be healed. I confessed publicly, "I see workaholic tendencies creeping back into my life. I hate what I see it doing to my family. I'm convinced the stress level I put on myself is against God's will for me, yet I tend to make excuses and deny it."

Then I had us all break up into groups of three or four and get as honest and open as we could and pray for healing for each other. It felt very risky, but on the other hand, to not intercept the tendency leaders have to hide their struggles felt like a greater risk.

"I still smoke pot," Dave admitted. "I've been doing it on and off for nearly eighteen years now, since I was a teenager. I know it's not what God wants."

Dave and his wife had both come to faith in Christ over the three years of attending Gateway. They both grew in knowledge and zeal for God at a rapid rate in their small group. Together, they had recently started leading a group of their own. Dave had lied on his leadership application about having any addictions because he thought, "I'm not like people who go to AA meetings. I just do it to relax, but it doesn't affect my behavior." Dave's bold confession had been prompted by Pete's own admission of secret struggles with watching sexually explicit shows on cable and the Internet.

Dave realized he needed to step back from leadership and do some work—he was telling others to be honest, yet he was living a dual life. He and Pete began meeting as running partners to help each other, and Dave got into counseling. But still, there was resistance to get into recovery. So the addiction continued.

As Dave recalls, "I just didn't see myself as one of 'those people' in AA meetings. It still felt manageable to me." Finally, the denial broke. His wife confronted him that pot was the center of his world—what he depended on to relieve stress and to not have to deal with real life. It cut him to the core.

Then one day not long after, as he was driving along he noticed a bud of pot on the floor of his car. "I pulled over and picked it up," Dave recalls, "and the thought came, 'I've got to save this little nugget.' When I heard myself say those words, I realized 'this is my god.' Marijuana is the most precious thing, like a nugget of gold. I'm worshiping pot!"

Dave went to a friend who had been through recovery and told him. The friend asked, "Do you want to be free of this addiction?"

"I do, but I'm afraid," Dave admitted. "I'm afraid of failing, and I'm embarrassed that I need help. I'm embarrassed to admit openly that I lied to the church staff, and I've lived a lie with my small group."

The friend started talking about grace. Dave had accepted God's grace through Christ and been baptized, and he had read Philip Yancey's book about grace. "But that day, I experienced grace specifically. Feeling so fallen, yet still loved. It was like a spiritual awakening for me," Dave recalls.

"How do I do it?" Dave asked his friend. "How do I recover?"

"First, just say it. Say, 'I'm in recovery from my addiction to marijuana.'" Dave said it out loud and they prayed. Dave's friend went with him to his first recovery meeting.

"I needed constant accountability from those who had been there," Dave recalls. "The first ninety days is the hardest part, and I had to attend lots of meetings and have a sponsor to call 24/7 who could help me apply the Twelve Steps in the moment."

Today Dave lives clean and honest. It started with loving confrontation in the context of grace, but only when denial cracked could he get the level of support he truly needed to recover. Dave now sponsors others in Gateway still struggling with not wanting to be "one of them" but starting to see the light.

I am aware of the messiness and fear this story may cause for some. The truth is, if we are reaching the broader culture around us and helping them become the leaders of tomorrow, like Peter, James, and John, they too may fall. If Jesus' disciples struggled, what makes us think our leaders-to-be won't struggle? But as we walk in the light together, the blood of Jesus cleanses us and like Peter, we too can become the rocks on which he builds his church.

Tobacco Addictions

If your church or group reaches the broader culture, you will deal with many people addicted to tobacco. According to the Department of Health, 30% of all Americans age twelve and older used tobacco during the previous month. But among young twenty-somethings (where the rate peaks drastically), tobacco use jumps to nearly 45%.[17]

This means one out of two or three people you reach could struggle with a substance that the Surgeon General declared was as difficult to quit as cocaine or heroin for many users.[18] Nicotine is a narcotic drug that elevates blood pressure and combines with certain chemicals in the brain to enhance feelings of pleasure. Other narcotics such as heroin and crack have identical effects in the brain. The addictive nature of tobacco enslaves many people as it slowly destroys their lives. Currently it is the number one cause of all preventable deaths in America.[19]

So how has the church helped addicts? I may be wrong, but it appears we have either made it clear that if you smoke, you're bad and not welcome here, or we've just ignored it. Instead, we need to provide both the grace and the truth along with spiritual direction and support that people need to overcome their addictions. Unfortunately, our culture does not provide the same support systems necessary for recovery of nicotine addiction that it does for substance abuse, yet it requires a more concentrated effort to stop smoking since it's so socially acceptable and equally as enslaving.

The sad reality is that most smokers want to stop. A study conducted by the Centers for Disease Control found that 70% of smokers want to quit.[20]

So how do we provide the right culture where the church can truly help? Kent and Larry provide some needed insights.

Kent grew up in a church where you would often see people standing around smoking after the service, elders included. It was acceptable behavior. "I never thought there was anything wrong with it until coming to Gateway," Kent confides. "I knew it was bad for my health, but I had already had cancer in my twenties, and I had smoked right through treatment, almost to prove I could laugh in the face of cancer and defeat it. I felt undefeatable. It was actually in Gateway's financial seminar that I saw it for what it was. The guy said that whatever we spent money on indicated our priorities. When I looked at my cigarette and alcohol budget, I realized it equaled a car payment. It forced me to see how important it was to me, and I started to realize I had an addiction."

Larry did not become a Christian until coming to Gateway and had smoked years prior. "If I had felt like people were judging me and looking down their noses because I smoked, I never would have stuck around to come to faith in Christ," Larry admits.

During our series on the Twelve Steps to Spiritual Growth, when we taught on the biblical underpinnings of the Steps, Kent and Larry started meeting as running partners to help each other quit. They shared, "We were shocked when we looked for Christian resources to help quit smoking—we found very little. Most people said they just lump smokers in with AA groups. The problem is, most AA meetings are filled with people smoking. And if you told a smoker to get in a Twelve Step group, he will probably balk because he doesn't want to be viewed as having a problem with alcohol or drugs."

"There's not really anything you can tell a smoker that he hasn't already heard," Larry said. "He knows it's nasty, unhealthy, expensive, and addictive. But if you tell him that, it will probably just annoy him unless he's really ready to quit." But as Kent and Larry met together, they voiced things about their struggle that gave new insights.

"I wanted to quit smoking to be closer to God," Kent said. "But I didn't want help. I wanted to do it cold turkey. I wanted to overcome it on my own. What I really realized is that I didn't want to let God help. I wanted to do it on my own because then I could maintain some control . . . just in case I decided to go back to it."

"When you quit smoking," Larry said, "it creates an incredibly painful, stressful experience. Smokers think they need to smoke to relieve the stress; the truth is that smoking causes the stress. But when you're quitting, those around you get the brunt of your impatience. I stopped smoking for five days, and my chest felt so tight I thought it would cave in. People don't understand how hard it is to quit."

■ ■ ■

It seems the best thing the church can do is help smokers grow spiritually and let them know that God desires that nothing enslave them. I challenge people to ask God, "Is there anything in my life keeping me from experiencing your life? Give me willingness to trust you with it." I find if someone is willing to ask God sincerely, he always will show her, and she will be more willing to let him remove it. Providing examples of others who have quit also helps smokers know quitting is possible (and may provide a sponsor). Finally, we can offer ongoing smokers' recovery programs based on a Christ-centered version of the Twelve Steps, so that people know where to go and what to do when they're truly ready to stop.[21] Tobacco addiction cannot be treated as a milder addiction just because it's more socially acceptable.

Sexual Addictions

It was 5:20 and I was still at my desk. I knew I was supposed to be home, and I would have hell to pay, but I had to look at one more picture. I knew the next image would be the perfect one. The one that really let the endorphins flow. I'd been saying this to myself for the last half hour. What was I doing looking at porn at work? I had a great job as an engineer; I could lose everything if caught. It didn't matter though, all that mattered was the adrenaline rush of the lust — the risk only increased the excitement. The addiction brought powerful shame, which made the highs really high and the lows really low. The only guarantee it brought was the internal isolation and the promise ... I'd do it again.

—Randy

With the rise of the Internet, sexual addictions spurred by pornography or chat-room fantasy will likely grow. A nationwide survey of 1,031 adults conducted by Zogby International found that 20% of the respondents admitted visiting a sexually oriented website, but that jumps to 37% for males in their early twenties.[22] Although this does not represent the rate of sexual addiction (around 10% currently for all ages[23]), it does uncover the growing problems to come in the emerging church—especially when studies show that nearly 70% of teens, and many untended children, have been exposed to pornography while searching on the Internet.[24] Already annual rentals and sales of adult videos and DVDs top $4 billion, and the industry produces twenty times as many titles a year as Hollywood.[25]

And it's not just males affected, Christian psychologist Mark Laaser points out:

It's abundantly clear that sexual addiction does not discriminate with respect to gender. It's an equal opportunity addiction. Two weeks ago we did the first intensive workshop that I'm aware of in the Christian community for female sex addicts. The women who came had essentially the same kinds of problems which male sex addicts experience—problems with pornography, compulsive masturbation, multiple affairs and so on.[26]

Today, cybersex activities include not only viewing pornography but also meeting in sexually oriented chat rooms, and having interactive online affairs with real-time video. People will do things online they would never do in the "real" world, not realizing the destructive addiction cybersexual fantasy often creates.

The Feelings of Addiction

Most all addicts try to escape or medicate unwanted feelings. The recovery movement wisely realized that making amends with broken relationships of the past (Steps 8 and 9) yielded powerful release from the need to escape. With sexual addiction, it is even more of an issue. According to recent research, 81% of sex addicts were sexually abused in the past, and 97% experienced emotional abuse growing up.[27] This does not take away responsibility for their actions, but often these unresolved relational pains drive them. Because sex addicts can't tolerate painful emotional feelings, they seek to escape the feelings through sexual activity.

Research has shown that sexual activity and sexual fantasy physically alters brain chemistry. Peptides such as endorphins get released from sexual stimulation. These peptides parallel the molecular construction of opiates like morphine, but are many times more powerful.[28] When sex or pornography moves toward an addiction, the person uses sexual stimuli to temporarily alter brain chemistry, and thereby their mood. The craving for the feeling crescendos into an obsession, until the addict has a mind constantly occupied with sexual fantasy, driven to find the next high.

One of the main ways the church can help our sex-crazed culture is to begin to help people understand that lust and fantasy and pornography are just imposters of the real thing they desire. Shaming people for their sexual behavior does not help—it drives them into hiding. What helps is when they realize what it takes to get what they really want—a lasting, truly loving, faithful marriage relationship where sex is a loving, satisfying part of a holistic, intimate relationship.

So we must teach them that contrary to popular opinion which says "no harm, no foul" in fantasy, it actually trains us in ways that keep us from the ability to enter into a growing, fulfilling sexual relationship in a marriage. And for singles or marrieds, fantasy actually decreases contentment and inhibits relational intimacy. Pornography trains a person's mind to need a constantly changing image, person, or position to gain that sexual-stimulus high. As I said in the last chapter, we are a generation training ourselves to be discontent and unsatisfied with one partner for life.

Leaders in the emerging church must also realize that just saying, "That's morally wrong—stop it," isn't enough to help people break free. Lust is wrong and they need to know it, but they also need to know that God's vision for sexual wholeness gets them what they truly want. Knowing the moral law by itself, without God's gracious power, will merely drive addicts deeper into acting out as they feel worse and worse about themselves.

Mark Laaser, psychologist and author of the book *Healing the Wounds of Sexual Addiction,* talks about his own story in the church.

> When I came into recovery I was a minister. I'd been saved since I was a child and I felt like I had surrendered my life to God. But as I look back on it, some of the spiritual stuff that I was doing was an attempt to try to manipulate God. One of the things I desperately wanted God to do was to remove all [temptation to lust]. I wanted God to take away the problem completely so that I'd never have to struggle with it again. And I became angry with God that he wouldn't do that. That's part of the nature of the spiritual problem. Many addicts when they come to the Lord have an agenda for what they want the Lord to do. That's why the first step is to admit that I have no control over my life, or over God or over my addiction.[29]

Maybe the best thing leaders can do for those struggling in this area is create a safe place to talk about these struggles. Ask the hard questions through your messages or small group times that force strugglers to see that they are out of control and powerless to stop. (For example, if you have a regular habit or repeating pattern but don't think it's a problem, stop for thirty days. If you can't, or won't, what does that tell you?) Then, as we provide support groups and resources, when the light breaks through, people can get the help needed to work toward recovery.

Stages of Recovery

The stages of recovery can be very similar for every addiction. Randy came to Gateway as an agnostic, in the first stages of recovery. Today as a Christ-follower, he helps others struggling with sexual addictions. Listen as Randy describes his experience and gives suggestions of ways to support others through each stage.

My Denial

In counseling, I started tracing back to how I spiraled down so low. Pornography and addiction to masturbation had been a pattern in my life since early childhood. My first sexual experience was in late high school, but in college I began going to strip bars. Sexual fantasy had been a part of my life since puberty, so I just thought it was a normal guy thing. I figured once I got married, that would cure my lustful desires—how wrong I was. I never understood that lust and sex are two different things.

When my wife told me she thought masturbation was sick and if I ever did it she'd leave me, I felt tons of shame and vowed to stop, but it only got worse. My counselor later told me sex addicts usually have a capacity for intimacy of three on a scale of ten. I thought I was so intimate, yet I was emotionally isolated from my wife and even my friends—no one knew my secret.

I continued to feed my lust with pornography even after marriage. Then one night, I picked up a hitchhiker who turned out to be a prostitute. The shame of what I did was unbearable. It drove me deeper into isolation and made my marriage more tumultuous. I knew I'd crossed a line. The fear of injury, arrest, disease, and discovery kept me from acting out this way for quite a few years. I would have been better off if one of those had happened so I'd break my denial, but the addiction was still in control. It took me six more years and several more affairs before my addiction would take me to the edge and cost me everything.

You can tell that people are in the denial acting-out phase if they are defensive and tend to joke away their behavior. Though my wife was willing to go to counseling after the affairs, I would say, "I'm not going to masturbator's anonymous." I would blame my acting out on her lack of sexual expression. I would redirect conversations to focus on other people's "worse" behaviors. All of these are expressions of denial. The best thing you can do in this stage is let addicts hear your own story of brokenness before God even if in some other area of struggle. Creating a grace-filled environment where people are getting ruthlessly honest allows an addict to crack through the denial.

Totally Broken

Six years later . . . one night after a wedding, I was drinking and met a girl at a bar. I didn't come home until 7:00 a.m. I left my wife and one-year-old daughter four days later. The next six months of acting-out were hell. I'd finally hit bottom the day I pushed my wife out of my office. Life was out of control. I was suicidal and I couldn't take any more. My wife and daughter deserved better, and I had to do something to change. I agreed to start real counseling.

After our first counseling session, I had a sense of relief. I vowed to never act-out with another woman again. Less than twenty-eight hours later, I got a call from a woman I'd met a couple weeks before. Separated from my wife, I held out as long as I could, then decided one drink wouldn't hurt. She left early the next morning—Thanksgiving Day—leaving me with nothing to be thankful about. I felt nothing but pain. This was the third woman I'd committed adultery with in six months. "What's wrong with me?" I thought. "I have a beautiful wife and baby girl, and I've lost it all for nothing." It took that much pain to seek the help I needed. I went to my first SA (Sexaholics Anonymous) meeting two days later. It was so hard to think of myself as a well-respected professional in my career, and then sit among sex addicts sharing how powerless they were with sex, pornography, and masturbation. I felt shame, confusion, and association as I heard pieces of my story told over and over.

Over the next thirty days, I understood why one Twelve-Stepper called sexual addictions the Vietnam of addictions. I found myself shaking, craving orgasm, and filled with uncontrollable fantasies continually. My sponsor told me, "I don't know how it works, but just ask God to remove your sexually compulsive thoughts. Repeat it as many times as you need to." I started a continuous chant to this God I didn't even believe in. Later, I realized I'd been thinking about something else—a small miracle.

It took constant support those first ninety days. I remember five weeks into it, feeling released, like the addiction broke. I remember thinking, "Oh my, this is how normal people think." The people there around me loved me when I could not love myself, and they asked for nothing in return.

This is what the church must be for addicts. In this broken stage, I could not handle the thought of anything related to more condemnation, judgment, or punishment. Embedded in my psyche was a strong guard against Christians, symbols of the cross, discussions of the devil, even certain words like sin, Satan, heaven or hell. I had already condemned myself to hell and I wanted a way out. I knew trying harder was not an option. My sponsor once asked me to write down everything I was taught to believe about God or my father's role in the family. Then on the other side of the page, he had me write down all I wanted to believe about God. Looking back, I see that I had a very distorted view of God due to my family and prior religious misconceptions, and ironically, what I was looking for is what I found in Christ. I decided to learn more about God . . . that's when I came to Gateway.

Seeking

I got in a men's small group. Through this experience, I realized it was okay to pray out loud, to ask questions and challenge Scripture, and I found other men outside recovery who would be vulnerable as Christians. Six of the seven men in my group struggled with sexually compulsive behavior, and we talked openly and prayed for each other. I was able to share insights from my other recovery group. For me, fear of never being good enough because of my sexual sins and the idea of Christ being the only way were huge impediments to becoming a Christian. But after being in the small group and actually learning to soak in God's love and acceptance, then reading *Mere Christianity*, I opened my heart to Christ and got baptized.

In this stage, addicts are looking for new possibilities in life. They need to be encouraged to seek truth. I was told to pray for truth, and as I did, I found greater and greater freedom. I began to long to explore and study about spiritual growth. I was hungry.

Giving

I now sponsor others who seek recovery. Once you've had such a life-changing spiritual awakening, Step 12 says you need to take the message to others. As you do, you find it accelerates your spiritual growth as well. In this stage, a person needs to be put into service to others. Addiction is a very self-centered pursuit, so giving to others and helping others find faith and find recovery is the most healthy way for people to stay out of the addiction.

We must remember that all addictions share common roots and common solutions regardless of outward expression. Although substance abuse, nicotine, and sexual addictions are the most prevalent, a broken generation will struggle with many compulsive behaviors that follow similar patterns. Eating disorders, gambling, and compulsive spending are three other compulsive behaviors that seem to be on the rise, which the emerging church must prepare to encounter if we want to create a healing culture.

The trail of brokenness following the Postmodern Experiment is littered with a generation of addiction. The church needs to become a healing community and minister to those around us who are consumed with the addictions that enslave them. We must make use of the resources available to support those needing recovery. As we understand both addiction and the path to recovery, we can better nurture a healing culture where God's grace and truth work together powerfully to set people free.

As the recovery movement realized, healing and spiritual growth require support and connection. In a generation longing for connection but wired to stay isolated and alone, the church must be a place where nobody stands alone. Without connection, healing and growth rarely happen.

So how does the church create a culture of connection? That's our next topic.

STUDY GUIDE

Culture Check

1. Does the culture of your church or group provide a place where Jesus can do his healing work in a broken, addicted world? If not, why not? How might you move toward forming a healing culture?
2. Read over the Twelve Steps and think of the biblical basis for each step. In the past, have you viewed the recovery movement more as an ally or enemy? Why?
3. Take a minute to assess which addictions are most prevalent in your ministry context. What might you do to minister to these people in need of a healing culture?

Small Group Questions

1. Have you ever tried to control something out of your control (an addiction, compulsive thoughts or behaviors, a person, or even a situation)? Talk about why you struggled and how that felt.
2. Read 1 John 1:8–9. The key to overcoming any sin pattern begins with admitting you are powerless to stop the behavior or control the situation (you're not God). Can you think of an area you are powerless over right now? Most people can, but tend to deny it. Discuss why it is so hard for us to admit our powerlessness.
3. Read Exodus 20:3. The recovery movement says to overcome an addiction, first we have to give up playing God (idolatry which breaks the first of the Ten Commandments). Next we have to turn our will and our lives over to the care of God. This is a daily decision for an addict struggling to stay clean, but it's also a daily struggle for every honest Christ-follower. Discuss: If every day you resigned from trying to make life and people go according to your will, and instead you decided only to do God's will for your life, how might your life be different?

4. Read over the Twelve Steps listed on page 245 in this chapter. These are incredibly biblical steps to a healthy, God-honoring spiritual life. After looking at each, discuss which Step or Steps would be good next steps for your growth.

The Struggle with Aloneness

Artist: Jessica Gilzow

Nobody Stands Alone: Creating a Culture of Connection

There is no better way to dismantle a personality than to isolate it.

The Princess of Wales, BBC TV's *Panorama*

Keith Miller called me this morning: "Just called to see how you're doing and how the writing's coming along" was his entire message.

My first thought was, *why does he care about me? He's a very successful author, busy writing and speaking.* It kind of felt too good to be true that this important, older man would actually think I was worth "just checking in on." And ironically, my first reaction was emotional defensiveness, pushing away something I long for.

Later this morning, I was rereading the book *A Generation Alone.* One of its authors worked extensively with Vietnam vets, recovering from posttraumatic stress disorder (PTSD), a condition resulting from a stressful incident beyond the normal functional range of human experience (combat, terrorism, genocide, torture, rape, violence, or long-term less extreme incidents). Entire generations of soldiers show similar signs of PTSD.

The author William Mahedy writes about college students he works with who show many of the same PTSD symptoms.[1] He explains that such high percentages of young people have endured traumas of abandonment due to divorce, psychological or sexual abuse as children, rape as young women, overexposure to media violence and sexual exploitation, and it appears that we've bred a PTSD generation. Mahedy says, "I can find no other explanation for the widespread problems with stability, self-image, feelings of emptiness, depression, suicidal thinking, fear of the future, and lack of hope among the young."[2]

267

But here's what ambushed me. He said, "Abandonment is the fundamental component of these [generational] disorders . . . the young have been abandoned by parents, loved ones, teachers, political leaders, even the culture itself. No one is really 'there' for them now. . . . More than any of their predecessors, they have been since birth a generation alone."[3]

I sat back in my chair, pondering that last statement—definitely true of what I've experienced ministering to people my age and younger. Then I started thinking about my own life, thinking back to when my father died when I was a teen. If I'm honest, I've always longed for someone to "see me," a mentorlike person to see something in me worth blessing and believing in and encouraging like my dad did. I have had other men around me who really knew me and encouraged my development. It always felt like coming home whenever I met with them. Yet we hardly ever talk or see each other anymore. In fact, I hardly see any of my close friends. Suddenly I realized how hard it is to maintain close connections and even harder to make new ones, and I was overwhelmed with the sadness of it all.

Then it hit me: I internally push Keith Miller away because I'm afraid I'll feel let down. I desperately want connection with others, but I am so afraid of the pain of admitting my need then feeling rejected and left alone. And what I realize is that I have a tendency to get so caught up in my busyness, that I'm sure there are others around me looking to me for the same things, yet I can't give them what I want others to give me. How messed up is that?

A Generation Alone?

Honestly, it's not easy letting you inside my raw reflections, but maybe the Lord allowed me to feel this longing this morning so he could expose it for us all—because I have to believe this is what most people feel in our broken world if they're honest. I didn't have anything close to abuse, neglect, or a father who intentionally left. I had a father who breathed belief and love into me, and a nurturing mother who sacrificed in amazing ways for her children. I've had more close friends than most, so if I feel this push-pull longing for connection coupled with a fear of getting close . . . I'll just bet I'm not alone. Growing up in a culture so isolated and alone, the attitude of relational distrust rubs off even on those who didn't experience severe trauma.

I'm convinced that to be effective, the emerging church must create a culture of connection for a generation alone. If the Boomer generation valued anonymity above all else when coming to church, emerging generations value connection above all else. It doesn't matter how hip the music, how funny the pastor, how postmodern the vibe, if a person comes and sits alone, feeling unconnected as an "outsider" week after week, she won't come back. This is especially true of spiritual seekers. Nobody wants to feel alone.

I attended a church not long ago that had a very cool, postmodern feel to the service. I loved the band, the worship, the message, and every external thing about it. But even though there were less than two hundred people there, and I probably stood out as a newbie, not one person made an effort to talk to me though I came thirty minutes early and stayed to hang out, awkwardly, thirty minutes after the service. I know this is not what the pastor intended, but a culture of connection requires lots of effort to maintain. I'm a pretty confident person, but I felt so alone standing there in a crowd, I could hardly stand it. I forced myself to stand there alone as a reminder of how visitors in my own church may feel trying to "break in."

Ben sent an email that reminded me how important it is for people to feel connected in community.

> My wife and I had been out of church for many years. Something inside kept pulling us to find a church. But in our search, it was hard to find one where we truly felt welcomed. We felt like "outsiders" no matter how hard we tried to feel a connection. From the first Sunday at Gateway, we felt welcomed. After attending the welcome lunch and especially after Kenny called us that same week, we started plugging in. In fact, since we knew we could cook better BBQ for the welcome lunch than the frozen lasagna we ate, we took over the welcome lunches and now serve as the official Gateway chefs. When J.J. said, "Dude, your food's bringing people into God's kingdom!" it gave us new understanding of what serving means in church, no matter what you do. For us, there has been no better way to get to know people, experience community, and see God's work among us.   —Ben

A Painful Lack of Connection

But lest I paint too rosy a picture, it doesn't always happen this way. Creating a culture of connection requires ongoing leadership energy. And some people have left Gateway feeling disconnected and hurt during phases when entropy set in to the culture, and we didn't intercept it soon enough. Once you desire connection but feel let down, all those voices of fear scream, "Get out before you get hurt worse." Listen to one honest email I received from Jose, a guy hurting and needing connection at a critical time in life, yet wanting to run when it didn't happen.

> I spoke with you briefly after your sermon on anger. I don't think it was a coincidence that I showed up again since I have a problem with anger. I've

heard that anger is like a loaded gun that can go off and seriously hurt people. Right now my family looks a lot like Swiss cheese. Lately, my anger has been directed at Gateway. Dark spirits whisper in my ear, "Those people at Gateway don't give a damn about you! Remember when Peter was supposed to call about a golf game and never did? And remember when they said someone would call about joining a small group and never did?" I know it was my fault for not being more proactive, but I find myself making lots of excuses for not attending Gateway functions. I currently have no desire to join a small group. My plate is full enough dealing with my failing marriage. There have been many times I've just needed someone to talk to or counsel with, but those dark spirits would remind me, "they're too busy, or they don't care, or they would never understand."　　　　　　　　　　　—Jose

Our generation longs for deep connection yet often settles for shallow ways of relating. In the wake of such high rates of divorce, neglect, and abuse, emerging generations long for connection, yet have been programmed for aloneness. Aloneness goes deeper than just being alone. Aloneness comes from longing for people to see you and know you yet still feeling isolated and alone on the inside even with lots of friends around you.

If churches do not help connect people into the community of Christ in meaningful ways, then we have failed in the full ministry of reconciliation— of restoring authentic relationship—that the Lord has entrusted to us.[4]

Nobody Stands Alone

From the beginning of Gateway, we have had the value that nobody stands alone. Yet creating a culture where that becomes a reality requires dogged determination. Here are some of the principles leaders must continually pay attention to if we want to provide a culture of connection.

Vision-Cast for Connection

It will be a constant leadership challenge in every small group and every Christian community to lead people to become a culture where nobody stands alone. The irony is that although we long for people to reach out to us, we fear appearing needy. So we long for others already connected to reach out and include us, but then once they do and we feel connected, our mental blackboard gets erased. We forget how horribly alone we felt trying to break in, and so we fail to do for others what we longed for them to do for us. The art of leadership requires that we never forget. And we can never let others forget. We must constantly remind those in our small groups and serving teams not to become an ingrown clique.

From the start, we have told our leaders over and over, "Our secret weapon for reaching people far from God will not be rockin' music, relevant messages, awesome kids programs, or crazy video . . . our secret weapon is *you!*" We would constantly remind our leaders to be on the watch for people standing alone, feeling isolated, or disconnected. And we help them know how to be friendly and welcoming, yet at the same time respect people's nonverbal signs for space. It's a tricky task to master because although people long to be connected, seekers really don't want to be singled out, put on the spot, or assaulted. They want opportunities to connect if they desire it, but they want the option of an "out" as well.

We never make newcomers stand up or identify themselves in a service, but we may give permission and encouragement to meet someone new. Often that permission is all people need. We teach about the importance of relationships— what Jesus meant by loving others as the second most important commandment—and we expose people's real needs and fears surrounding connection and community. We teach to create the kind of openness and safety described in the previous chapters, and with the ground plowed in this way, the soil is fertile for growth in connection. And then we keep on teaching and motivating people to get connected and reach out to others.

During a season of connection crisis, right after a surge in growth numerically, people weren't feeling connected. I started to vision-cast for getting connected in a small group every chance I could. Finally, I got an email from a new person saying, "Stop pushing small groups. You talk so much about the value of getting connected in community, it almost feels like church on Sunday isn't important—only getting connected in a group."

That's when you know they finally got the vision, when people get sick of hearing it. You have to keep on saying it, and then find ways to catalyze

My first day at Gateway, everything was incredible: the people, the music, the message. I found it very easy to plug into a small group (I was hesitant but dived in nonetheless) and started making friends. To this day I cannot imagine being who I am without their impact and their love in my life. This church has meant a great many things to me. It has meant great friendships that I feel comfortable sharing my all with, growing in my knowledge of Scripture, better understanding of true compassion, the comfort of a place where anyone is welcome and everyone reaches out. It's a church where talents are embraced and people are given a chance to share their gifts. It is no surprise to me that Gateway has been so successful in bringing so many to love our Savior, Jesus Christ.

—Jane

people to take next steps if the message motivates. This requires coordination between what's taught and our organizational ability to help people take steps to connect.

Organize and Reorganize

The second leadership principle in a culture where nobody stands alone is recognizing how much organization does matter. The more successful a church or small group becomes connecting others, the more you have to pay attention to reorganizing how things work so that new people can also be connected.

I once had the privilege of being in a meeting with Peter Drucker, organizational business guru of the twentieth century, as he consulted a small group of executive pastors from around the country. He said, "Whenever an organization grows by 30% or more, you must reorganize in order to be prepared for the next leg of organizational growth."

We have tried to apply this principle to connecting people into community. As a result, connection strategies that worked in the early years no longer worked the more people we connected. We try to regularly assess whether those who want to get connected find it easy or difficult, and we try to adapt organizationally as needed.

Some people resist organizing for connection, feeling it should just be spontaneous or it will feel forced and impersonal. But what you have to realize is that a lack of organization or vision for connecting others can actually create the most unfriendly, uncaring of communities, because that's where people drift if not led proactively the other way.

Conversely, the Body of Christ functioning as a healthy organism can minister in powerful ways as Emily describes:

> I started attending Gateway, I had just asked Christ in my life. I had moved to Austin to live with my atheistic boyfriend, I knew I was heading for disaster. Living together proved to be a wrong decision. Not knowing anyone in Austin, I followed the sign off of Loop 1 to Gateway. The first few months I didn't say a word to anyone. I then realized if I wanted God to transform me, I would have to make an effort. I filled out the info card with much hesitation. A week later, I got into a car accident. Scared and not talking to my now ex-boyfriend, I had no idea what to do. As soon as I walked in my apartment the Gateway Connections team called. They spoke to me for forty-five minutes, letting me cry and vent along the way. Finally, someone I could talk to without judgment! My boyfriend is now my husband and we attend Gateway regularly. We were both baptized earlier this year, went on the mis-

sion trip to Mexico, and we are looking forward to leading mission trips in the future. God is doing amazing things, and we are so grateful that he led us here.

As Emily's story shows, organization allows the Body of Christ to function as it should, connecting those who need the ministry of Christ's community.

Involve People Early

Another principle of leadership for connection is getting people involved early. We found more spiritual seekers coming to faith our first year than we would have ever predicted, simply because they felt involved, needed, and valued. But it gets messy. Often people were put in positions of service before they found faith. Though we would never allow a person to be in a position of spiritual leadership without going through our leadership application and interview process, we created many opportunities for involvement serving, regardless of where a person was spiritually.

The funniest story of the power of involvement comes from our core-building days when the church consisted of twenty-four people. Christy†† was a sharp young schoolteacher, but she did not know much at all about Christ. Desperate for help one week, my wife, Kathy, asked Christy if she would help teach the toddlers' class. Christy felt honored, but said she knew nothing about the Bible. Kathy said, "Can you read Bible stories enthusiastically from a children's Bible?" Christy thought she could handle it, and for the next six months, Christy and Kathy worked side-by-side serving the children together. Christy came to faith shortly after that. Christy jokes, "I think God knew I needed things on a preschool level." Now as devoted Christ-followers, she and her husband, Jody††, still faithfully lead our two's class five years later!

Create Need-Based Connection Points

The ultimate purpose of getting people connected is to help them find community and follow the way of Christ. But we realize that not everyone feels ready to dive into spiritual community, and often simpler, low-commitment connection fosters the trust needed to move forward into community. So we have tried to organize opportunities to connect based on people's perceived immediate needs. Although the number of ministries and serving teams has grown from zero to over fifty in five years, we've always tried to think of connecting opportunities in several broad areas:

- connection through compassion
- connection through pain

■ connection through service
■ connection through affinity

Let me show you why these four broad areas are important initial points of connection particularly for our postmodern generation.

Connection through Compassion

Maybe due to empathy with others who have been broken by this evil world, our generation cares deeply about the needs of the poor, the forgotten, and the marginalized. In a postmodern mind, a church that does not do these acts of compassionate extension could not possibly represent God. Unfortunately, it is the secular culture more than the prophets of the Old Testament who are influencing a change in the church toward social concern. But either way, this turn is for the better.

From the beginning, we have seen compassionate extension as a way to express God's love in a tangible way to a hurting world. We have tried to serve those less fortunate in ways that empower them rather than just benefiting those serving. Partnering with other ministries and forming relationships in the city remains key to this effort, though we are still far from where we long to be in coordination with the larger Body of Christ. Our vision is for our city to see churches working together as a transforming presence of community development. But as we have mobilized people into compassionate service, what we've noticed is a secondary benefit of connection as well.

Kylie, whom you read about in an earlier chapter, came to Gateway only because her husband grew up in church, had wandered far away, and really missed it. She said, "Of all religions, Christianity was the last one I thought I'd ever identify with." She was willing to "do church" if she had a say in picking which one. "I looked for community involvement," Kylie said. "I saw that Gateway had an impressive Compassion Ministry. If a church didn't serve the community, I wasn't going to go. Because Gateway obviously cared for people in need, I was more open to attend."

Our compassion ministries (homebuilding, mentoring kids, visiting the elderly, serving the homeless, and our clothing closet and food pantry) have all been led by people who came to faith at Gateway, partly by getting connected serving those less fortunate. Compassionate service is not only a command for all churches,[5] it is also an easy way for people to connect with others as they serve together. You don't have to be a Christian to serve those in need, but often those serving alongside Christ-followers see a supernatural love and motivation that attracts them to Christ and his community.

Connection through Pain

No greater motivator for change exists than pain. Pain, as C. S. Lewis once said, is God's megaphone to a deaf world. In a broken, isolated world, the church must provide ways for people to connect in a healing community at their greatest point of need. In the early days of our church, we did not have trained leaders to help others in sensitive areas like depression support, crisis care, drug and alcohol recovery, divorce recovery, or healing from sexual abuse or abortions. Most of it fell to the few pastoral staff. But as we would talk about issues like these, we tried to connect people to outside resources and into small group communities as places to find prayer and support—it was the best we could do.

But as the church grew, the pastoral staff alone could not provide the care and connection needed for healing, so we prayed for leaders who could provide more direct support groups for people facing pain or crisis. Hoping for mature Christ-followers from other churches who would be led into the mission of serving the needs of our broken generation, we waited and waited.

Then one day, God started showing us that he was going to answer our prayers in a more biblical way. He got me thinking back to the year Kathy and I lived in Russia, right after their liberation from seventy years of atheistic communism. We didn't have the option of waiting around for equipped, mature believers to serve and lead others. We only had a year to see Russians come to faith and begin to lead others. But God was faithful, and a decade later that ministry continues on, led entirely by those Russians who came to faith and began to lead that year.

I was born and raised a Muslim. I became a Christian three years ago. For the first year, I went from church to church, feeling the fire and desire that I had at the beginning dying down. I prayed for God to show me the way to overcome this struggle. That's when a friend told me about Gateway. That first Sunday, I loved the service and worship music so much, I prayed to God that this could be my home church. I started to get involved with the greeting team. Later I became one of the greeting team leaders. Then I joined a small group. The group has been a great blessing to me. I got to know a group of awesome guys. Finally, I heard stories of the mission trips and how they change people's lives. On the trip to Matamoras, Mexico, God changed me more than I ever expected. Now I am thinking of becoming a team leader for the next mission trip.
—Behroz[††]

As we opened up our minds to the potential leaders all around us, the Lord began to show us what Paul meant when he wrote to the messy church of Corinth, "Praise be to the God and Father of our Lord Jesus Christ, the

Father of compassion and the God of all comfort, who comforts us in all our troubles, so that we can comfort those in any trouble with the comfort we ourselves have received from God."[6] Within a couple of years, ministries serving as points of connection around people's pain were springing up from the very people God had comforted through Gateway in the same way.

Kylie, who came due to our Compassion ministries, felt so included as she served that she soon volunteered to meet a need no one was meeting. Having a heart for women who had been sexually abused or traumatized through domestic violence, she approached us about helping start a support ministry. The only problem—Kylie still was not a Christ-follower. But instead of discouraging her, we encouraged her to pursue answers to her faith questions and gave her permission to see what interest was there—with her understanding that this was not an official Gateway ministry until we had an approved Christian leader.

> I got involved in Gateway's Depression Support group and made some wonderful friends who have helped me learn to grieve and experience laughter and joy again. When I was diagnosed with Leukemia, Jo and the support group were there for me, bringing meals and praying for me. God used Gateway to save my life and the Christ-followers there have given me so much— you've opened my heart to the Lord.   —Jake

Rachel, the Goth woman you met earlier, recalls, "I had been coming to Gateway for three weeks, and I was about to give up because no one had said anything to me. But the message that week was on connection through service, so I went up to the Compassion ministry table motivated by the message. I picked up information about a meeting to discuss sexual assault and domestic violence. It was the weirdest thing," Rachel said. "I went to this meeting to talk about a potential support ministry, but of the three people there, I was the only Christian. As we began to talk and meet over the weeks, Kylie, Sandra, and I became close friends as we shared stories of the pains of our pasts."

As Rachel shared her story with Kylie and Sandra, God began to do an unexpected thing in their hearts through her story. "My father was an evangelist and Bible college teacher," Rachel explained. "It began when I was four years old. Unable to find Mom or Dad, I left the apartment looking for them. We lived on the college campus where my dad taught. When my dad found me, he took me to my room and I thought I was going to get a spanking. The room was real dark, shades drawn. As I walked into the room, I didn't see it coming, a blow to the back of my head knocked me onto the bed. When I rolled over in shock, he smacked me on the face. He kept hitting me for about two or three minutes. I was so in shock I wasn't crying. He said, 'Don't ever do that again. Don't make me hit you again.' I looked at him, and burst out in tears. I climbed up to the top shelf of my closet and stayed there all day. That was the beginning of fourteen more years of physical and sexual abuse from a man who supposedly led thousands to faith in Christ."

"Why in the world would you believe in Christ now?" Kylie asked dumbfounded. "Didn't the school or church nail him?"

"Not until he was accused of sexual assault on campus, and I was a teenager at that point. The church didn't want to see and tried to cover it up. When he finally divorced my mother for another woman, it was too late. It was a mess. I hated God, hated my father, hated the church, and hated myself. I was suicidal. Because my dad had always said I made him do it because I was so bad, I sincerely thought I was evil personified. I believed I was the Devil himself. I was a horrible, evil little girl because I made my dad, the evangelist, do bad things. Even when my fifth grade teacher questioned all the bruises, I covered for him, because I knew it was all my fault."

"So you say that now you're a Christian?" Sandra questioned. "Why?"

"As a teenager, my mom wanted to send me to a Christian camp. I absolutely refused and, after a huge fight, ran to my room. As I lay there on the bed, I heard a voice say, 'Rachel, go to the camp.' So I went. The first days at camp I nearly got thrown out. But I felt surrounded with God's love and began to soften. I felt like a little girl, reconnecting with the God I once loved in my innocence. I knew he was there, and I opened my heart to Christ. When I returned home, my father was scared of me. He would mock me saying, 'You think God loves you? You think he cares about you?' For six months, he didn't touch me. Then his fear wore off and the abuse and molesting began again.

"Finally," Rachel explained, "I told a woman I respected at the church that my dad hit me . . . a lot. She told me to be quiet, that I was dishonoring my father. I retreated again from God and people after that. Years later when my father left, I was still confused and angry with God. I kept asking God where he was all that time and why he didn't stop my dad. One night I had a dream. I was back in my old house. I heard a knock on the door, and ran to open it. At the door stood Jesus—and I thought, *cool*. As I opened the door to let him in, my father came up behind me, slammed the door and locked it. I saw Jesus go to the back door and knock. My dad ran to that door and locked it. Then I saw Jesus knocking on the window, but Dad pulled the shades down. This happened window by window until the whole house was pitch dark . . . but I could still hear Jesus knocking. Then I heard him say: 'I was there, but your father would not let me in.' I knew it was true, that my father had been given responsibility, but he had not let Jesus in. He had let in something very dark instead. I realized Jesus had been there all along, my prayers weren't bouncing back, but people can lock him out. People can make choices against God that hurt others. That realization began an intense healing journey for me."

Rachel's story had a profound impact on the other two women. Within six months, Sandra had come to terms with the guilt from her past that kept her hardhearted toward God, confessed it, and accepted God's grace. Kylie too worked through her struggles and found faith. Today, these women together have been instruments leading many other women to faith in Christ and onto a path toward healing of the soul through our Comfort and Hope ministry.

I am amazed to see how God has raised up leaders where there were none. Our Divorce Recovery ministry got its start from a woman who found faith and healing at Gateway through her divorce. A couple in the divorce courts when they came to our church reconciled, and later started our Before You Divorce ministry. Trent found healing and faith at Gateway, and he and his wife began our Recovery ministry. A woman suffering through depression came to Gateway and began our Depression Support Group. Women who had abortions found faith and healing and began counseling those considering abortion or seeking recovery.

God has stayed true to his Word, comforting others with the comfort they received from him. All we had to do was be willing to take a risk at times, guide and equip along the way, and God's Spirit raised up wounded healers so that nobody stands alone in their pain.

Connection through Service

One of the easiest ways to help people connect and feel included comes through simple serving opportunities. All our serving opportunities are organized in teams with a team leader, from our greeting team to our children's ministry teams. Though we may begin with a serving team leader who primarily helps connect people through serving together in a particular area, our goal is to lead that serving team leader into becoming a serving *group* leader. Not just leading a task, but spiritually developing people who serve on the team. In some cases a team will have one team leader (who focuses on task leadership) and another group leader (who focuses more on spiritual development).

When I first started working at Willow Creek Community Church, my job was to spiritually develop serving groups in the food service ministry where some 350 volunteers chopped food and made change. Not exactly exciting, visionary stuff! Yet I love to tell the story of the Thursday team who stayed together serving for seven years. They met and served together all those years for one reason only: community. I started by convincing them not just to do the task but meet twenty minutes early to simply pray for each other. After much resistance, they gave it a trial run. Getting in each others' lives created better interaction and deeper conversations while serving together. Before long, I suggested they come forty-five minutes early and discuss a passage of Scripture, pray, and then serve. That simple combination kept that group going for seven years because they became close friends. Friends who not only served together but helped each other grow.

Early on in our portable church days, we had all kinds of spiritual seekers helping serve with setup, teardown, greeting, hospitality, and truck driving. People don't want to feel like outsiders, they need to feel included. So we found ways to get them involved.

Aaron hadn't been to church in years when his wife, Beth, who grew up Jewish, invited him to this "movie-theater-church" she had been attending. Beth and Aaron started helping out with setup and teardown. Soon Aaron saw we needed help with our portable trailer and volunteered his truck to help. As they got to know us and felt included through serving, soon Beth came to faith in Christ and Aaron renewed his faith in Christ from his lapsed Catholic background. As we got to know Beth, we discovered she had acted on Broadway. Beth started our drama team and continues to lead it today.

People want to get involved and connect. Often jumping into a small group discussion feels too intimidating, but serving and feeling useful can be a great first step of connection with surprising spiritual results.

There's a woman volunteering in our office who grew up Jewish. She and her husband and son would always try to beat the church crowd to the restaurant on Sunday. One Sunday at lunch her son asked, "What do church people do in church?" And they both agreed they needed to at least let their son experience church, so they decided to do a "church tour Sunday."

She later told me, "First we went to a church I called 'The Church of Yoga,' but we ended up leaving early because we were falling asleep and didn't understand the meditation thing. Then we went to another one that felt like 'Church of the Rich and Famous.' On our way home," Deborah said, "we heard the Gateway ad and came to the twelve-thirty service"—they did this all in one morning! She walked in and said, "Ahh, the Church of Starbucks and Rock-n-Roll, and people are wearing shorts—this I relate to."

They kept coming, understood what was being taught, and she decided to volunteer. The first day in the office she was asked to assemble our *Investigating the Way of Christ* books. She said, "You've got to be kidding, I'm Jewish and you want me to make Jesus books?" But she not only *made* the "Jesus books," she read one, along with about twenty other books on Christianity over the next four months. Over lunches with new-found friends on our administrative staff, she conversed about all she was learning. This week as I was walking through the office Deborah said to me, "Hey, I'm getting dunked." She has now made Jesus her Messiah and wants to be baptized.

We encourage seekers to plug in and serve in ways that don't require spiritual maturity, and we find that it often helps them sort through their questions in community and find an authentic faith.

Connection through Affinity

People long to connect with those to whom they can relate. Whether as singles, newly marrieds, new parents, dads, moms, single parents, cycling enthusiasts, rock climbers, Harley riders, soccer players, or even Xbox junkies (yes, we've had 'em all). Again, in all of our affinity-based connections, what we find works best are opportunities to connect requiring minimal commitment first, followed by ongoing invitations to connect deeper into community. At our retreats or seminars, people can "show and go." But we always try to give them a next-step opportunity to meet others and connect deeper in a small group.

As I mentioned before, you must continue to create organizational capacity to connect people into community. And as the church changes, organization must change. At one point in year three of our church, we had 110% of our weekend attendance meeting each week in small groups.

A close friend of mine, who wasn't even a Christian, invited me to Gateway. Though I was a Christian, I had wandered far from God for about eight years. I was intrigued by this unpretentious place where the focus was put on growing internally through Christ rather than external appearances. I started playing on various sports teams and met many wonderful people. For the first time in my life, I joined a small group during the Taste of Community. Our group has been incredible and we have really bonded. My relationship with God is growing and I see changes in my life. Thank you for making this a place where people feel welcome and for fostering a community where people can grow together in Christ.

—Jeremy

But soon our growth outstripped our leadership to connect people. To meet the challenge, we started short-term, six-week groups we call Taste of Community. What we found is that people fear commitment when they don't know what they're getting into. Nobody wants to show up at a small group with a group of people they don't know and then have to tell them they feel no affinity and don't want to come back. Also, our rapid growth has supplied more people desiring to join small groups than we have trained leaders to lead them.

One day I was talking to my friend Brett Eastman, and he shared with me something we used to talk about together while at Willow Creek—something that he had actually done at Saddleback. I talked to our staff about it the next week by asking this question to introduce the dangerous idea: "If we could get ten people who don't go to church and probably have never studied the Scriptures to meet together in a home, open the Bible, and have a spiritual discussion about it, would we do it?" The answer was a no-brainer—of course! "Then let's do it," I said.

Since then we've planned a weekend series once or twice a year to catalyze people toward connection. We recruit hosts to lead Taste of Community groups. A host[7] simply has to be a Christ-follower, who opens his or her house to meet, serve food or drinks, and tell friends and neighbors to come if they're not connected to a church. We do a crash-training course with the hosts, provide curriculum,[8] and ask them to simply facilitate a group for six weeks. When people sign up for a Taste group, we get affinity information and try to connect them in affinity-based groups. During this six-week period, our small group staff meets with the hosts for ongoing training, and to see if the host or another member of the group has the spiritual maturity and potential to become an official small group leader.

I grew up in a strict Muslim household having moved from Pakistan as a kid. After becoming a Christian, I was growing strong in my faith (a very hidden faith), but I was missing a community of believers. After I moved from my hometown to Austin, I prayed to find a church. A friend told me to check out Gateway. I loved it. But after some weeks of attending, I started to feel very discouraged and alone. I thought about leaving, but instead I prayed, "Lord, I want to be involved in this church. Point something out to me, help me open up." Soon after I prayed that prayer, I saw a flyer for the first ever men's retreat at Gateway. I signed up. Ever since that weekend, I have had that community I longed for. Guys to hang out with, grow in faith with, support and encourage as well. Because of this experience in a men's small group, I wanted to help others have the same. When Gateway started doing the Taste of Community, I volunteered to host one. It has just been awesome. All these guys, mostly new to faith loved it so much, they invited friends as well, and now we are an official small group. I know what it feels like to experience your Christian faith alone, and I know what it's like to have community. The safe, authentic Christian community Gateway has given me is one of the things I cherish most in life. —Amir

Taste of Community groups have allowed seekers and believers freedom to check out a group with permission after six weeks to decide whether to keep going or stop. The strategy may not work forever, but for now, we've found that close to 75% to 80% of Taste groups tend to keep going and become official small groups. We dream of a day when more people are connected in community than we have room to seat in our services. I believe our generation is ripe for this side-door entrance into the church through a small-group community.

In a day and age when so many stand alone, leaders need to take risks and get creative. Creating a culture where nobody stands alone must be a priority for every leader, whether in a church or small group. Our generation is desperate for it.

When you bring together all the cultural factors we've been discussing in prior chapters, and you connect people in community, what you find forming is nothing short of the family environment so many longed for but never had growing up. And in his family, God restores what was lost for his beloved children, as we will see in the next chapter.

STUDY GUIDE

Culture Check

1. How do you balance respecting people who want to remain anonymous, yet making sure nobody stands alone if they want connection? How do you continue to vision cast and organize to create a culture where people connect? List the ways people can get connected right now in your church culture.

2. Early involvement makes new people feel at home. What avenues do you have to involve new people who are believers? Seekers?

3. Take a straw poll. Start asking every new person you meet two questions: "Are you connected yet?" "Do you know how to get connected when you're ready?" These two questions will tell you a lot about your culture.

Small Group Questions

1. Think back to a time when you were a newcomer to church or another group. Discuss what that felt like. What made it difficult or easy for you to connect and feel at home?

2. Read Galatians 3:28, James 2:1–9. The community of Christ is called to break down walls of separation, and to reach out and connect people to Christ and his community from all backgrounds and

differences (racial, gender, socioeconomic). How can we become more of a connecting group in our church? In the world around us?

3. Why is it that once a group gets established, it's difficult to invite others in? How do we feel about inviting others into our group? What concerns do you have? Are there creative solutions to address those concerns?

4. Read Matthew 9:10–13. One way to connect those outside the church is to have a "Matthew Party" as a small group. Matthew invited his "unchurched" friends to hang out and meet Jesus. Brainstorm Matthew parties you could do as a group to include spiritual seekers or newcomers to your church.

The Family I Never Had: Creating a Culture of Family

I kneel before the Father, from whom his whole family in heaven and on earth derives its name.

Ephesians 3:14–15

Y ou know, I've never really been at peace, if I'm honest." The statement hung in the air as Brett,[††] Gary,[††] and Rick[††] simply listened. The clamor of restaurant noise filled in the space between my awkward admissions. "I want to love my little girl and my wife. I want to be able to relax and spend time with them, but I feel guilty for just enjoying life with them. For some reason I always have to be accomplishing something tangible or I get anxious."

Why did it feel so difficult to admit my powerlessness? My lack of peace? Maybe because I had grown up wired for a definition of success that forced me to prove my worth, to play the game of life to win, even if it cost me peace and love and the enjoyment of that life. Admitting to failure had never been part of my definition of success. Now actually doing so felt like emotional bungee jumping. And yet, this honest transparency felt sweet to my soul.

It was 1995, and this small group of men had become like family to me over the course of a few years. Every Tuesday, I found myself anticipating hanging out with my friends, experiencing spiritual transparency like I never had before. As I would walk into the restaurant from the bitter Chicago cold, my friends' presence somehow transformed that place into the warmth of a family dinner table—it felt like coming home should feel.

"As I was studying the fruits of the Spirit," I continued, "I realized I'm not growing in peace—never have. I live out in the future, always needing to climb the next hill, accomplish the next goal; always taking on a little more | 285 than is humanly possible. I know enough to realize that I might accomplish a lot in ministry yet destroy my family and God's work in me in the process. I've heard too many horror stories of well-meaning pastors who fell into that trap."

"Well, why don't you start saying 'no' to some things?" Brett asked.

"I can't. I've thought about it, and there's nothing I can cut out right now," I argued.

"Then why don't you feel at peace if you're living as you think God wants you to?" Rick countered.

"Because I have no time for my family, and I can't seem to relax when I'm spending time with them," I replied.

"So what do you get out of these other things?" Brett asked. "They must give you something or you wouldn't keep saying 'yes' to them and 'no' to your family. What do they do for you that enjoying time with family doesn't?"

"Nothing," I volleyed back in defense, "but if I don't study for my finals, I'll fail! If I don't do my job, I'll get fired!"

"Who says you have to get a masters degree, much less two masters degrees?" Brett pushed on me to force my thinking in a new direction. "So what if you fail? What does that mean if you fail?"

"What if I fail? I'm not going to fail!" I couldn't even conceive of it. The thought of not accomplishing my goals, not succeeding seemed so foreign; I couldn't even imagine it. It just wasn't possible.

"Well I think Brett's right," Rick chimed in. "How many times have we had this conversation where you're frustrated and anxious about all you have to do, but you won't say 'no.' You say you hate it, but I think you like living this way. There must be something you get out of red-lining your life that you value more than spending time with your family, or you wouldn't do it. You've got to figure out what that is."

"Seems to me you're frustrated," Brett interjected, "because what you want to value doesn't match how you actually live. Maybe you ought to pray for clarity on why trying to do so much is so important."

Normally, I would have resented Rick's and Brett's comments. My defenses would have attacked such a straightforward challenge, but I knew these guys really loved me as a brother in Christ. And besides, I knew all their junk as well! I didn't feel the need to pretend because I didn't feel judged or alone. We had all been incredibly honest about all our struggles in living the truths of Scripture, and we had built up a deep reservoir of trust. I knew confidentiality was sacred to them. I knew they cared. I knew they were on

my side.

They had stood by me, cheering me on when I got a promotion. They listened with empathy and prayed for me when I felt overwhelmed in my new job. When my family went through a medical scare, they showed up at our house the night we heard. Their families were with us in heart and prayer all the way. I trusted them.

Although it took another year of soul searching and spiritual prodding, God used this small group to lead me to an awareness of the truth and start me down a path of spiritual growth that has set me free in amazing ways. But it only happened because I felt the confidence that they loved me, despite the fact that I kept on doing what I didn't want to do.

During a two-day retreat, God used these guys to put another piece of the puzzle in place. Still feeling like God's Spirit was trying to teach me to live with his peace, I talked openly about what I was learning so far.

"So think about this," Brett suggested. "Jesus said when you know the truth, it will set you free, right? I think many times when we are stuck and enslaved to destructive patterns, it's because we've believed lies that may be buried deep within from things we learned in our families growing up. What messages did you guys get about your worth or accomplishments growing up?"

"I felt totally built up by my dad and mom," I chimed in. "They believed in me like crazy. My dad really valued work. He'd have me out working in the yard and say things like, 'My son will never be lazy, he'll know the value of a buck.' I think it's because he grew up so destitute in the wake of the Great Depression." Then something else came to mind. "Growing up in the sixties and seventies, I remember my dad would get visibly angry when he spotted a hippie, and he would say to me, 'Son, you will never be a bum like that.' Come to think of it, he said that a lot, 'You'll never be a bum, you'll know the value of hard work.'"

"Maybe that's a clue," Brett suggested. "Do you feel like you're not worth enough unless you prove something to your dad?"

"No," I honestly said. "I felt totally loved and valued by my dad." It didn't seem to connect at all. I never had to doubt how much my dad valued and believed in me.

Convergence!

Three months after that conversation, my grandmother on my dad's side passed away. Sitting at my grandmother's old house in Dallas, I was talking to my aunt about my grandmother, when it hit me that I knew nothing about my grandfather. My father never talked about his father because he hated him so much for abandoning the family. And since my father died when I was a teenager, my aunt was my only connection left to my grandfather. "What was your father like?" I innocently asked my aunt.

A look of intense anger and pain transformed her naturally pleasant face into an expression of long-buried rage. I remembered times when the fleeting shadow of that look darkened the face of my father. Her forceful words hit me like a knockout punch: "He was a bum!"

The phrase reverberated in my head, *"He was a bum." "He was a bum."* She had used the exact phrase, with the same boiling tone. Convergence! It was as if God's Spirit had led me down this path, preparing me to rip back the curtains of my psyche and show me something so ingrained that I was blind to it . . . I lived subconsciously afraid of ever being a bum. That's why I could never do enough. How could I ever prove I'm not a bum?

Back home, I told my small group of my discovery. The pain my father's father inflicted on his family through his alcoholism and irresponsibility had somehow transferred through my father's unresolved anger, right into my soul. I didn't understand it, but it made sense. I knew my dad loved me, but what if I were a bum? What if I didn't work hard enough? What if I didn't succeed like he thought I would? The lie that had been sown into my mind was that I had to keep accomplishing more and more to be worth loving, to prove I am not a bum. And the problem was that no amount of accomplishment was ever enough. Once I understood the lie I had swallowed, this small group family helped me begin to purge that hidden fear of failure with God's truth. I experienced a breakthrough to peace and love and enjoyment with my family that has continued to give me a life no amount of accomplishment could ever match.

The Power of Family

People have an immense mystical power to shape one another in profound ways. God made us that way. Growing up, our families shaped us for better or worse, actually for both. Our family of origin sowed into our conscience ways of living life, some ways that align with God's design, some that conflict. All parents pass on to their children good ways of doing life—but also broken ways. Just as God declared to Moses, the sins of the fathers pass from generation to generation.[1] But that's not the end of God's story about family.

God has a plan to create a new family, a redemptive family—a family with the power to heal and restore what humanity lost by going its own way. Ephesians chapter three says this is the mystery of God, that through Christ we can reconnect to the Father as a new family. A family that "being rooted and established in love, may have power, together with all [God's people], to grasp how wide and long and high and deep is the love of Christ."[2] I have come to believe that God's plan is really simple; to reconnect people to the Father and to brothers and sisters who learn how to act toward each other as his loving family. "Be imitators of God, therefore, as dearly loved children and live a life of love,"[3] Paul says.

The devastating effect of all sin is alienation—alienation from God, from others, and from ourselves. God's prime directive is to love God and love people as his new family because this heals our aloneness and restores what we lost. Incredibly simple, yet so difficult to do.

Christian psychologist Larry Crabb, after a quarter century of puzzling over how people heal and grow, came to this conclusion:

> When two people connect ... something is poured out of one and into the other that has the power to heal the soul of its deepest wounds and restore it to health. ... In recent days, I have made a shift. I am now working toward the day when communities of God's people, ordinary Christians whose lives regularly intersect, will accomplish most of the good that we now depend on mental health professionals to provide. And they will do it by *connecting* with each other in ways that only the gospel makes possible.[4]

God's restored family changes people in unbelievable ways.

■ ■ ■

It was the first night of our capital campaign. My nervousness could be seen in my pacing about. We had to raise money to build a facility because we were getting kicked out of the old synagogue we had been leasing. But how would this often skeptical, cynical generation respond? We called it our "One Life Journey" because that felt true to why we were doing it. One Life mattered enough to Christ to give his One Life, and we all have One Life to use to impact other lives. After an introduction video, Ted opened the floor to the hundred or so in the room. "Tell us what God has done in your life through our church family."

Jeff jumped up, unable to contain his excitement. "Ever since I was five years old, I have been confused about my gender. I was medically diagnosed as a male to female transsexual. I tried hormones a couple of times but life got worse and worse. I tried marriage, but that ended in tremendous pain. I tried the gay lifestyle but that didn't work for me either."

As Jeff opened up without reservation, I am ashamed to say my first thoughts were, "Oh no, this is going to freak people out. They won't be able to handle it. Don't let this derail the night, Lord!"

"Now that I have found my place with Jesus," Jeff continued on, "I have noticed a remarkable change. In the past five months I've been at this church, I have found a community of people who accept me and love me, who have helped me begin to explore my songwriting and musical gifts, who have helped me grow closer to the Lord than I ever imagined possible."

Jeff paused, fighting to control his emotions, as he said, "I used to blame God for this horrible burden and could not understand why God would do such a thing to a five-year-old boy. That part's still confusing, honestly. But for the first time in my life, I seldom feel the need to be a woman. God has used this church in a profound way in my life. Now that Christ is in my life, I have a suspicion that God allowed this because he now wants me to reach out to others that have the same problems. I can show them the love and forgiveness that he is beginning to show me through others, and I know that if I stay strong and do God's will, I will be rewarded for all the pain and suffering I have been through my whole life."

Instead of freaking out, people were in awe of the power of God, working through his church family. Others stood and shared powerful stories of healing and hope they too had found in his family. When we are connected to God's family, we can truly become ourselves.*

The Functional Family of God

What intent does God have for this renewed, restored family of Christ-followers? How do leaders help people live in the power of Christ's redeeming, healing love?

It doesn't happen because you start a small group ministry as another add-on to millions of other programs. Everything must align, from the teaching, to the leading, to the organization in order to point people toward creating this culture. All the culture creation discussed so far is prerequisite to creating a culture of family. It all interconnects like the individual strands of a net that only together have strength to catch people in the free fall of aloneness. When we study all the "one another" commands of Scripture and consider what healthy families do, we can see several traits that we must inspire Christian communities to strive for as part of God's redemptive family.

---

* When all was said and done, our church raised over seven times our previous year's annual budget, almost two times what we projected, and no contribution made up more than 3% of the total. With nearly 80% participation of our weekend attendance, it demonstrated to me an amazing spirit of family unity and evidence of God's Spirit at work among us.

Giving Value

"You matter, and we love you and won't give up on you, even when you fail." This is the message that reflects God's grace, which conveys our worth. God intended every parent to pass this truth down to every child. But many times people received the opposite, "You're worthless, and unless you can get it right, you don't deserve to be loved." God can use his new family to correct the lies with the truth. Carrie tells of the journey of restoration she's been on and the power of God's family to restore what was lost.

> I have traveled and lived in many different places trying to find "home," first alone, then with my son. "Home" seemed to die with my mother when I lost her at a very young age. My father remarried, and for some reason my stepmother saw me as a threat to her intimacy with my dad. As a result, I felt I lost not only my mom but my father as well. I could never do enough to get his affection or her kindness. Following many abuses and loss of family ties, I felt abandoned by the God my mom introduced me to.

> Once out of my home, I ran as far from God as I could go. I only wound up even deeper in the pit, pregnant and despairing. Now, as a single mom, I faced unrelenting challenges, feeling even more like I didn't fit. I didn't fit with other mothers; I didn't fit with other singles. Finding myself pregnant a second time, I made the hardest decision of my life. I gave my second son up for adoption.

> After years of going my way, I realized how much I needed Christ as well as the fellowship of the church. I started praying for Jesus to rid me of all of the things that kept me from finding rest and a home. I came to Gateway feeling very hurt, rejected, and defensive, and therefore afraid of people. My feelings of judgment, hurt, and rejection had only followed me into the doors despite my hopes that I would find my family and my home.

> I am still hanging in there and have found others who see my value in Christ and that do love and encourage me. I have found a core group of people who have looked beyond my rough edges and have found the jewel that Christ put me here to be. I praise God for them. I have stopped looking at the negative and have learned to stop trying to make people love me. Through my experiences at Gateway I'm learning to open up and receive the love and acceptance of those who offer open hearts and arms.

> I will be at Gateway for four years this December; that is a long time for me to stay anywhere. I have wanted to bolt many times. I don't know if it is possible for me to feel at home anywhere after the things that life has thrown my way; but I am grateful that Gateway has tilled the ground and

planted the seeds so that those with Christ's heart could be available to love me, even when I have acted or felt unlovable. This in turn has shown me how to be lovable, and God is restoring all of the things that I thought I had lost forever when I turned my back on him. —Carrie

God can use his new family to re-parent and restore what was lost due to the "sins of the fathers," so that we can begin to pass down something better.

Enjoying Life Together

Some of the greatest memories I have of growing up came from being with my family. Just enjoying life together, laughing together, playing together, taking trips together. I'm convinced one of the reasons sin has such appeal in our generation is because we don't know how to enjoy life together as God intended. God is a God of immense joy. His Spirit gives joy and life overflowing when he fully has his way with us. And one of the tasks of God's new family needs to be teaching each other how to enjoy life as God intended. When we experience more and more enjoyment of life together, the last thing we want is to turn away from the Source of this new life.

A man who got involved in our recovery support group opened up about his new spiritual journey when asked why he was there. He said, "Since I've opened my heart to Christ, I've found this new life with God that's been awesome. I just don't want to do anything to screw it up." The best deterrent against sinful acting out—is joy! But growing up far from God, we often don't know how to enjoy the pleasures of life *with gratitude* and *without sin*. Small groups can be like families who teach each other to enjoy life with God.

We encourage new small group leaders to work primarily on one thing the first three months with their groups—opening up and having fun with each other. What I've found in the past twenty years of leading small groups is this: if you help people feel at ease and enjoy being together, opening up to each other early on, you'll have years of time to truly go deep in study and prayer. If your group fails to achieve that homestyle, laughing-around-the-dinner-table feel, your group will never become the healing, life-giving family environment God intended. Groups who do life together, share a meal together, play sports together, have game nights, and serve others in need describe the early church community who "worshiped together . . . and shared their meals with great joy. . . ."[5]

Encouraging Development

Fear holds us back from becoming all God intended us to be. That's where God's family can play such a powerful role encouraging development. When brothers and sisters in Christ learn to celebrate each other's God-given gifts, encourage each other to develop these gifts, and support each other through feelings of failure, that's the family every single person longs to find.

I don't know why I feared it so much, but more than anything else in life, I feared public speaking. I've since learned I'm not alone as it's the number-one fear of most people. Although recognized for leadership growing up, I would resist the promptings of others to run for student government for only one reason: the speech! I successfully avoided addressing any group larger than ten people until I was twenty-five years old.

In the late eighties while working as a project engineer, I volunteered to help Dave,[††] JP,[††] and Donna[††] start a campus ministry at the University of California Santa Barbara (UCSB). I was single, and I had time nights and weekends, so I led music and a small group Bible study. Serving together, we became close friends and made lots of crazy memories filled with late-night laughter. They encouraged my development continually. They motivated me to use my hour-long commute to listen to teaching tapes they loaned me. They inspired me to memorize Scripture to help me live out of the truth. They recognized and encouraged me to develop my God-given gifts.

One night I was hanging out with Dave, telling him something I had discovered in my studies, when out of left field he said, "You know, I think God's given you the gift of teaching." I laughed in his face.

"Me, teach? No way! If I have the gift of teaching, God's made a mistake," I said, "because I hate public speaking."

But he kept saying, "I see it! You really do have a love for learning and a contagious excitement for explaining it. You may just need to overcome your fear of communicating."

Dave took it on himself to encourage and motivate me to overcome my fear. I kept resisting him. Finally, he set up a seminar for me to teach a group of twenty-five students. I told him I wouldn't do it. He kept insisting, and I kept resisting. "I can't put college students through that kind of torture," I said. That night as I prayed, I had a strong sense that I was resisting God's Spirit, not Dave. The thought that kept coming to me was, "If they have to suffer through your failures, that's my business. You just be faithful to do what I ask you to do." I decided to accept in faith.

My first teaching experiences were nightmares. I felt terrified, which made those students nervous for me. It wasn't good or helpful, and I felt like an embarrassing failure. But Dave, JP, and Donna kept encouraging me, telling me how I was improving. With their love and support, I actually came to believe I could be a useful teacher some day, and my attitude shifted from fear of failure to one of wanting to learn and grow. As Dave began giving me more specific instruction for improvement, I took more and more risks to develop.

Those two years, surrounded by these life-giving friends, were the most pivotal, developmental years for me. I began taking new risks everywhere, with speaking, with creativity, song writing, in relationships, at work. I felt more alive than ever because I knew I was becoming more of whom God intended me to be. When I think of where God has led me since then, I find myself in awe of the power of God, working through his family.

The Scriptures command us as God's family to encourage and build up one another, instruct one another, teach and admonish one another, prompt one another toward love and good deeds, serving one another in love. We teach people how to relate to each other in these ways, telling stories of the powerful abilities they have to develop one another. When small group communities learn to be the voice of God, looking for the potential God sees in each person, encouraging the development of each other, amazing things happen. People realize they're not alone, and gain new courage to try new things.

That's the kind of family the whole world wants. A family that provides the love and support, encouragement and prodding to develop into the people God intended us to be. Just like no natural family can be perfect, no small group family and no church family will be perfect either—but as we continually lead the culture toward this vision for God's intended community, people will develop and help others to develop.

Bearing Burdens

"Carry each other's burdens, and in this way you will fulfill the law of Christ . . . for each one should carry his own load."[6] A healthy family teaches responsibility. God has made every individual with a certain capacity to take on responsibility (that is, "carry his own load"). We've all been given a backpack worth of responsibility to carry—it's manageable. If a person refuses to work when perfectly capable, it would not be loving for the church to support him.[7] He would never learn to handle the responsibility God has made him capable of carrying. In this fallen world, however, troubles come that can burden a person more than he or she can carry alone. This is when God intended his family to rally. When a person gets saddled with the big, heavy, trunk-load of trouble he can't lift, God's family plays an important role in sharing that burden.

Jim had "been there, done that" when it came to Christianity. Not only had he been a Christian for decades, as a very effective communicator he had traveled the globe with well-known Christian speakers. He had heard it all and said it all. But despite all the biblical knowledge he still had a huge hole in his heart. Feeling isolated and alone, constantly pitching Christian faith like a traveling salesman yet unable to talk openly about personal demons, he crashed emotionally.

Sinking into deep despair, Jim looked for relief by diving deeper into a pornography struggle he had never truly addressed. Eventually, he found himself sexually involved with a woman he had just met. Feeling so ashamed and guilty, he confessed. After feeling cast out and abandoned by those he once ministered with, he ran far from God and Christian community.

Years later, Jim found Gateway and began to open up to a growing group of trusted friends. He began to heal and feel a renewed love for God. He met a woman who was also rebuilding her life after a painful, failed marriage. After Jim and Shelly married and experienced growth together, they opened their home for a small group, desiring to minister to others once again. Little did Jim know, his small group would grow most by ministering to his own family. Here's what Jim says looking back:

> It wasn't until after we were married and began to go through trial after trial that we really began to learn that Gateway people aren't just quirky and fun, they live what they believe. They put shoes on the gospel so that they might literally LOVE you through good times and bad. In some of our worst moments—losing my job, losing our baby, and suffering a never-ending custody battle, Gateway people came through for us in practical ways. People drove four hundred miles to testify on our behalf. They loaned us their mobile phones when our phones were turned off. They brought us food, money, and checked on our home while we were gone. So many people attend church each week and sit next to people they will never ever know, much less care for. Who cares if you have memorized the entire canon of Scripture if you have never lived out the ideas themselves? Thanks for being Christ to us.
>
> —Jim

I have honestly been blown away at the outpouring of tangible burden-bearing that people have demonstrated to one another at Gateway. We celebrate examples like this publicly, and we teach what it means to tangibly help one another, but only God's Spirit at work can truly lead people to be family. When people bear one another's burdens, they experience family as God intended.

Sharing Joys and Sorrows

Julie and Ross are one of many couples who were hit hard by the "dot-bomb" layoffs, where Austin's high-tech community went from boom to bust. As engineers with a family of four to feed, in a six-month period both were unemployed. Before that time, Julie said, "Gateway had become our second family. We found people here to 'do life with'—to hang out with, talk to, watch football, have 'jazz nights,' you name it." But Julie admits how she came to a crisis of faith after two years of unemployment.

> God has kept us on the edge of our seats with our job situations, but over and over he's been faithful; bringing temporary jobs along the way and providing an amazing support system. It's very humbling to depend on God and his family so much, but also a great way to build faith. Dozens of people have been faithfully praying for our family. Every time we come to church, people ask how we're doing and tell us they're praying for us. At critical times, God has provided through his family. One time at a point of crisis need, an usher at church came up to hand us an envelope anonymously addressed to us with 160 dollars in it. Months later at another critical time, we found an anonymous envelope taped to our garage with 200 dollars. In September, we totaled our minivan in an accident. Wondering how we could fix it, J.J. (our music director) approached us saying someone wanted to pay our deductible for us. Not long after that, our alternator died, and we just couldn't replace it. Another Gateway angel stepped up with a new one someone else bought, and he lent his expertise to help Ross install it.
>
> A sermon given during this time talked about how God gives to us through others. The one-sentence summation was, "If God wants to give you a gift, for crying out loud, take it!" Boy, did we learn to receive from God with gratitude. A few days before Christmas, two Gateway friends handed us another anonymous envelope. Inside was a machine-printed statement with the Scripture "Bear one another's burdens, and so fulfill the law of Christ," next to it was $300 for our kids' Christmas.

After all the financial trials of two years, Julie got the shocking news that her mother had a brain aneurysm and would die within days. Before sunrise the next morning, she was at the airport, taking the first flight to Lubbock with barely any time to process all the grief and confusion. On her way to the women's restroom, Julie ran straight into Dianne. The first year Dianne and Stuart came to Gateway, both lost their mothers the same month. Looking back on that time, Dianne had said, "In the middle of the grief, God showed us he was smack dab in the middle of our lives in the form of all the people praying for us, preparing meals for us, helping us."

Julie began to sob as she poured out her heart to Dianne, realizing God had arranged this encounter. As it turned out, Stuart and Dianne were on the same flight Julie was taking to Lubbock! "God knew exactly what I needed," Julie recalled, "and Dianne and Stuart knew exactly what I was feeling. They shared my sorrow and comforted me like angels all the way to Lubbock."

After all the trials she had been through, Julie's crisis of faith finally took its toll.

> You'd think that maybe I'd hide my lack of faith from my friends at Gateway, but really, just the opposite was true—I told several close friends, all of whom prayed for me and many of whom had gone through similar experiences. Their support was a huge comfort to me in a very dark time. I don't think you could count on that kind of support in just any church. My church is pretty special in that way. This is a crazy, mixed-up world we live in. God is really the only thing that makes sense to me. His way is the only way for me, and my church family was a huge catalyst in my journey to reach that conclusion. Although I can't say the last years have been the easiest in my life, I've certainly grown more spiritually in that period than in any other. Calling Gateway "God's family" isn't just some catch phrase to me; Gateway is the very embodiment of God's love and care for me and my family.

I remember how many people celebrated with Julie and Ross when they each finally landed jobs. But that's the beauty of God's family, having a group of people who "mourn with those who mourn and rejoice with those who rejoice"—that's just what family does.

Giving Life to New Families

Healthy families give life to new healthy families. As kids grow up and mature, they naturally tend to want to create the same life-giving experience through a family of their own. And in God's family, as people develop and mature spiritually, those with gifts of spiritual shepherding, leading, and teaching need to be given the encouragement and freedom to lead others. When groups get larger than ten to fifteen people, it becomes difficult for people to feel as connected and known. Quiet people tend to get quieter and loud people tend to make their voices heard more.

We believe this life-giving community must give life to others when it is healthy. At the same time, a very real tension develops that emerging churches must struggle to resolve. We've fought hard against the idea of splitting a group into two when it reaches a certain size. In a generation fearful to trust due to failed relational connections of the past, once they feel like they've found a family of friends, to insist on splitting the group due to size feels destructive, like a divorce.

On the other hand, when groups become ingrown for years and years and never reach out to others, never provide connection and support to others, generally they stagnate and disband because the individual members are not growing to be more Christlike by extending life to others. For that reason, we have encouraged the development of apprentice leaders who first subgroup into two groups within the same home. This allows a natural bridging of one group into two without tearing apart important relationships.

The other major way we've seen new life come from existing groups is when leaders encourage other group members to be Taste of Community hosts for six weeks. Jared was an apprentice leader who took over a small group I had led. Jared encouraged Claire and Drew from his group to host a six-week Taste Group. With Jared's support, God used Claire and Drew in ways no one could have predicted. Two of the men who joined their six-week Taste group with their wives were not Christ-followers at the time (and reluctant to go to a small group) but felt completely safe with Drew, who had not been a Christ-follower when he joined our original small group two years before. Claire and Drew created such a warm, trusting environment that this new group decided to keep meeting after the six-week trial period. All these couples are now growing in faith together. Claire reflects back on her experience and sums up the power of God's family to reverse the negative effects of broken families.

> I have had more love in my life since I came to Gateway than I ever have. I was looking for something, but did not know what it was. When I finally got plugged into church, I felt like I had come home. Since then, I have moved closer and closer to God. He has shown himself to me in so many ways! I have experienced so many "God things" and been open to seeing these things for what they are. I have changed the way I am raising my children, the way I interact with my husband, and the way I relate to my parents. I feel so much better about myself knowing that I am not alone! I have confidence and strength that I never had before. I attribute my Gateway family with my newfound love. I know God is with me and he has put the people of Gateway in front of and all around me so that I never have far to look for him.
> —Claire

And that, I have come to believe, is how God's story of family comes full circle. In every generation, many people find themselves broken and isolated by families of individuals who turned away from God and his ways. But as we reconnect to the Father through the grace offered in his Son, he teaches us to love one another with a new kind of love. And as we grow up into his family, he heals and restores us, and we, in turn, have the chance to be a redeeming influence in our family of origin, and to pass on to our children something a little closer to what God intended all along.

Christ's church still holds the hope of the world in its hands. The hope that a distrustful, cynical, relativistic, broken, isolated group of people can be restored by the grace of God into a beautiful portrait of his family—not yet perfect—but undeniably more at home! I only pray his family will wake up and unite to move his kingdom vision forward, before it's too late for the church in our post-Christian society.

STUDY GUIDE

Culture Check

1. Families can build up or tear down a person. Do you see negative family-of-origin issues being addressed and repaired through your church family? How? If not, why not? How can you change the culture if needed?

2. As a leader, think of specific ways (vision casting, organizing, telling stories) you can help create a culture where small, family-size communities can function as God's family in these ways: To give value to one another. Enjoy life together. Encourage development. Bear burdens. Share joys and sorrows. Give new life to new "family environments."

Small Group Questions

1. Read Exodus 34:6–7. God gives authority to parents, and their decisions to turn away from God's path can bring negative consequences that pass from generation to generation until someone breaks the chain. How have you seen generational patterns evident in your own experience?

2. Read Matthew 12:46–50, Ephesians 3:14–19. Fortunately, God has a plan to restore what was lost through a new kind of family—a family of people willing to follow their Heavenly Father. How might God want to use us in this way with each other?

3. Think about the functions of a healthy spiritual family: To give value to one another. To enjoy life together. To encourage development. To bear burdens. To share joys and sorrows. To give new life to new "family environments." Talk about each function of being a spiritual family—think of examples of when we've done this well and ways we can grow to be more functional as God's family.

4. What are one or two practical next steps for our group to focus on in order to become more functional as a spiritual family?

The Struggle
Forward

Artist: Tonia Plasencio

Life or Death?
Creating a Culture for
Emerging Leaders

The righteous man is the one who lives for the next generation.

Dietrich Bonhoeffer

t was 1996. I had just finished reading reports of the largest yearly drop in church attendance this half-century.[1] Having studied the trends of post-Christian Europe, I had the overwhelming feeling North America was headed toward the death of the church in my lifetime if trends didn't reverse. The Gallup study said the younger generations in the U.S. were successively more unchurched than the previous generation.

That day I felt troubled and began to pray that God would reverse that trend in our country. I longed to see his church effective in providing hope and healing and spiritual direction to this generation of seekers I had been diligently trying to reach for a decade.

I believe God answered that prayer partially by leading us to start a church *out of* the culture rather than *for* the culture. We had to grapple with how to contextualize the message of Christ (which you've read about in this book), just as the early church had to do in the transition from a Jewish to a Gentile culture.[2] In that first-century Jerusalem meeting on contextualization, James declared, "We should not make it difficult for the Gentiles who are turning to God."[3]

With every new culture since, the church has wrestled with how to stay true to the message of Christ without putting cultural barriers up that make it difficult for people to turn back to God.[4] And what we have experienced in our come-as-you-are culture is God's Spirit using the soil we've plowed and watered to cause amazing growth in people.

303

Other churches across America report similar stories like the ones you've been reading of a generation turning to God. Their churches may look different externally, but what they have in common is a church culture that bridges effectively to the surrounding unchurched culture.

This is encouraging, but a handful of churches reaching our generation are not enough. The trends have not changed for the better this decade, as off in the distance the death bells toll for the church in North America. The Barna Group's most recent research indicates, "Since 1991, the adult population in the United States has grown by 15%. During that same period the number of adults who do not attend church has nearly doubled."[5] Barna also notes that the unchurched are more likely to be younger than the norm.

Others following research on religious trends in the western world observe:

> Christianity has been largely abandoned in Britain and the rest of Europe. . . . Christianity has partly faded in Canada, where only 20% of adults say that they attend church regularly, and only about 10% actually do. In about the year 1990, Christianity started to lose market share in the U.S. The percentage of American adults who identify themselves as Christians is dropping by about 1 percentage point per year. The percentage who say that they attend church on most weeks is 40%.[6] [Sociological research in the U.S. and Canada shows that self-reporting of church attendance in polls overestimates actual weekly attendance by around 80%, indicating 20–30% of the population of the U.S. actually attends church as of 2004].[7]

The point of course is not church attendance; the point is to see Christ's vision of his Body, the church, making an impact in our world. But if trends continue in North America, the church will be virtually dead within the next three to four decades as it already is in most of Europe.

What worked effectively in previous generations does not work now. Currently, only 6% of Americans over the age of eighteen will find faith in Christ.[8] Barna says, "Studies we have conducted over the past year indicate that a majority of the people who made a first-time 'decision' for Christ were no longer connected to a Christian church within just *eight weeks* of having made such a decision!"[9] That means the American church has already lost its impact on emerging generations. Just because someone prays one prayer of faith accepting Christ does not mean they are following Christ.

The church is ineffective in helping new generations follow Christ as his family, his Body, his redemptive community. Something's broken. The church will continue this decline toward death in North America unless something changes. So which way forward from here?

Is There Hope?

Although the church appears statistically to be less and less of an influence in our postmodern, post-Christian world, God has not given up on his vision for his church. After all, the church was his idea, and he sees it as his beautiful bride when functioning as he intended. The church, functioning as his Body, can still influence our world one life at a time as you have seen through the stories told in previous chapters. But we need thousands of churches with a come-as-you-are culture, following the Scriptures under the Spirit's guidance, formed *out of* the messy, unchurched culture of our postmodern context.

The hope for the resuscitation of the church lies in the hands of its future leaders. Leaders create culture—in churches, in small groups, wherever they lead—and culture determines how people function together. Leaders serve and empower others to use their unique gifts together to fully function as the Body, so that every part functions effectively in his or her unique way, re-presenting Christ to the world.[10] But that's part of the problem. We have a broken paradigm for envisioning, equipping, and empowering new leaders.

According to recent surveys, only 5% of current senior pastors said they have the gift of leadership.[11] Most pastors have the primary gift of teaching, which is essential for the health of the church, but teaching alone cannot create culture or mobilize all the gifts needed for the Body to function effectively. We have operated according to a modern model of church, where the church is seen primarily as an educational institution. And so we have raised up teachers, and seminaries to equip teachers to teach, but we have no model or path for raising up or equipping leaders. As a result, naturally gifted leaders have no vision for starting new churches.

I'm convinced that it will take new leaders, starting new churches, for successive new generations to overcome the current decline and see the church resuscitated. I believe thousands of local churches with a come-as-you-are culture can and should be started over the next decade to effectively reach successive generations. But this vision is dependent on the right emerging leaders responding to God's call, and the right existing churches banding together to envision, equip, and empower a new generation of leaders.

Existing churches must consider the legacy they will leave for successive generations. That's what Paul was doing in the two letters to Timothy, his emerging leader/teacher. Paul knew the future of Christ's church would one day be in the hands of young leaders of his day, so he gave young Timothy a vision to lead Christ's church into the future, equipping Timothy in a residency-style rather than purely academic-style apprenticeship. And Paul empowered Timothy to lead and teach others and equip other emerging leaders so that a multiplying empowerment of leadership would occur for generations to come.[12]

Emerging Leadership Initiative

This has been our vision from day one at Gateway—not only to start a new church but to partner with other like-minded churches to raise up emerging leaders to start new churches in a multiplying effort. As I have spoken with pastors all over our country who are successfully reaching this generation, I see that God has clearly put a common desire for empowering emerging leaders and starting new churches on the hearts and minds of many.

Multiple movements of God's Spirit seem to be developing in an effort to lay aside individual church fiefdoms to cooperate together across denominations and traditions in unprecedented ways.[13] We all realize that emerging leaders are our only hope for turning the tide so that Christ's church exerts a compelling influence once again. And we believe this is an effort that all existing churches can participate in to successfully breathe new life into church for generations to come.

Together with Gateway, a group of like-minded churches has established a collaborative effort called Emerging Leadership Initiative (ELI) as a way to partner with other churches and leaders to do our part to turn the tide around.[14]

Let me spell out for you what we think needs to change in this transition from a modern context into a postmodern context, and how you might join with us in working together as his church, for his greater kingdom purposes.

A New Way To Envision Leaders

We believe the old paradigm for finding emerging church leaders is broken. Out of the modern context, which grew up over the past few centuries out of the Enlightenment, we inherited an educational and institutional view of the church. As a result, the people most attracted to the role of pastor were predominately teachers and educators. The way we identified future church pastors was to find those with a gift for teaching and a love for learning and send them off to seminary to "prepare" them to lead a local church. The gift of teaching is extremely important in the effective functioning of the church Body. But without leadership the church becomes a giant brain full of knowledge without a coordinated Body to live out the re-presentation of Christ in the world.

In the new postmodern paradigm, leadership is not passé as some claim; it is more necessary than ever. As cultures change at an ever-accelerating pace, innovative servant-leaders will be needed to lead culture creation to contextualize the church in new ways. Leaders will be needed to mobilize and organize teams of people so that all of the gifts of the Spirit function to re-present the Body of Christ in the world. And in order to start new churches, leaders with an entrepreneurial spirit must be found. But currently, many of those leaders have a compelling vision and a clear path to start high-tech businesses, consulting firms—anything but innovative, high-impact churches. That needs to change!

Existing church leaders must partner together to identify emerging leaders. Together we can accomplish something that no one of us can do alone. We must inspire successive generations of young leaders who understand the context of their culture. Even if your church feels called to minister in a more traditional or more modern context, we all have a responsibility to raise up the next generation of leaders. Truly, this is the legacy of one generation—not what we can accomplish in this short life, but what we pass on from generation to generation even after we are gone. The church in the postmodern context must reclaim this vision and inspire future leaders to lead the greatest endeavor of all history—the reclamation of humanity through the Body of Christ, his church.

A New Way to Examine Leaders

Through ELI, we provide a new way to help potential emerging leaders assess whether they have the natural leadership initiative vital for starting a new church. Through our online assessment center, emerging leaders anywhere in the world can benchmark their temperament, giftedness, and experiences against other young emerging leaders who are leading innovative churches to effectively reach emerging generations.

A New Way to Equip Leaders

We believe the old paradigm for training church pastors is broken. Seminaries equip teachers to teach the Scriptures, but they are not able to truly give leaders the contextualized training necessary. Book knowledge alone can never equip a leader for the challenges of culture creation.

What we need is a residency-style model of equipping. Where emerging leaders are equipped in the context of relationship with other leaders in the cultural setting closest to his future church.

To do this, ELI is establishing Training Churches where emerging leaders can be immersed in an effective come-as-you-are church culture. The curriculum focuses on practical leadership/teaching experience necessary to start a new contextual church, personal spiritual formation necessary to be a lasting leader, and online seminary education (which forward-thinking seminaries are moving toward)—all matched to the needs and past experience of the emerging leader.

A New Way to Empower Leaders

We believe the old paradigm of empowerment will not work for what this new world needs. We need thousands and thousands of churches started everywhere to reverse this decline, but starting a new church takes money. In the old denominational paradigm, funding usually came from a central denominational source with many denominational strings attached to it. This centralized funding source does not lend itself to the multiplying effect that will be needed to start the numbers of new churches needed. The other common funding mechanism came from taking a large group of people from the mother church to start the daughter church, but usually, the post-partum recovery tends to be long. It often takes years before a church wants to daughter another church. The result is that very few American churches plant more than one or two new churches in a decade.

What we need is a new funding model that multiplies resources at the same rate we multiply new leaders. To empower a multiplying number of leaders, a funding network is needed to spread out the burden. But this can be accomplished if existing churches partner together to empower young emerging leaders, practicing the same principles of tithing that the Lord gave for the functioning of every local church.

From conception, Gateway has set aside 10% of every dollar as a "tithe" to meet kingdom needs beyond our overall church needs. Half goes toward church planting and half to benevolence and mission efforts for people in need. It was difficult to "give it away" when we were a small start-up church, and it still takes faith to "give it away" when there are so many unmet opportunities within our congregation. But we believe church leaders should "practice what we preach to church members," to give back to God's larger kingdom-building efforts, not because it serves us, but as an act of faith to serve God's purposes in the world. As a start-up church, this greater-kingdom commitment enabled us to start two more churches and set aside funds for a third, all within our first four years of existence. We could do much more in a unified effort together with other like-minded churches.

Just imagine if existing churches began to cluster together, each giving an equal percentage in a regular way, in line with how the Lord has blessed each church. No church would be overburdened, and every church regardless of size could participate in a movement of leadership empowerment. In this way, clusters of local churches could empower new leaders in an ongoing way, so that eventually every representative church could plant a new church every year or two. And as new churches are started, they too become a sending agent contributing toward the funding and empowerment of others. We have modeled out how this could effectively produce a multiplying funding base to support a new church started out of every training church every year.

A New Way to Expand Across Denominations

We believe the old paradigm, of denominations unable to work together, cannot accomplish the unity Christ pictured for his whole church in his final prayer on earth.[15] Christ's vision clearly is for his whole church functioning as one, just as he and the Father are one, so that the world might believe! The addition model of one church working alone and independently to daughter another church maybe once or twice a decade will not change the course of history in the postmodern world.

It is time for a radical new paradigm of cross-denominational coordination to create a multiplying effort of churches starting church-planting churches. Not from a top-down, central controlling entity, but out of individual willingness to partner in a unified kingdom-building effort.

Potential Church Multiplication-Enabled by a Single Church

(Assumes 2 Emerging Leaders training at the church at all times)

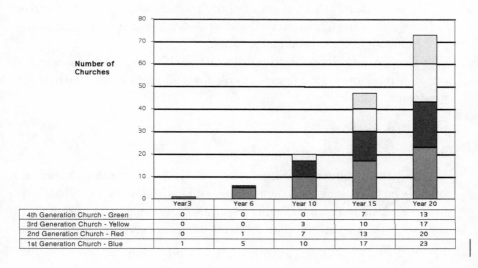

	Year 3	Year 6	Year 10	Year 15	Year 20
4th Generation Church - Green	0	0	0	7	13
3rd Generation Church - Yellow	0	0	3	10	17
2nd Generation Church - Red	0	1	7	13	20
1st Generation Church - Blue	1	5	10	17	23

In this new paradigm (which is actually as old as the church itself), coded in the DNA of every new church planted would be the vision to multiply new leaders to start new churches. With this vision, every church could eventually reach a stage of starting a new church every year or two, and in this way one church could see fifty to seventy churches multiplied out from it in a twenty to thirty year time span (see graph). Literally thousands and thousands of effective, contextual churches could be started in the next thirty to forty years, reversing the potential demise of Christ's church. Apart from this happening, I cannot imagine another way to reverse current trends.

More Than Just a Dream?

I realize you may be thinking this sounds great theoretically, but it could never happen. The truth is—it has always happened this way. Jesus said this is exactly how God's kingdom spreads, like a tiny seed that multiplies out many branches that give shelter to many birds and then produces new seeds that produce new trees.

If you trace the history of the growth of Christ's church, the first three hundred years it multiplied to spread its influence over the entire Roman Empire. The church-planting movement of the 1800s produced a multiplying church-planting effect that grew today's mainline denominations. The parachurch movement of the 1950s mobilized literally tens of thousands of young leaders because of a multiplying paradigm. And recently, an unprecedented cross-denominational effort in the Philippines has multiplied 50,000 new churches in twenty-five years.[16] And the church can multiply in the same way into an influential, compelling force in our postmodern world—*if*—we unite to empower new leaders to start new churches for new generations.

My heart beats fast to think of churches functioning as the effective Body, re-presenting Christ everywhere, so that many more spiritually hungry people can find the food that satisfies.

So let me end this book with a call to action. If you've stuck with me this far, you're probably ready to put the book down and get involved. So here are some ways to do so:

A Call to Action

Current Church Pastors and Leaders

Hopefully throughout this journey across the pages of one church context, you've been evaluating your own culture and context as a church leader. If you are seeking to reach emerging generations, evaluate your current culture and make a transition plan for areas of culture creation that you find lacking or nonexistent.

Not everyone has been called to focus on reaching emerging generations, and other people groups are equally important. If this is the case with your church, I would encourage you to reevaluate how well your church culture is suited to truly impact those people God has called you to reach. What kind of transition plan needs to be put in place so spiritual seekers can come as they are and truly grow spiritually from there?

Even if your church's main focus will never be emerging generations, every church must leave a legacy of next-generation leaders or you're signing your own death certificate within one generation. You *can* play a vital role in empowering the next generation of leaders. Consider how you can identify and empower young leaders to start new churches or even contextual ministries on or off the campus of your church.

While at Willow Creek, we started Axis, a church-within-a-church focused on emerging generations, which has grown to minister to thousands of young adults under the umbrella of Willow Creek. Visit ELI's website* for more ideas and collaborative partnerships that could increase the impact of the legacy you leave.

Emerging Leaders

If you fall into the emerging-leader category, I hope your heart has been beating fast as you've seen how God can use his church to reach our generation. When I looked at the most effective churches of previous generations, I noticed that many were started by leaders in their twenties. They made lots of mistakes, but they persevered and were able to see God cause great growth in thousands of people as a result. Don't let your age be a roadblock in taking steps toward the vision God's giving you.

Successfully starting a church *out of* the surrounding culture is the most challenging yet rewarding endeavor you could partner with God to accomplish. Yes, God can use your leadership in the business world in amazing ways as well, but don't forget, there are many Christ-followers willing to go into business; there are not as many willing to join him full time in building his organization—the church. The harvest is still huge; the laborers are still few, just as Jesus said.[17]

My prayer is that you can hardly wait to take the next step in figuring out if starting a new church is God's will for you. And even if you don't feel equipped to point lead, find ways to get involved in new churches starting near you, because the Body is not complete without what you have to offer.

---

* *www.elichurchplanting.com*

We want to do all we can to encourage and help you. Visit ELI's online assessment* to see what next steps make sense.

Small Group or Ministry Leaders

Evaluate the culture of your small group or ministry. Every group can function as Christ's Body to some degree, since he promises that when two or three gather he is there in your midst. Consider ways you can continue to shape the culture of your group so that it has an influence in the world around you and every member can minister to others. (Consider going through this book as a group and utilize the discussion questions at the end of each chapter.)

If your group's culture is not really suited to impact the emerging post-modern culture, as a group, consider starting a new group with this mission in mind. Small groups are a great way for even more traditional churches to reach out to emerging generations. Maybe God is prompting you to start a new group with your neighbors or coworkers, or maybe he will prompt another member of your group as you talk and pray together about the need. Use the principles of this book and other available resources to get started.[18] Take a risk, and watch how the Lord uses you to create the soil in which amazing growth can occur, even in the lives of those you least expect to follow Christ.

Passionate but Not a Leader

If you have gifts other than leadership and you have found yourself passionate about creating a come-as-you-are culture for emerging generations, here are some ways to get involved. Consider becoming a part of a local new church start. Even though you may not be the point leader or teacher, you could be the catalytic voice of a core to start a vital new church.

I think about Crossroads Community Church in Cincinnati, pastored by a friend of mine. It has reached over five thousand people in the past eight years, all because a small group of nine twenty-somethings caught a vision to start a church to reach their generation. For a year, they met weekly as the church, they studied Scripture and talked about creating a come-as-you-are culture for their unchurched peers—and they tithed into a bank account they had set up. Finally, they started the search and used their money to hire Brian Tome to be their lead pastor. They have seen amazing fruit, all because a few people—not any of them point leaders—had a compelling vision and a willingness to sacrifice. Maybe you will be the impetus for God's vision of a new church to address unmet needs in your area!

* *www.elichurchplanting.com*

The Party's Open!

Jesus once told a parable of the kingdom of heaven, saying a king prepared a great wedding party for his son. All those originally invited made excuses for not attending, so the king ordered his servants to "invite to the banquet anyone you find. So the servants went out into the streets and gathered all the people they could find, both good and bad, and the wedding hall was filled. . . ."[19] Not everyone invited to the party will come, and God alone decides who remains, but our job is to let everyone know that the party's open—all are invited, *good and bad.*

"Come as you are." That's where God starts with every person—right where they are, "as is," then grows them up from there into his Body, the church. I often wonder how in the world God has created the beautiful, messy, work of art I see taking shape all around me in people learning to be his church. But one thing I'm quite sure of—it's his doing! He alone causes the growth. I don't always understand it. I can't often predict it. I surely can't control it. And I know God could have done it completely without me, yet by his loving kindness, I get to co-labor with him. And so do you!

The people you've read about in this book live all around you. They may not look fit for God's kingdom party at first glance, but God can make anyone ready. And I'm convinced that this is a party no one will want to miss.

But one question remains: Will we create a culture where all are invited?

■ ■ ■

The party's open . . . come as you are!

STUDY GUIDE

Culture Check

1. Do you feel a sense of urgency to raise up leaders for the emerging church? Why or why not?
2. Is church-planting a part of your strategy for building the church for successive generations? Why or why not? How will you leave a legacy that outlasts you?
3. Have you considered partnering with others (like ELI or other new-church initiatives) to increase your impact? Why or why not?

Small Group Questions

1. If trends continue in our country, what do you think the influence of the church will be like by the end of our lifetime? How do you feel about that?

2. Read Matthew 28:18–20. What is our responsibility individually and as a group according to Jesus? How might we creatively help each other live out this command?

3. Read 2 Timothy 2:2. In this passage, Paul reveals a pattern. What is it? How can we better develop emerging leaders around us who will be faithful to develop others?

4. Are there creative ways our group can participate in a new paradigm of starting new churches? Brainstorm creative ideas to be a part of the solution.

5. From reading *No Perfect People Allowed*, what has had the biggest impact on you? What are some practical next steps you can take? What practical next steps could we take together as a group?

ACKNOWLEDGMENTS

This book was written first through the lives of people who are dedicated to following Jesus and building his church in and through our generation. First I need to acknowledge and thank those who formed the early culture of our church, for without them, this story would not be the same. My wife, Kathy, showed incredible faith when she moved across the country with our two small children to plant a church with me, developing and directing our children's ministry the first three years as unpaid staff. Ted and Stephanie Beasley and JJ and Tonia Plasencio moved to Austin on faith to help start and establish Gateway that first year, and we wouldn't have survived during those roadie days without Angie Bare, our admin "glue." Our interns, Matt and Michele, and early core group believed in the vision of what could be—thanks, guys, for bringing the vision to life. And to those who walked into a dark movie theater church that first year, just checkin' things out, yet you stayed and served sacrificially every week during those portable days—you are our heroes. And a huge thanks to our awesome Gateway staff, who continue to form and shape a life-giving, come-as-you-are culture. It is an honor to serve Christ with all of you.

To my editor, Jack Kuhatschek—I cannot thank you enough for taking time out to hear our story and even fly to Austin to meet the people of Gateway in person. Thanks for the early sculpting and molding to insure that readers experience the culture through real lives and stories. And Kathy, what can I say except that I do not have the room to acknowledge fully your partnership in this project—from late nights talking over ideas, to collecting stories and permissions, to reading and editing, you have always been my constant source of encouragement and life partner in every way.

I owe Kayla Covington a huge debt of gratitude for her meticulous work in combing through the manuscript and endnotes to give helpful editorial comment—thanks so much, Kayla. And to Keith Miller—God brought you into my life to coach, encourage, and at times coax me down out of the "writer's block tree"—thanks, Keith! And others who read my first draft, Ryan Pazdur and Jennifer Carson, your editorial input and encouragement were invaluable. And to Steve B., thanks so much for your content contribution. And to all of you at Gateway who shared your One Life stories with us, thank you for allowing God to touch other lives through your personal journeys of faith.

Several people influenced the beginning of our church (and thus this book) from a distance: Hal and Sue Rich, Bill and Renee Curtis, Ron and Diane Nobles—thank you for investing in a vision and trusting God to multiply all you've given in time and treasure. Bill Hybels mentored me as a leader and teacher, and Dieter Zander shaped my philosophy of church in profound ways for which I'm grateful. Thank you both for your examples as we worked together. Dallas Willard, Henry Cloud, Philip Yancey, and Keith Miller mentored me through their books. I pray it inspires them to see the theology they've taught lived out in a church culture. And to my family of prayer warriors—my mom and sister, Martha and Alison, and my in-laws, Mary Lou and Clarke Covington, thanks for being a lifeline for our family throughout our Gateway journey and the writing of this book.

Finally, I want to thank Ashley and Justin, the two most wonderful kids in the world. Thank you for your patience and words of encouragement during Daddy's "homework" crunch. Your love and support have enabled me to cross the finish line.

NOTES

Introduction: God's Story in Our Stories

1. "Best Cities for Singles," *Forbes.Com Magazine* (June 5, 2003): *www.forbes.com/ 2003/06/04/singleland.html* (accessed September 27, 2004); and "Austin Named Country's Coolest City," *Austin Business Journal* (June 24, 2004): *www.bizjournals.com/ austin/stories/2004/06/21/daily48.html* (accessed September 27, 2004).

Chapter 1: The First Corinthian Church of America

1. John 18:38.
2. George Barna, *The Second Coming of the Church* (Nashville: Word, 1998), 7–8.
3. "We Believe But Not in Church," *BBC News*, UK edition (May 18, 2004): *news.bbc.co.uk/1/hi/uk/3725801.stm* (Accessed September 19, 2004).
4. Barna, *Second Coming of the Church*, 68.
5. Leighton Ford with James Denney, *The Power of Story: Rediscovering the Oldest, Most Natural Way to Reach People for Christ* (Colorado Springs: NavPress, 1994), 43.
6. Tom Clegg and Warren Bird, *Lost in America: How You and Your Church Can Impact the World Next Door* (Loveland, Colo.: Group, 2001), 25.
7. 1 Corinthians 9:22b NLT.
8. 1 Corinthians 12:1–14 paints a beautiful picture of the church as Christ's Body, made up of diverse people who form its various parts by each one's unique gifting and ministry.
9. Jesus said it first in Matthew 9:37.
10. Ephesians 4:11–16 is a passage we will consider in more depth later. It outlines this picture of the church re-presenting Christ in culture.
11. James A. Alexander, "Creating a High-Performance Culture: Leadership Roles and Responsibilities," *AFSM International S-business, Professional Services Leadership Report* (Ft. Myers, Fla.: AFSMI, Q4 2001), 6. *www.afsmi.org/pdf/content/PSLRQ/pslr_q4_01.pdf* (accessed September 19, 2004).
12. Edgar H. Schein, *Organizational Culture and Leadership*, 2nd ed. (San Francisco: Jossey-Bass, 1992).

Chapter 2: Cynical and Jaded: Results of the Postmodern Experiment

1. Neil Howe and William Strauss, *13ᵗʰ Gen: Abort, Retry, Ignore, Fail?* (New York: Vintage Books, 1993), 24.
2. "The Sixties," *Wikipedia: The Free Encyclopedia* (May 7, 2004). *en.wikipedia.org/ wiki/The_Sixties* (accessed September 19, 2004).
3. William Strauss and Neil Howe, *Generations: The History of America's Future, 1584 to 2069* (New York: William Morrow and Company, 1991). Howe and Strauss demonstrate

a fairly predictable eighty-year cycle around outer-directed and inner-directed periods of generational history. The postwar (WWII) economic boom was marked by a mood of unanimity of purpose (outer-directed). Many great institutions were formed and grew larger, and a spirit of conformity and national pride prevailed as suburbia with its Beaver Cleaver families spread like wildfire. The Baby Boomer generation was coming of age. During a time of such outer-directed social conformity required to build up the external world, an inner hunger often begins to rumble. In reaction to the lack of attention to the concerns of the inner world, a rejection of the high level of social conformity ensues. The inevitable outcome gives birth to an inner-directed "spiritual hunger." In U.S. history, the late sixties through the seventies marked such a time according to Howe and Strauss.

4. Howe and Strauss, *13th Gen*, 44.
5. Howe and Strauss, *13th Gen*, 55.
6. "Advance Report of Final Divorce Statistics 1983," *Monthly Vital Statistics Report* 34, no. 9 (December 26, 1985), Table 1. *National Vital Statistics System*: *www.cdc.gov/nchs/nvss.htm* (accessed September 19, 2004).
7. Howe and Strauss, *13th Gen*, 59.
8. Ibid.
9. Donald J. Hernandez, *America's Children: Resources from Family, Government, and the Economy* (New York: Russell Sage Foundation, 1993).
10. Frank E. Furstenberg Jr. and Christine Nord, *Washington Post*. Cited in Howe and Strauss, *13th Gen*, 60.
11. Everclear, "Father of Mine," on *So Much for the Afterglow* Audio CD (Hollywood: Capitol, 1997).
12. Lynette and Thomas Long, *The Handbook for Latchkey Children and Their Parents: A Complete Guide for Latchkey Kids and Their Working Parents* (New York: Arbor House, 1983). Cited in Howe and Strauss, *13th Gen*, 61.
13. Howe and Strauss, *13th Gen*, 59.
14. Cited in Howe and Strauss, *13th Gen*, 65.
15. Howe and Strauss, *13th Gen*, 66.
16. Bruno Manno, "Outcomes-Based Education, Has It Become More Affliction Than Cure?" Center of the American Experiment: *www.amexp.org/Publications/Archives/manno080194.htm* (accessed July 20, 2004).
17. Romans 2:4 (italics mine).
18. Jane's Addiction, "Ain't No Right," on *Ritual De Lo Habitual* Audio CD (Burbank, Ca.: Warner Bros., 1990).
19. Travis, "Side," on *The Invisible Band* Audio CD (New York: Epic/Independiente, 2001).
20. George Barna and Mark Hatch, *Boiling Point: It Only Takes One Degree: Monitoring Cultural Shifts in the 21st Century* (Ventura, Ca.: Regal, 2001), 193.
21. Ephesians 4:16.
22. Howe and Strauss, *13th Gen*, 88.
23. Stanley K. Henshaw, "Unintended Pregnancy in the United States," *Family Planning Perspectives* 30, no. 1 (1998). *The Alan Guttmacher Institute*: www.guttmacher.org/pubs/journals/3002498.html (accessed September 19, 2004). Note: The Alan Guttmacher Institute says 43% of women will have had at least one abortion by the time they are forty-five years old if trends continue.
24. Patricia Tjaden and Nancy Thoennes, *Full Report of the Prevalence, Incidence, and Consequences of Violence Against Women: Findings from the National Violence Against Women Survey* (National Institute of Justice, November 2000), iii–iv. www.rainn.org/fullnvaw-survey.pdf (accessed September 20, 2004). Robert T. Michael, *Sex in America: A Defini-*

tive Survey (New York: Warner Books, 1994): reports one out of five women had been sexually molested in 1994 survey. Other surveys indicate as high as two out of five. Whatever the actual statistics, my counseling experience is that it's way too high a percent.

25. David Popenoe and Barbara Dafoe Whitehead, "Should We Live Together?" 2nd ed. (Rutgers National Marriage Project, 2002), 3: *marriage.rutgers.edu/Publications/swlt2.pdf* (accessed September 20, 2004).
26. "Substance Dependence, Abuse, and Treatment," *Results* from the 2002 National Survey on Drug Use and Health: National Findings (2003). Substance Abuse and Mental Health Services Administration: *oas.samhsa.gov/nhsda/2k2nsduh/Results/2k2Results.htm#chap8* (accessed September 20, 2004).
27. "Tobacco Use," *Results* from the 2002 National Survey on Drug Use and Health: National Findings (2003). Substance Abuse and Mental Health Services Administration: *oas.samhsa.gov/nhsda/2k2nsduh/Results/2k2Results.htm#chap4* (accessed August 10, 2004).
28. Robert Putnam, *Bowling Alone: The Collapse and Revival of American Community* (New York: Simon & Schuster, 2000), 27.

Chapter 3: Doubters Wanted: Creating a Culture of Dialogue

1. Jeremiah 29:13.
2. Matthew 5:44–46.
3. David K. Clark, *Dialogical Apologetics: A Person-Centered Approach to Christian Defense* (Grand Rapids, Mich.: Baker, 1993), 195.
4. Luke 11:46b.
5. Luke 7:34 NLT.
6. Philippians 2:3–11; Luke 19:10.
7. Mark 7:6, 8.
8. Matthew 22:36–39.
9. Mark 10:17–22.
10. See Matthew 11:2–3.
11. Psalm 42:9.
12. Psalm 89:46.
13. Psalm 22:1.
14. The three wise men, called *magoi*, were likely Zoroastrian priests (or at least of the priestly caste) from Persia. Note other mysterious ways God breaks out of the box of the expected in Scripture: Peter seeing the unclean animals that God says to eat (Acts 10), Baalam hearing God's words from the donkey (Numbers 22), or Christ coming as the Suffering Servant.
15. Matthew 16:23.
16. Mark 9:24.
17. Hebrews 11:6.
18. 1 Corinthians 12:3; John 16:8–11; 2 Chronicles 16:9.
19. In Acts 10, Peter is sent by God to complete the work God was already doing in the heart of the Gentile, Cornelius, by leading him to faith in Christ. We find that same work in many who began seeking God through recovery or even other faiths, and we let them know that we believe God led them here so they might truly come to know who he has revealed himself to be through the prophets and the Christ.
20. Mark 12:34.

Chapter 4: Losing My Need to Pretend: Creating a Culture of Authenticity

1. Luke 11:42.

2. Mark 10:35–40.
3. John 17:21a.
4. I first heard this from Vince Antonucci, the pastor of Forefront, a church very similar in philosophy and style to Gateway, which reaches many non-Christian people. Vince combined it with the phrase "Nobody Stands Alone," which we came up with at Axis (Willow Creek's church-within-a-church). Since Forefront started in a dark movie theater, Vince would tell people, "The three things you need to remember about Forefront: No perfect people allowed, nobody stands alone, and no making out on the back row."
5. Matthew 5:48.
6. Matthew 6:12.
7. 1 John 1:8.
8. James 5:16a.

Chapter 5: Come as You Are: Creating a Culture of Acceptance

1. Romans 7:15 NLT.
2. Gordon MacDonald, quoted by Philip Yancey, *What's So Amazing about Grace?* (Grand Rapids, Mich.: Zondervan, 1997), 15.
3. Yancey, *What's So Amazing about Grace?* 45.
4. Romans 2:4 (italics mine).
5. Romans 8:1.
6. Romans 8:16.
7. Romans 8:31b.
8. Yancey, *What's So Amazing about Grace?* 42.
9. 1 Peter 3:18 NLT.
10. Romans 15:7.
11. Ted Beasley word-crafted this vision-casting statement printed in our programs.
12. Romans 5:20, 7:4,10; Galatians 2:17–21.
13. See Romans 8:1–6. Our only chance of fulfilling the law is with God's help. We can't do it alone! And Galatians 3:24–25 says the law was to serve as our tutor, to show us our need for Christ, not to make us better.
14. J. Keith Miller, *A Hunger For Healing: The Twelve Steps as a Classic Model for Christian Spiritual Growth* (San Francisco: HarperSanFrancisco, 1992), 50–51.
15. Luke 15, Matthew 22:1–10.
16. Romans 13:8b NLT.
17. J. J. Plasencio, "Just the Way I Am," *We Will Remember: The Songs of Gateway Community Church* (Plasenciomusic, Sesac, 2001).
18. Romans 6:15 NLT.
19. Matthew 13:28–30 NLT.

Chapter 6: But Don't Stay That Way: Creating a Culture of Growth

1. 1 Corinthians 3:6 (italics mine).
2. John 15:5 NLT (italics mine).
3. Galatians 3:3.
4. Galatians 5:1–6.
5. Patrick M. Morley, *Man in the Mirror: Solving the 24 Problems Men Face* (Brentwood, Tenn.: Wolgemuth & Hyatt, 1989).
6. Romans 8:4 NLT.
7. Romans 8:5.
8. Matthew 22:36–39; John 13:34–35.

9. 1 John 4:19.
10. 1 John 4:20.
11. Luke 14:25–26, 28 NLT.
12. Hebrews 10:24–25.
13. Henry Cloud and John Townsend, *How People Grow: What the Bible Reveals about Personal Growth* (Grand Rapids, Mich.: Zondervan, 2001), 122.
14. 1 Peter 4:10–11.
15. Cloud and Townsend, *How People Grow*, 69.
16. Ibid., 70.
17. Dallas Willard, *The Divine Conspiracy: Rediscovering Our Hidden Life in God* (San Francisco: HarperSanFrancisco, 1998), 322.
18. Romans 6:12–13 NLT.
19. Romans 8:1–5 explains how grace forms the context where the intent of God's law can be fulfilled, as we learn to set our minds continually on what his Spirit wills.
20. Romans 5:3–5; James 1:2–5.
21. Consider all of the exhortations of the Old Testament to not forget God's works. Israel used everything from monuments to yearly celebrations, from storytelling to songs, in order to reflect and celebrate God's works in their lives.

Chapter 7: What about Other Religions? The Tolerance Litmus Test—Q1

1. Romans 2:14–15.
2. This way of understanding God's extra-dimensionality or supernatural capabilities was inspired by a century-old book called *Flatland: A Romance of Many Dimensions* by Edwin A. Abbott.
3. Acts 26:17b–18a.
4. Acts 17:22–23.
5. Acts 17:24–28 (italics mine).
6. Mortimer J. Adler, *Truth in Religion: The Plurality of Religions and the Unity of Truth* (New York: MacMillan, 1990), 89.
7. Romans 2:14–15 NLT.
8. This list adapted from C. S. Lewis, *The Abolition of Man, Or, Reflections on Education with Special Reference to the Teaching of English in the Upper Forms of Schools* (New York: MacMillan, 1947), 95–121.
9. Romans 1:20–21.
10. Adler, *Truth in Religion*, 104.
11. Mormonism might be included today as a world religion claiming divine revelation (although through an angel as does Islam) though Adler did not include Mormonism in his assessment for some reason.
12. John 14:6–7. For other verses where the writers of Scripture report Jesus making claims equating with divinity see: John 10:31–33; Matthew 9:3–8; in Matthew 28:17–20 Jesus accepts their worship though he earlier said to worship God only in Matthew 4:10; in Revelation 1:17 Jesus claims to be the first and last as does God in Revelation 22:12–13.
13. 2 Chronicles 16:9 NLT.
14. Romans 1:16–2:16.
15. Hebrews chapter 11 and Romans 4:16–17 make this clear.
16. John 8:56.
17. Revelation 5:9b, 7:9.
18. Acts 10:34–35 NLT.

19. I first read of this idea from C. S. Lewis though others have written similar ideas, derived from the notion that God allows us to forever reject him, which defines the worst part of hell—eternity separated from the very Source of love and life.
20. Matthew 7:21–23.
21. 1 John 5:13.
22. John 8:41–43.
23. These points were adapted from an open-air talk I heard Cliff Knechtle give years ago at UCSB. Cliffe Knechtle is the senior pastor of Grace Community Church in New Canaan, Connecticut. He speaks at many college campuses all over the country. His website has streaming videos of many of his campus dialogues: "Give Me an Answer! Real Answers to Tough Questions about Christianity" at *www.GiveMeAnAnswer.org*.

Chapter 8: How Do You Feel about Gays? The Tolerance Litmus Test—Q2

1. Luke 10:25–37 (my paraphrase).
2. Walter L. Liefeld, "Luke," *The Expositor's Bible Commentary*, ed. Frank E. Gaebelein (Grand Rapids, Mich.: Zondervan, 1984), Luke 10:25–37, Vol. 8, 943–44.
3. 1 Corinthians 6:9–11 (italics mine).
4. Matthew 21:31.
5. Here are a variety of resources discussing potential causation of homosexual orientation:

    Brian D. McLaren and Tony Campolo, *Adventures in Missing the Point: How the Culture-Controlled Church Neutered the Gospel* (Grand Rapids, Mich.: Zondervan, 2003), 180–181.

    Matt Ridley, *Nature Via Nurture: Genes, Experience, and What Makes Us Human* (New York: HarperCollins, 2003).

    N. E. Whitehead, "Born That Way Theories," NARTH: *www.narth.com/menus/born.html* (accessed September 20, 2004).

    Don Knapp, "Male Hormone Levels in Womb May Affect Sexual Orientation," *CNN.com Health* (March 29, 2000): *www.cnn.com/2000/HEALTH/03/29/* (accessed September 20, 2004).

    R. Blanchard & L. Ellis, "Birth Weight, Sexual Orientation, and the Sex of Preceding Siblings," *Journal of Biosocial Science*, no. 33 (2001), 451–67.

Chapter 9: The Humble Truth about Truth: Creating a Culture of Truth-Telling Humility

1. Stanley Grenz, *A Primer on Postmodernism* (Grand Rapids, Mich.: Eerdmans Publishing, 1996).

    Lesslie Newbigin, *The Gospel in a Pluralist Society* (Grand Rapids, Mich.: Eerdmans Publishing, 1989).

    Stanley Grenz and John R. Franke, *Beyond Foundationalism: Shaping Theology in a Postmodern Context* (Louisville: Westminster John Knox, 2000).

    Brian McLaren, *A New Kind of Christian: A Tale of Two Friends on a Spiritual Journey* (San Francisco: Jossey-Bass, 2001).

    Dennis McCallum, ed., *The Death of Truth: What's Wrong with Multiculturalism, the Rejection of Reason, and the New Postmodern Diversity* (Minneapolis: Bethany House Publishers, 1996).

2. Philippians 2:1–11; John 1:14–17.
3. 1 Corinthians 8:1.

4. John 8:31–32.
5. Acts 18:28b, 17:2–3.
6. Acts 17:2–3.
7. Acts 17:30–31 NLT (italics mine).
8. John 16:13.
9. 2 John 1–2 NLT.
10. Gideon's fleece, Balaam's talking donkey, a suffering Messiah, Zoroastrian astrologers (Magi) finding the Messiah in the stars, Peter's strange unkosher dream, Paul's Damascus road encounter—all represent just a quick perusal of downright mysterious, unpredictable acts of God.

Chapter 10: Tribal Truth: Creating the Culture of Incarnational Truth

1. Ralph D. Winter and Steven C. Hawthorne, eds., *Perspectives on the World Christian Movement: A Reader* (Pasadena, Ca.: William Carey Library, 1981). See chapters 40, 63, 64, and 71 for various examples of how social ties in tight-knit people groups effect people's decision-making regarding beliefs.
2. Ethan Watters, *Urban Tribes: A Generation Redefines Friendship, Family, and Commitment* (Bloomsbury: New York, 2003), 54.
3. Watters, *Urban Tribes*, 8.
4. Ephesians 4:11–16 NLT.
5. Hebrews 1:3.
6. 1 Corinthians 12:27.
7. Ephesians 4:21 NLT (italics mine).
8. John 14:6 (italics mine).
9. Our mission has always been "to help unchurched people become a unified community of growing Christ-followers" (defined by the Great Commission—Matthew 28:18–20; Great Commandment—Matthew 22:34–40; and Jesus' Great Prayer—John 17).
10. John 17:20–21 (italics mine).
11. Galatians 4:4 NLT.
12. 1 Thessalonians 1:5–8.
13. 1 Thessalonians 2:7–8, 11–12.

Chapter 11: All God Intended You to Be: Creating a Culture of Hope

1. Romans 15:4 (italics mine).
2. Luke 4:18–19.
3. John 10:10 NLT (italics mine).
4. 1 John 4:9 (italics mine).
5. Dallas Willard, *The Spirit of the Disciplines: Understanding How God Changes Lives* (San Francisco: HarperCollins, 1988), 80–81.
6. Luke 11:46.
7. Matthew 9:12–13.
8. Christian Schwarz and Christoph Schalk, *Natural Church Development* (Carol Stream, Ill.: ChurchSmart Resources, 1998).
9. David Walsh and Douglas A. Gentile, "Slipping Under the Radar: Advertising and the Mind," National Institute on Media and the Family: *www.psychology.iastate.edu/faculty/dgentile/Walsh_Gentile_WHO.pdf* (accessed September 20, 2004).
10. Suzanne Tedesko, "Family Planning Media: Now That's Entertainment," *In Context: A Quarterly of Humane Sustainable Culture*, no. 31 (Spring 1992), 42. Last updated June 29, 2000: *www.context.org/ICLIB/IC31/Tedesko.htm* (accessed September 20, 2004).
11. Suzanne Tedesko, "Family Planning Media: Now That's Entertainment," 42.

12. Luke 9:1–2.
13. Tom Allen, "Postmoderns value authenticity, not authority, pastor says," *The Baptist Standard* (April 19, 2004). For an online version: *www.baptiststandard.com/ postnuke/index.php?module=htmlpages&func=display&pid=1620* (accessed September 20, 2004).
14. See 1 Corinthians 12:28.
15. I heard this statistic at a communications seminar. There is a Chinese proverb that says the same thing without percentages: "Tell me and I will forget. Show me and I may remember. Involve me and I will understand."

Chapter 12: Mental Monogamy: Creating a Culture of Sexual Wholeness

1. John 4:24.
2. John 4:28–29 (my paraphrase).
3. Ethan Watters, *Urban Tribes: A Generation Redefines Friendship, Family, and Commitment* (Bloomsbury: New York, 2003), 28.
4. "Sexuality, Contraception, and the Media," *Pediatrics*, vol. 107, no. 1 (American Academy of Pediatrics Committee on Public Education, January 2001), 191–94. *aappolicy.aappublications.org/cgi/content/full/pediatrics;107/1/191?fulltext=sex+tv&searc hid=QID_NOT_SET* (accessed August 8, 2004).
5. "Teenagers' Sexual and Reproductive Health," *Facts in Brief* (New York: The Alan Guttmacher Institute, 2002): *www.guttmacher.org/pubs/fb_teens.pdf* (accessed September 20, 2004).
6. David Popenoe and Barbara Dafoe Whitehead, "Should We Live Together?" 2d ed. (Rutgers National Marriage Project, 2002), 3: *marriage.rutgers.edu/Publications/swlt2.pdf* (accessed September 20, 2004).
7. Matthew 15:19 (italics mine).
8. Prepare and Enrich is the assessment tool we currently use. For more information see: *www.lifeinnovations.com*.
9. Hebrews 13:4.
10. Popenoe, "Should We Live Together?": *http://marriage.rutgers.edu/Publications/swlt2.pdf* (accessed September 13, 2004).
11. Popenoe and Whitehead, "Should We Live Together?" 4.
12. Popenoe and Whitehead, "Should We Live Together?" 5.
13. Carin Gorrell, "Live-in and Learn," *Psychology Today* (November/December 2000): *cms.psychologytoday.com/articles/index.php?term=PTO–20001101–000012* (accessed September 20, 2004).
14. I heard this analogy from Brian Wells at Crossroads Community Church, Cincinnati.
15. Matthew 19:4–6 TNIV.
16. Here is a partial list of references for further study: Leviticus 18; Matthew 15:19; Acts 15:20; Romans 1:24; 1 Corinthians 6:13, 18, 7:2, 10:8; Galatians 5:19; Ephesians 5:3; Colossians 3:5; 1 Thessalonians 4:3–6. I'm often asked what the term "sexual immorality" actually means, that is, "How far can you go until it's sexual immorality?" I explain that God apparently created sex to be progressive and climactic. There's a line you cross that causes only frustration if not completed in climax. So to answer the question, once you cross the line from expressing emotional intimacy into foreplay, you're into sexual immorality if outside of marriage. You know it because it's not very fun or fulfilling to stop—you want more because you did cross the line. The God-honoring approach is to not cross that line of sure frustration, and that line is different for every person (though petting and oral sex clearly cross the line).

17. "The Science of Love," *Science and Nature: Hot Topics* (BBC News, February 8, 2002): *www.bbc.co.uk/science/hottopics/love/index.shtml* (accessed September 20, 2004).

18. Like Solomon wisely said, "There's nothing new under the sun," and this illustration is not original with me. I heard it from Steve Tarr who heard it at another church as he traveled the country visiting emerging churches. I could not locate its original source.

19. David H. Olson and Amy K. Olson, *Empowering Couples: Building on Your Strengths*, 2nd ed. (Minneapolis: Life Innovations, 2000), 124.

20. "Advance Report of Final Divorce Statistics 1983," *Monthly Vital Statistics Report* 34, no. 9 (December 26, 1985), Table 1. *National Vital Statistics System*: *www.cdc.gov/nchs/nvss.htm* (accessed September 19, 2004).

21. David Popenoe, "Teen Pregnancy: An American Dilemma" (Testimony before the House of Representatives, July 16, 1998): *marriage.rutgers.edu/Publications/pubteenp.htm* (accessed September 20, 2004).

22. "Unmarried Childbearing," National Center for Health Statistics, last updated March 25, 2004 (Centers for Disease Control, 2004): *www.cdc.gov/nchs/fastats/unmarry.htm* (accessed September 20, 2004).

23. "Unmarried with Children," *USA Today* (May 16, 2001): *www.usatoday.com/news/opinion/2001–05–16-edtwof2.htm* (accessed September 24, 2004).

24. Stanley K. Henshaw, "Abortion Incidence and Services in the United States, 1995–1996," *Family Planning Perspectives*, vol. 30, no. 6 (November/December 1998): *www.guttmacher.org/pubs/journals/3026398.html* (accessed September 20, 2004).

25. "STD Statistics," American Social Health Association (2001): *www.ashastd.org/stdfaqs/statistics.html* (accessed September 20, 2004).

26. Jerry Ropelato, "Internet Pornography Statistics," *Top Ten REVIEWS* (2004): *www.internetfilterreview.com/internet-pornography-statistics.html* (accessed September 21, 2004).

27. Patricia Tjaden and Nancy Thoennes, *Full Report of the Prevalence, Incidence, and Consequences of Violence against Women: Findings from the National Violence against Women Survey* (National Institute of Justice, November 2000), iii–iv: *www.rainn.org/fullnvawsurvey.pdf* (accessed September 21, 2004).

28. Kathleen Coulborn Faller, "Prevalence of Child Sexual Abuse," *Child Sexual Abuse: Intervention and Treatment Issues* (Administration for Children and Families, U.S. Department of Health and Human Services, 1993): *nccanch.acf.hhs.gov/pubs/usermanuals/sexabuse/index.cfm/* (accessed September 21, 2004).

29. David H. Olson and Amy K. Olson, *Empowering Couples: Building on Your Strengths*, 2nd ed. (Minneapolis: Life Innovations, 2000), 124.

30. Karen S. Peterson, "Affairs Rare Despite Rumored Popularity," *USA Today* (December 21, 1998): *www.dearpeggy.com/announce4.html* (accessed September 24, 2004). A 1994 study done by the University of Chicago indicated about 28% of men and 17% of women admitted to an extramarital affair. Since it was a random survey, assuming none of the men randomly surveyed were married to the women surveyed, it appears an estimated 45% of marriages were affected. Others have estimated much higher rates of infidelity: Bonnie Eaker Weil, *Adultery: The Forgivable Sin* (Hastings House Book Publishers, 1994), 3. She estimates 30–50% of wives, 50–70% of husbands have had an affair, but this appears too high considering research that still indicates most people are faithful most of the time.

Chapter 13: Recovering an Addicted Generation: Creating a Culture of Healing

1. Mark 2:16–17.
2. Matthew 5:3.

3. Henry Cloud and John Townsend, *How People Grow* (Grand Rapids, Mich.: Zondervan, 2001), 264.

4. Luke 18:9–14.

5. Wendy Kaminer, *I'm Dysfunctional, You're Dysfunctional: The Recovery Movement and Other Self-Help Fashions* (Reading, Mass.: Addison-Wesley, 1992), 3.

6. Dick B., *The Good Book and the Big Book: AA's Roots in the Bible* (Kihei, Hawaii: Paradise Research Publications, 1997). For Dick B.'s online history of AA: *www.dickb.com/archives/history.shtml* (accessed September 20, 2004). Ernest Kurtz, *A.A: The Story*, 1st Harper & Row ed. (San Francisco: Harper & Row, 1988). A revised edition of *Not-God: A History of Alcoholics Anonymous* (Center City, Minn.: Hazeldon Educational Services, 1979).

7. Acts 10:34–35 NLT.

8. Acts 8 and Acts 10 tell the stories of the Ethiopian and Cornelius—spiritual seekers who apparently believed in God but needed to learn of Christ.

9. 1 Corinthians 6:12 NLT.

10. Taking Centers for Disease Control stats, 40% or more use tobacco (among 18–25-year-olds), 20% struggle with substance abuse, approximately 10% struggle with sexual addictions, not to mention Rader Programs that say an estimated 19–30% of college women have eating disorders—it indicates that potentially half the young adult population—if not more—struggle with addictions. For stats see: "Substance Dependence, Abuse, and Treatment," *Results from the 2002 National Survey on Drug Use and Health: National Findings*. 2003. Substance Abuse and Mental Health Services Administration: *oas.samhsa.gov/nhsda/2k2nsduh/Results/2k2Results.htm* (accessed September 16, 2004).

11. Gerald G. May, *Addiction and Grace* (New York: HarperCollins, 1988), 24.

12. Ibid., 26–28.

13. Patrick Carnes, *Don't Call It Love: Recovery from Sexual Addiction* (New York: Bantam, 1991), 105.

14. Carnes, *Don't Call It Love*, 106. Carnes found that 2/3 of addicts grew up in rigid, disconnected families.

15. "Substance Dependence, Abuse, and Treatment," *Results from the 2002 National Survey on Drug Use and Health: National Findings*. 2003. Substance Abuse and Mental Health Services Administration: *oas.samhsa.gov/nhsda/2k2nsduh/Results/2k2Results.htm#chap8* (accessed September 16, 2004), chapter 8.1–8.2.

16. "Trends in Lifetime Prevalence of Substance Use," *Results from the 2002 National Survey on Drug Use and Health: National Findings*. 2003. Substance Abuse and Mental Health Services Administration: *oas.samhsa.gov/nhsda/2k2nsduh/Results/2k2 Results.htm#chap5* (accessed September 16, 2004), chapter 5.

17. "Tobacco Use," *Results from the 2002 National Survey on Drug Use and Health: National Findings*. 2003. Substance Abuse and Mental Health Services Administration: *oas.samhsa.gov/nhsda/2k2nsduh/Results/2k2Results.htm#chap4* (accessed September 16, 2004), chapter 4.

18. "You Can Quit Smoking: Consumer Guide," *Tobacco Cessation Guideline* (June 2000). Office of the Surgeon General: *www.surgeongeneral.gov/tobacco/consquits.htm* (accessed August 1, 2004).

19. "Targeting Tobacco Use: The Nation's Leading Cause of Death, 2004," *Tobacco Information and Prevention Source (TIPS)*. 2004. Centers for Disease Control and Prevention: *www.cdc.gov/nccdphp/aag/pdf/aag_osh2004.pdf* (accessed August 10, 2004).

20. "Survey finds most smokers want to quit," *CNN Health* (July 25, 2002). *CNN*: *www.cnn.com/2002/HEALTH/07/25/cdc.smoking/* (accessed July 31, 2004).

21. Setting Captives Free has an online, Christ-centered, sixty-day program to quit smoking called Breath of Life: *www.settingcaptivesfree.com/breath_life/*. I would also recommend the *NIV Recovery Devotional Bible* and *A Hunger for Healing* by Keith Miller as resources for any recovery group.

22. "Zogby/Focus Survey Reveals Shocking Internet Sex Statistics." *Legal Facts: Family Research Council*. Vol. 2. No. 20. (March 30, 2000).

23. "Pornography Addiction," News Stories. Last updated April 25, 2003. KFSN-TV Channel 30: *abclocal.go.com/kfsn/news/042403_nw_pornography_addiction.html* (accessed August 8, 2004).

24. Victoria Rideout, *Generation Rx.com: How Young People Use the Internet for Health Information*, The Kaiser Family Foundation Survey 2001, 3. *kff.org/entmedia/loader.cfm?url=/commonspot/security/getfile.cfm&PageID=13719* (accessed September 16, 2004). Found 70% of fifteen- to seventeen-year-olds viewed pornography.

   Sonia Livingston and Magdalena Bober, *UK Children Go Online: Surveying experiences of children and their parents* (Economic and Social Research Council, 2004), 3. *personal.lse.ac.uk/bober/UKCGOsurveyexec.pdf* (accessed September 16, 2004). Found 68% of twelve- to nineteen-year-olds in the UK have viewed pornography.

25. Ralph Frammolino and P. J. Huffstutter, "The Actress, the Producer, and Their Porn Revolution," *Los Angeles Times Magazine* (January 6, 2002).

26. "Recovery from Sexual Addiction: An Interview with Mark Laaser," *Library*. (Last updated November 6, 2001). International Association of Christian Twelve Step Ministries: *www.iactsm.com/dox/sexaddic.htm* (accessed August 10, 2004).

27. Carnes, *Don't Call It Love*, 109.

28. Carnes, *Don't Call It Love*, 22.

29. "Recovery from Sexual Addiction: An Interview with Mark Laaser," *Library*. (Last updated November 6, 2001). International Association of Christian Twelve Step Ministries: *www.iactsm.com/dox/sexaddic.htm* (August 10, 2004).

Chapter 14: Nobody Stands Alone: Creating a Culture of Connection

1. William Mahedy and Janet Bernardi, *A Generation Alone: Xers Making a Place in the World* (Downers Grove, Ill.: InterVarsity, 1994), 25–26.

2. Mahedy and Bernardi, *A Generation Alone*, 28.

3. Mahedy and Bernardi, *A Generation Alone*, 29.

4. 2 Corinthians 5:16–19, 6:11–13.

5. Isaiah 58; Matthew 25:34–40.

6. 2 Corinthians 1:3–4.

7. I believe Rick Warren actually came up with the "H.O.S.T." acronym. I heard it from Brett Eastman of Lifetogether.

8. *Lifetogether.com* website has small group resources.

Chapter 15: The Family I Never Had: Creating a Culture of Family

1. Exodus 34:6–7.

2. Ephesians 3:17–18.

3. Ephesians 5:1–2.

4. Larry Crabb, *Connecting: Healing for Ourselves and Our Relationships: A Radical New Vision* (Nashville: W Publishing Group, 1997), xi–xii.

5. Acts 2:46 (NLT).

6. Galatians 6:2, 5.

7. 2 Thessalonians 3:10.

Chapter 16: Life or Death? Creating a Culture for Emerging Leaders

1. Gallup announced a 5% drop in church attendance in 1996. For more information see historical charts and articles on the Gallup site: *www.gallup.com/poll/focus/sr040302.asp* (accessed August 7, 2004).
2. Acts 15 records the first conference on cross-cultural contextualization of the gospel.
3. Acts 15:19.
4. The work on contextualization that most influenced me is Ralph D. Winter and Steven C. Hawthorne, eds., *Perspectives on the World Christian Movement: A Reader* (Pasadena: William Carey Library, 1981).
5. George Barna, "Number of Unchurched Adults Has Nearly Doubled Since 1991," The Barna Update (May 4, 2004): *www.barna.org/FlexPage.aspx?Page=BarnaUpdate&BarnaUpdateID=163* (accessed September 20, 2004).
6. Bruce A. Robinson, "Religious Trends in the West," Ontario Consultants on Religious Tolerance: *www.religioustolerance.org/index_tren.htm* (accessed September 20, 2004).
7. Penny Long Marler and C. Kirk Hadaway, "Testing the Attendance Gap in a Conservative Church," *Sociology of Religion Journal* (Summer 1999): *www.findarticles.com/p/articles/mi_m0SOR/is_2_60/ai_55208518/pg_1* (accessed September 20, 2004).
8. The Barna Group, "Evangelism," *www.barna.org/FlexPage.aspx?Page=Topic&TopicID=18* (accessed September 20, 2004).
9. Barna, *Second Coming of the Church*, 2.
10. Ephesians 4:11–16 paints this picture of this team of gifted leaders equipping and mobilizing the body.
11. Barna, *Second Coming of the Church*, 36.
12. 2 Timothy 2:1–6 (also refer to 2 Tim 1:6–7).
13. Efforts similar to Emerging Leadership Initiative (ELI) have been springing up all over, as if God's Spirit has put the same vision in leaders across our country with a new freedom to collaborate together. A few I'm aware of currently: Passion for Planting out of New Life Church in Washington D.C. (ELI partner, *www.church-planting.net*), 20/20 out of Kensington in Detroit (ELI partner), Acts 29 Network out of Mars Hill in Seattle (*www.a29.org*), Glocalnet and New Church Initiatives (*newchurchinitiatives.org*). I'm also intrigued with the vision of Neil Cole and others who seem to have cracked the code for house churches in the Western world. All types of culture-engaging churches will be needed in our diverse world.
14. See "Partnerships" on ELI's website for a bio on church partners collaborating to start new churches: *www.elichurchplanting.com*
15. Read John 17 for Jesus' final prayer for unity.
16. Dr. James Montgomery, "Never Before in Church History," *Dawn Report*, no. 45 (October 2001): *www.dawnministries.org/resources/dawn_report/issue45/never_before.html*.
17. Matthew 9:36–38.
18. Several great resources to help you in this endeavor can be found through Lifetogether, an organization seeking to empower small group movements (*www.lifetogether.com*). Gary Poole's book *Seeker Small Groups* is also a great resource.
19. Matthew 22:9–10.

WILLOW
Willow Creek Association

Willow Creek Association
Vision, Training, Resources for Prevailing Churches

This resource was created to serve you and to help you build a local church that prevails. It is just one of many ministry tools that are part of the Willow Creek Resources® line, published by the Willow Creek Association together with Zondervan.

The Willow Creek Association (WCA) was created in 1992 to serve a rapidly growing number of churches from across the denominational spectrum that are committed to helping unchurched people become fully devoted followers of Christ. Membership in the WCA now numbers over 10,500 Member Churches worldwide from more than ninety denominations.

The Willow Creek Association links like-minded Christian leaders with each other and with strategic vision, training, and resources in order to help them build prevailing churches designed to reach their redemptive potential. Here are some of the ways the WCA does that.

- **A2: Building Prevailing Acts 2 Churches—Today**—an annual two-and-a-half day event, held at Willow Creek Community Church in South Barrington, Illinois, to explore strategies for building churches that reach out to seekers and build believers, and to discover new innovations and breakthroughs from Acts 2 churches around the country.

- **The Leadership Summit**—a once a year, two-and-a-half-day conference to envision and equip Christians with leadership gifts and responsibilities. Presented live at Willow Creek as well as via satellite broadcast to over one hundred locations across North America, this event is designed to increase the leadership effectiveness of pastors, ministry staff, volunteer church leaders, and Christians in the marketplace.

- **Ministry-Specific Conferences**—throughout each year the WCA hosts a variety of conferences and training events—both at Willow Creek's main campus and offsite, across the U.S., and around the world—targeting church leaders and volunteers in ministry-specific areas such as: evangelism, small groups, preaching and teaching, the arts, children, students, women, volunteers, stewardship, raising up resources, etc.

- **Willow Creek Resources®**—provides churches with trusted and field-tested ministry resources in such areas as leadership, evangelism, spiritual formation, spiritual gifts, small groups, stewardship, student ministry, children's ministry, the use of the arts-drama, media, contemporary music —and more.

- **WCA Member Benefits**—includes substantial discounts to WCA training events, a 20 percent discount on all Willow Creek Resources®, *Defining Moments* monthly audio journal for leaders, quarterly *Willow* magazine, access to a Members-Only section on WillowNet, monthly communications, and more. Member Churches also receive special discounts and premier services through WCA's growing number of ministry partners—Select Service Providers—and save an average of $500 annually depending on the level of engagement.

For specific information about WCA conferences, resources, membership, and other ministry services contact:

Willow Creek Association
P.O. Box 3188
Barrington, IL 60011-3188
Phone: 847-570-9812
Fax: 847-765-5046
www.willowcreek.com

We want to hear from you. Please send your comments about this book to us in care of zreview@zondervan.com. Thank you.

GRAND RAPIDS, MICHIGAN 49530 USA

ZONDERVAN.COM/
AUTHOR**TRACKER**